General
George E.
Pickett

in Life &
Legend

CIVIL WAR AMERICA

Gary W. Gallagher, editor

General George E. Pickett in

Life &

Legend

Lesley J. Gordon

The University of North Carolina Press

Chapel Hill and London

© 1998
The University of North Carolina Press
All rights reserved
Manufactured in the United States of America
The paper in this book meets the guidelines for
permanence and durability of the Committee on
Production Guidelines for Book Longevity of the
Council on Library Resources.
Library of Congress Cataloging-in-Publication Data
Gordon, Lesley J. (Lesley Jill)
General George E. Pickett in Life and Legend /
by Lesley J. Gordon.
    p. cm. — (Civil War America)
Includes bibliographical references and index.
ISBN 0-8078-2450-x (cloth : alk. paper)
1. Pickett, George E. (George Edward), 1825–1875.
2. Generals—Confederate States of America—
Biography. 3. Pickett, La Salle Corbell, 1848–1931.
4. Generals' spouses—Confederate States of
America—Biography. 5. United States—History—
Civil War, 1861–1865—Biography. I. Title. II. Series.
E497.1.P57G67   1999
973.7'13'092—dc21   98-13058
[B]   CIP

02 01 00 99 98   5 4 3 2 1

FOR MY PARENTS,

Robert and Frances Gordon

CONTENTS

MAPS AND ILLUSTRATIONS

ACKNOWLEDGMENTS

There are a number of people to thank for helping me complete this book. I thank especially my teachers. At East Granby High School, Pat Metzner first encouraged my early interest in the Civil War. At the College of William and Mary, Robert Engs and Ludwell Johnston supported and directed my initial study of George Pickett. Cam Walker and Judith Ewell were inspiring and important female role models. At the University of Georgia, William S. McFeely, Laura Mason, Miranda Pollard, Peter Hoffer, William Leary, and Jean Friedman each helped me to broaden my assumptions and conceptions of history. John Inscoe gave his sound editorial advice, enthusiasm, and good humor. I thank especially Emory M. Thomas, my dissertation adviser, who continues to provide invaluable guidance and support as a mentor and friend.

Gary Gallagher has encouraged me and my work on Pickett since I first pitched the idea to him in an elevator at an SHA meeting. He read this manuscript more than once with his careful and critical eye and improved the final product immensely.

Other scholars have critiqued various parts of this book and made it better. These include Gaines Foster, Steven H. Newton, Steven Woodworth, Carol Bleser, and Eugene Genovese. Peter S. Carmichael, John Y. Simon, Catherine Clinton, Richard McMurry, Thomas Dyer, Shirley Leckie, William Piston, Robert Krick, Carol Reardon, R. E. Stivers, Jeff Dygart, Steve Hoffman, Mart Stewart, Gil Hill, Martha Boltz, and Rand Jimerson each contributed additional support to me and this project.

I remain in debt to friends and classmates from my years at Georgia. These include: Elisabeth Hughes, Karin Zipf, Jonathan Sarris, Mark Clark, Brian Wills, Keith Bohannon, Jill Severn, Chuck Barber, Amy Forbes, Liz Walsh, Mary Hershburger, Jenny Lund Smith, and Frank Byrne.

Michael Vouri of the San Juan Island National Historical Park generously opened his private collection of notes and books to me, answered many questions, and shared his own extensive research on George Pickett in the West.

At Murray State University I thank history colleagues Bill Mulligan, Charlotte Beahan, Ken Wolfe, and Dean Joe Cartwright for their encouragement while I revised and completed this book for publication. A Presidential Fellowship from Murray State helped greatly in enabling me to finish important research in the summer of 1996.

I thank Mary Tripp Reed, Kevin Dupre, and Darla Kremer for their friendship, humor, and ability to make Murray seem more like home. I especially thank John Murphy for listening, cooking, critiquing, and generally keeping me well anchored during the final stages of this book.

I owe a special thanks to archivists and librarians who assisted me in my research through the years. These include Michael Meier at the National Archives; Charles F. Bryan, Nelson Lankford, and Frances S. Pollard at the Virginia Historical Society; Guy Swanson, formerly at the Museum of the Confederacy; Gary Lundell at the University of Washington Libraries; and Drew Crooks, formerly at the Washington State Capital Museum. I also wish to thank the staffs of the Manuscript Department, Henry E. Huntington Library; the John Hay Library, Brown University; William R. Perkins Library, Duke University; the Louis Round Wilson Library, University of North Carolina, Chapel Hill; the Manuscript Division, Alderman Library, University of Virginia; the Archives at the Virginia State Library; the New Hampshire Historical Society; Rare Books and Manuscripts Department, Earl Gregg Swem Library, College of William and Mary; Historical Society of Quincy and Adams County, Illinois; Quincy University; the Hargrett Manuscript and Rare Book Library, University of Georgia; the Center for Pacific Northwest Studies at Western Washington University; and the Manuscripts Department, United States Military Academy.

Jill Hungerford, her husband, David, and her parents, Chick and Nancy, have been generous friends and confidants. Scott and Joann Armistead, David and Shirley Armistead, and Bertie and Bill Selvey were gracious hosts during my jaunts to Richmond.

My parents have always had faith in me and my brothers, telling us to follow our dreams. They always said that we could do whatever we put our minds to, and this book shows yet again how right they were.

General
George E.
Pickett

in Life &
Legend

Introduction

A Widow, Her Soldier, and Their Story

LaSalle Corbell was married to Confederate major general George E. Pickett for only twelve of her eighty some odd years. She outlived her husband by five decades, spending much of her widowhood in public as a successful author and lecturer. Appointing herself General Pickett's official military biographer, she became a self-proclaimed authority on the antebellum and wartime South. Her many published books and short stories romantically recalled "dem good ole times" before the war, where all blacks were loyal slaves and all Southern whites were paternalistic planters.[1] She was a favorite at Confederate veteran reunions and battlefield commemorations. Touring a national lecture circuit, the vivacious and animated widow stirred packed audiences with her crowd-pleasing "Battle of Gettysburg." An advertisement for her lecture series attested that LaSalle Pickett was "fitted as no other woman to speak from the life of those heroic hours in the nation's history."[2] Justifying her authorship of *Pickett and His Men*, a combination division history and military biography, she maintained, "My story has been so closely allied with that of Pickett and his division, that it does not seem quite an intrusive interpolation for me to appear in the record of that warrior band." She asked: "How could I tell the story, and the way in which that story was written, and not be part of it?"[3]

How indeed? Civil War historians have tried to tell George Pickett's story without LaSalle and found it immensely difficult. Sallie Corbell seemed always to seep into the narrative. Her fabricated and romanticized tales have become accepted parts of not only the Pickett legend but also Civil War canon. Her adoring portraits of "Her Soldier," the long-haired cavalier honorably leading his men to certain death and glory, linger to this day. Historians and novelists as diverse as William

Faulkner, Michael Shaara, and James McPherson have incorporated the sentimental, sometimes foppish, but always fearless George Pickett into their narratives.[4] Civil War buffs and scholars continue to see General Pickett just as his wife intended: "The epitome of the mythic Southern soldier."[5]

In 1986, Civil War historian Gary Gallagher attempted to exorcise LaSalle's influence from George Pickett's life story and military career. He denounced her not only as author of the published George Pickett letters but also as plagiarizer of Walter Harrison's history of Pickett's division. Gallagher demonstrated convincingly that her *The Heart of a Soldier: As Revealed in the Intimate Letters of General George E. Pickett, C.S.A.*, published in 1913, and Arthur Crew Inman's edited *Soldier of the South: General Pickett's War Letters to His Wife* sounded suspiciously similar to LaSalle's other writings and contained information George could not have known at the time of the letters. Although not the first to suspect LaSalle as the author of the letters, Gallagher has written the most thorough indictment of her. Judging the published letters "worthless as a source on the general's Confederate career," he concluded that LaSalle's desire to inspire readers who honor "courage, loyalty and the love of man for woman" was a dismal failure. Instead of honoring him, Gallagher asserted, the doctored letters "cast a shadow on him that will only be lifted if a cache of genuine letters comes to light."[6]

Recent Pickett biographers Richard Selcer and Edward Longacre generally accept LaSalle's mythmaking role, depicting her as a misguided romantic who was "pretty handy with a pen."[7] Edward Longacre's 1995 popular biography *Leader of the Charge* condemns LaSalle's "hero-worship" and her violation of "the rules that guide the historian." LaSalle Pickett appears in these biographies as an obstacle to getting at the truth—sometimes an entertaining one, but an obstacle nonetheless. Longacre maintains that although "Mrs. Pickett has greatly complicated the efforts of would-be biographers to sift fact from fiction," there remain enough "authentic" sources to allow George to "speak for himself."[8] Yet both of these historians rely heavily on LaSalle Pickett's writings in their works, without providing any thoughtful analysis of her.[9]

LaSalle Pickett seemed abundantly aware of the power her pen and voice wielded, power that defied restrictions of time, space, and traditional gender conventions. But her determination to rewrite the past forces the critical scholar to consider questions of perception and memory and varying versions of the "truth." The infusion into history of postmodernist theory, literary analysis, and other interdisciplinary influences helps, but methodological problems remain for any historian trained to seek out hard evidence.[10]

Civil War history has been informed by a multitude of personal memories. The postwar period witnessed an outpouring of published and unpublished memoirs, and historians routinely rely on them as reliable sources. But as recent scholarship has demonstrated, memory by its very nature is subjective and fluid. Individuals and nations constantly reshape their perception of their past to align it with their present self-image. It is a way to make sense of the present.[11]

LaSalle Pickett wrote at a time when American society was undergoing a profound reconsideration of its national past. Victorians became adept at mythmaking, searching past lives and events not for cold "facts" but for didactic lessons that could instruct present and future generations. Public memory of the antebellum South and the Civil War focused on noble causes and honorable actions—old-fashioned virtues that seemed increasingly lacking in a rapidly modernizing world.[12]

LaSalle Pickett's writings both affected and reflected this change in public memory. And, while not always "factual," her writings give significant insight into the private dynamics of her marriage. She revealed as much about herself, her husband, and the time in which they lived as she hid. An early review of her first book, *Pickett and His Men*, recognized her worth: "As a contribution to the historical literature of the South," the reviewer wrote, "the work possesses little value." It was the amazing and passionate love story that impressed him: "The author has pictured as no other could have done the home life and the home love of one of the Confederacy's greatest leaders, and the book has all the interest of a beautiful, pathetic romance, around which glows the halo of truth."[13]

Despite LaSalle's efforts, the Picketts were no angels. A careful and critical study of their lives shows two individuals who faltered when faced with disturbing change, war, and defeat. Failure and disappointment distinguished George Pickett's military career more than victory. Fate happened to choose his Virginia division to spearhead the most famous failed frontal assault in American military history: Pickett's Charge at Gettysburg. He gained immortality but never lost his insecurities or his bitterness.

Yet the Picketts' shared and separate stories of war, defeat, and exile are compelling human sagas, rife with irony, tension, and tarnished ideals. Both husband and wife were products of the declining nineteenth-century Virginia planter elite, and both struggled to live up to the antebellum South's societal, cultural, and gender expectations. George tried all his life to be a good son, a courageous soldier, and a devoted husband. There seemed to be a constant fight within him between feminine and masculine traits and self-discipline and self-indulgence. He appeared devoted to women he loved: his ailing mother, his spinster aunts, and each of his three wives. These women all shaped and affected his personality, his sense of self, and his masculinity.

LaSalle Pickett's gender limited her options as an intelligent and ambitious young white woman. She transferred her hopes and ideals to her husband, George, who fell far short of her high expectations. During their marriage, she became a mirror into which George could project his fears and his hopes; through her eyes he became the man he always wanted to be. After his death, she made those images real through her short stories, books, and public lectures. She recast George as the courageous Confederate hero and ideal man, and herself as the loyal, submissive wife and elite Southern white lady.

Although this study explores questions of cultural and social identity and change, war and the military are central to it. From the age of seventeen, George Pickett looked to the army's all-male subculture, and the exhilaration of battle, for his personal identity. He found that the large-scale violence of war could complicate as much as clarify, but he knew of no other place to find answers and direction. Ironically, the Civil War destroyed his sense of place, forced him to return to the slaveholding South he had escaped, made his former comrades his enemy, and blurred the lines that he believed determined the "rules of war." He found himself accused of the very behavior he thought only the hated enemy capable of practicing: uncivilized warfare. LaSalle Corbell also discovered that war and marriage to a soldier changed her identity and gave her life different purpose and direction. In fantasy and in reality she was at the forefront of battle, assuming an active role in war rather than standing passively on the sidelines. Still, the horrors of that war left permanent scars, no matter how hard she tried publicly to celebrate the past.

Just as there were constant tensions in the Picketts' lives, there are tensions in this narrative between fact and fiction, image and reality. George and LaSalle Pickett thrived on the public arena, conscious of what others thought of their actions and behavior. Glimpses of their private selves are difficult to find, particularly since LaSalle made such special efforts to rewrite their past. In addition, a paucity of personal papers and the present-day Pickett family's stubborn refusal to cooperate with researchers have made conventional historical research highly problematic. There is even a chance that a collection of Pickett manuscripts at Brown University is fraudulent—perhaps fakes LaSalle created to promote the authenticity of those she published. This book sifts through the imagery, myths, and fragmented pieces of conventional evidence to present a convincing and consistent portrait of the Picketts. To be sure, there remain holes in the narrative, but where the historical record is silent, the author attempts to place George and LaSalle within the larger cultural and social milieus from which they came.[14]

This study is meant to be a retrospective reconstruction of two lives, united by love and war. LaSalle's inclusion in the text may seem at times awkward and distracting, her attempts at rewriting history frustrating. Her presence throughout the narrative is meant to emphasize and reflect the lasting influence she had on her husband's memory. As the reader will readily perceive, no one could satisfactorily write about either George Pickett or LaSalle Corbell without including the other; their identities were too entangled to do otherwise.

CHAPTER 1

Virginia, Illinois, and West Point, 1825–1846

Perilous Years

On August 31, 1837, Andrew Johnston wrote a long and rambling letter to his sister, Mary Johnston Pickett. Johnston, a native Virginian, had taken up residency in Quincy, Illinois, to practice law. He had only recently arrived there and had much to tell his sister back home in Richmond. Johnston discussed family matters, especially expressing concern for his sister's twelve-year-old son, George. "He [is] at an age," Johnston stated, "when his excellent disposition is to be confirmed or altered, perhaps for life." Andrew maintained that adolescence was a crucial time for southern boys to develop their independence and personal management. He closed his letter with the hope that his nephew "will pass with honor to himself & joy to all of us through these perilous years."[1] George spent the rest of his life trying to fulfill these expectations.

George Edward Pickett was born into Virginia's elite on January 25, 1825. His parents and grandparents were successful slaveholding merchants and farmers who traced their ancestry in Virginia to the seventeenth century. In 1814, George's grandfather Pickett purchased Turkey Island Plantation, twelve miles southeast of Richmond on the James River. Turkey Island quickly became a bustling farm and family home boasting a large brick mansion, numerous slave quarters, and 1,000 acres of land. Neighbors included several of the "first families" of Virginia: the Harrisons at Brandon, the Byrds at Westover, and the Carters at Shirley Plantation.[2]

As members of Virginia's ruling elite, the Picketts no doubt shared the dominant proslavery ideology of the antebellum South. They were self-conscious of their social status, protective of family honor, and paternalistic toward their many slaves. But as residents of the economically troubled tidewater region, George's parents were also probably anxious about the future of slavery and large-scale farming. By the 1830s, eastern Virginia was in transition, suffering from vast national and local change. An economic depression that swept the region soon after the War of 1812 showed no sign of abating twenty-five years later. Visitors often remarked on the bleak farming conditions, and slaveholders began to debate the feasibility of slavery. National expansion of a market economy, increased white male suffrage, soil depletion, and fresh land in the West made tidewater planter families like the Picketts more and more uncertain of their economic and political power. Slavery and the slaveholding aristocracy became problematic institutions in the growing republic.[3]

By the time George entered adolescence, it is not surprising that his family would worry about his future. His father, Robert, began to transfer energy and money away from tobacco farming to other economic endeavors. At one point he considered selling Turkey Island and joining family in the new slave state of Missouri. Instead, Robert remained in eastern Virginia and entered the coal business. He reduced his number of slaves by nearly half and took boarders at his second family home in Richmond. When George reached manhood, he could no longer rely on life as a planter.[4]

Being a white elite male in the antebellum South meant more than simply finding a viable occupation; it meant upholding strictly defined gender, class, and racial codes of behavior. Southern honor required men of George's race and class to display personal worth and self-mastery publicly, thereby reinforcing and demonstrating their power. A careful mix of independence and discipline was crucial toward maintaining the patriarchy that ruled the slaveholding South. Any crack in this veneer of racial, class, and gender control could bring down the whole social structure.[5]

As a boy, George showed few signs of model southern manhood. He could be fiercely independent but possessed little of the self-discipline or self-mastery that his class and status required. He was talkative and boisterous with a ready laugh and a melodious voice. He loved to hunt, sing, and dance. Gregarious and flirtatious, he was charming not only to his spinster aunts but also to a large number of male and female friends. His mother, Mary, called him indolent, and he certainly was, preferring play over work. Worn by poor health and the premature death of five other children, Mary became apprehensive about these perceived flaws in her son's character. She fretted over his lack of self-reliance and discipline, direction and ambition. She wondered if he would ever mature into a respectable gentleman.[6]

Robert and Mary tried to do all they could to ensure that George would make it safely through adolescence. From 1837 to 1839, they sent him to one of Richmond's most prestigious and oldest male academies. Founded in 1803, Richmond Academy offered college preparation courses in English, classics, and mathematics. Yet, even enrolled at such an auspicious institution, George was restless. While at Richmond Academy, he had his first taste of military life. The school organized students into corps of cadets and taught drill exercises and military tactics. George's private education proved short-lived; after only two years, the Picketts apparently could no longer afford the school's high tuition. His friends would later miss their mischievous classmate who reveled in disobedient and disrespectful behavior.[7]

In the winter of 1839–40, Robert and Mary sent George away to live with his uncle Andrew. Mary was pregnant again, and Robert's troublesome plantation and slaves took more and more of his time and attention. They probably hoped Andrew could serve as surrogate father and teacher to their son, especially if George could no longer enjoy the benefits of private schooling. They no doubt hoped that someone like Andrew could instill the boy with purpose and direction and a better work ethic. George boarded a steamer in March 1840 to embark upon a new stage in his life. He would not return to live permanently in Virginia for another twenty-five years.[8]

In many ways, Andrew Johnston embodied the new democratic spirit sweeping the nation. Twenty-seven and ambitious, he arrived in Quincy, Illinois, in 1837 and soon purchased a tract of land in the city. He joined a local law firm and advertised his services in a Richmond newspaper to encourage others to follow his example and buy Illinois property. He quickly made influential friends and became active in local politics. He served as Quincy's treasurer, joined the town's Whig Party and gained appointment on the library's board of directors. In 1838, Johnston became coeditor of the *Quincy Whig*, along with Connecticut native Nehemiah Bushnell. Far from his family's planter connections and influence,

Johnston made a name for himself in just three short years. Robert and Mary Pickett could not help but admire Andrew's enterprise and determination, traits that seemed increasingly important in a changing world, and traits George so badly lacked. Even though he was a native southerner, Andrew had little trouble fitting into Quincy's nonslaveholding society.[9]

In a moment of desperation, Mary confessed to her son that she wished they could give up the cumbersome Virginia plantation and slaves and "come to your Uncle's new country" to begin again. To struggling planters, who faced economic, social, and political decline, opportunities seemed to abound in new western states like Illinois.[10]

Robert and Mary Pickett wrote their son often.[11] They filled long letters with Richmond gossip, family affairs, and constant reminders of why George was in Quincy. Pickett's family never stated exactly what George did to cause such concern. Indeed, their letters concentrated instead on moral advice and didactic sermons. Their sheer number and emphasis on George's character is significant. "I feel very well convinced," George's father wrote, "that if you would only attend to the advice given to you and industrious examples set you by your uncle you cannot prove otherwise than a respectable member of society, honored and loved by all."[12] Robert urged industry and steadfastness to his wayward son, noting that there were a "number of instances of young men of the best families, throwing away their time, their fortune, their health, their honor, their all; and merely from want of proper arrangement of things in their youth." George must shun waste and idleness and look upon Andrew as an example to admire and emulate.[13] Aunt Olivia agreed and urged her nephew to fight the "indolence of disposition which, dear George, has always been your greatest fault."[14] He was to study hard, read his Bible regularly, attend church, and think seriously about his future.[15]

These letters expressed parental concern and love, but they must have made George feel self-conscious of his station in life and aware of his inability to live up to his family's expectations. Sophia Johnston told her nephew that the rest of the family was "all lost," but upon him they placed high hopes.[16] George appeared to chafe under these pressures, unwilling to conform to societal and familial expectations thrust upon him. He clung tenaciously to his former behavior during his months in

Quincy: dancing, hunting, and smoking, with little concern for serious study or occupation.[17] He had apparently already internalized aspirations of the privileged and powerful. Caught in a time of economic, social, and political stress, George seemed unwilling to face challenges of an uncertain future. He searched much of his life for the acceptance, approval, and stability absent from his younger years.

In his apparent quest for acceptance, George devoted his energy toward entertainment and an active social life. He had little trouble making friends and courting young ladies in Quincy. He also joined a local theater group that regularly produced plays for the community. A member of the "Young Thespians" later claimed that George had a particular liking and ability for female parts. There is no additional evidence to confirm that he enjoyed playing women's roles, but if he did, this may have been a form of protest for someone who excelled at roles different from those expected of him by his family and society.[18]

George was less successful acting the part of an attorney. Sometime during his stay in Quincy he began to study law with his uncle. His mother expressed her relief; she hoped that at least he was applying his mind.[19] But he could not hide his lack of interest in studying for the bar.

In December 1840, Robert Pickett hinted at securing his son an appointment to the United States Military Academy. Robert and Mary assured George that they would not force him into a career path he did not want to follow. Still, he had to make a decision. In January 1841 he would be sixteen, and the careless days of youth were fast coming to an end. His aunt wrote: "In five years you will be a man, and how much you have to learn in that time."[20]

Robert Pickett was not entirely convinced his son's purpose was to be a soldier. He had some serious doubts about the life of a professional army officer. His brother-in-law John Symington's military career hardly seemed appealing: "It really is a hard case to be knocked about from piller [sic] to post in this way. Scarcely is he fixed at one place before he has to take up a line of march in another."[21] George did not seem to need more uncertainty in his life.

In fact, the military was one of the few career options open to George Pickett. Southerners considered military service comparable in prestige to planting, medicine, or law. Robert himself was a colonel in the local militia, as was Andrew. Such a career would certainly bring no dishonor to the family name; it could even bolster honor.[22] As early as March of 1840, Sophia Johnston hoped her nephew would grow taller, because "a soldier should be tall, at least he should look [tall] as much as possible." She added, "I shall be proud of my nephew Pickett, not a militia captain but a real one."[23]

The "real" military George was about to join held a precarious place in antebellum American society. Civilians' views toward soldiers were full of contradictions. Fear of a large standing professional army dated to the colonial experience. Americans had put their trust in the militia system since the Revolution, believing that the best soldier was a semi-civilian. From its founding in 1802, the United States Military Academy had undergone constant public scrutiny. The egalitarianism of the 1830s and 1840s stirred a new wave of antimilitarism, and Americans feared and resented a publicly funded academy that trained professional army officers.[24]

Coexisting with the fear of a standing army and a military academy was a marked reverence toward soldiers and martial combat. Anxieties about the fate of the new republic already found an outlet in the celebration of an ostensibly simpler and more idyllic past. Sir Walter Scott's stories of medieval knights resonated among literate men and women North and South. Americans celebrated the Middle Ages as a time of strong traditional values and heroic combat. Such romanticism became closely linked to a mythical cult of martial chivalry where men fought bravely for ideals and principle. To mid-nineteenth-century Americans, war was an opportunity to display and test individual and national character. Northerners and southerners elected soldiers to public offices, showed a fondness for military titles, read and told tales of great warriors, and sent their sons to military academies. They enjoyed dress parades and celebrated militia training days as holidays and social occasions.[25]

Reverence for the military seemed even greater in the South. The hierarchy that divided southerners by race, class, and gender relied on controlled violence. Young white men learned early to shoot and fight, and proximity to the frontier further encouraged male admiration of violence and arms.[26]

Perhaps it is not so strange that a nation anxious about its capitalistic and democratic tendencies would have such ambivalent feelings toward its military. French observer Alexis de Tocqueville predicted that Americans would shun war because it was too costly to personal property. Yet war reinforced a nation's virility and power. Military success provided proof of strength and conviction for a people concerned with a weak or corrupt national character. Expressions of patriotism could not be separated from an almost giddy martial spirit, especially in times of war. When Tocqueville toured the United States in the early 1830s, he exclaimed: "How can one deny the incredible influence military glory has over a nation's spirit?"[27]

Military leaders responded to this mix of reverence and fear by professionalizing the armed forces. Superintendents at the United States Military Academy began to fashion the school after European models. Ambitious and upwardly mobile young men could look to the military as a career; and an elite officer corps evolved.[28] In the process, a military subculture developed, further separating professional soldiers from civilians in American society. By the 1840s, a combination of bureaucratization, civilian attitudes, and soldier estrangement made the United States Military Academy an effective institution of military socialization. The West Point experience inspired loyalty, created codes of behavior, and fostered a distinctive military subculture in American society. To be a West Point graduate and professional army officer was to be different from the rest of antebellum Americans, North or South.[29]

Despite the ambiguous and amorphous place the military held in American society, the army offered much to young men like George Pickett. Graduates gained a free education, income, professional purpose, and direction. The military also affirmed their masculinity. Being a soldier meant being a man: self-reliant and disciplined, dominant and aggressive. While the world changed around them, George Pickett and his classmates could find haven and reassurance in the conformist, hierarchical, all-male army.[30]

Before he could commence his military experience, George required a congressional appointment. Throughout the summer of 1841, Andrew Johnston worked his political connections to secure an appointment for his nephew. Congressmen often used such nominations to the academy as rewards to faithful constituents. Johnston's newspaper had been a vocal supporter of John T. Stuart, a Whig member of the House of Representatives. On August 19, 1841, he wrote Stuart that he and Captain

Symington understood their nephew's name to be "first upon the list of applications—that a vacancy at West Point from your district would make the nomination in his favor." Johnston, wanting more concrete assurance, added, "I write at present therefore to enquire whether we may certainly look for his appointment in next February."[31]

If the appointment was indeed imminent, George's parents faced a dilemma. They had not seen their son in two years and might not see him for several more while he attended the academy. Earlier that summer, Robert Pickett had assured George, "We all wish to see you very much, and look forward to the time of your return with great pleasure."[32] George's parents wanted him home for the winter, but as Johnston explained to Congressman Stuart, they were "willing to forgo [sic] that pleasure if his leaving this district would at all interfere with the nomination and appointment."[33] Existing records fail to tell anything about George's preference. No doubt he had mixed feelings: missing his family and friends but dreading continued reminders of his need to improve his character and habits.[34]

Evidently, Stuart assured the Picketts that their son's visit home would not jeopardize his nomination. George journeyed to Richmond in mid-February with stern warnings from his mother to be careful of a measles epidemic. Despite her anxiety about his health, she could not contain her excitement. He had a new brother whom he had never seen. Mary wrote: "I cannot tell you how I feel at the hope of seeing you, and presenting your dear little wild brother to you."[35]

By April, George Pickett received his "conditional appointment" to the United States Military Academy.[36] Still, nomination to West Point did not ensure acceptance, and Pickett first had to pass the entrance examinations. P. T. Turnley, a fellow nominee, recalled that candidates had to "read and write a correct and legible hand, understand the four grand rules of arithmetic, vulgar and decimal fractions, simple compound fractions, etc." He also remembered that there were great regional differences among the educational backgrounds of West Point nominees. Young men from the East, especially from cities, seemed better prepared than their classmates from the South and West.[37] Pickett had no difficulty fulfilling the requirements; apparently he had learned something during his years at private school and under his uncle's tutelage. He satisfactorily passed the examination and entered West Point's class of 1846. At the age of seventeen, George Pickett's military career had officially begun.

George was one of 116 young men to enter West Point during the summer of 1842. Four years later, only 48 of these men marched across the field at graduation ceremonies. The academy's "strict standards of scholarship and discipline" discouraged many.[38] Pickett's cousin Henry Heth remembered his own years at West Point as "abominable."[39] Dabney H. Maury, who was in the same class as Pickett, described his experience at the academy as "the only unhappy years of a very happy life."[40]

Pickett did not comment directly on his own West Point experience. His undistinguished academic record and accumulation of demerits spoke for themselves. Pickett was no scholar and, at this early stage, not much of a soldier. While Robert E. Lee, referred to as a "paragon among cadets," graduated without a single demerit, George Pickett earned an average of 165 demerits each year.[41] The troubling character traits his parents tried so hard to correct lingered. Pickett spent four long years bucking the system at West Point and indirectly resisting his family's expectations. A classmate explained, "George E. Pickett was a jolly good fellow with fine natural gifts sadly neglected."[42] By the end of his final year, he was just five demerits short of expulsion.[43]

Self-discipline continued to elude George. Throughout his four years, he was late repeatedly and caught "visiting" after midnight. His first demerit came within only three days of his arrival at West Point; he was late for roll call. He later earned demerits for using profane language, marching out of step, and other such "highly unmilitary conduct." He threw bread at dinner, wore a checkered shirt, chewed tobacco, and often wore his hair too long. On Christmas Day 1843, Pickett engaged in "highly unsoldierlike conduct walking out on the parade grounds, smoking tobacco and improperly dressed." He twice visited the hotel without permission and at least once wandered down to the steamboat landing.[44]

The formal delinquency register did not record Pickett's frequent visits to Benny Havens, the notorious tavern located temptingly close to West Point. The academy forbade drinking, and had he been caught at the tavern, even the most powerful family connections and political pressure could not have saved Pickett from dismissal. Two of Pickett's classmates recalled vividly his love of drink. William Gardner remembered: "[Pickett] was a devoted and constant patron of Benny Havens."[45]

Late one night, P. T. Turnley found George drunk and lying in a snow-drift. Turnley rescued his inebriated classmate from frostbite, and worse, certain expulsion.[46]

Pickett's academic performance was little better. During his first year he did well in French, standing 12 out of 83, but in mathematics he ranked below average: 49 out of 83. He finished the year ranked at number 218 out of an entire cadet corps of 223. Throughout the next three years, Pickett continued to slip in his studies. Varied courses in drawing, chemistry, English grammar, philosophy, engineering, artillery, and infantry tactics made little difference to him. By his fourth year he ranked at the bottom in every subject. George Pickett graduated from West Point fifty-ninth in a class of fifty-nine. Fellow cadet William Gardner characterized Pickett as someone who had "no ambition for class standing and wanted to do only enough study to secure graduation."[47]

At West Point, George scoffed at the self-discipline and study habits his parents lectured him about. In the fall of 1843, Andrew confessed, "I have been disappointed, I acknowledge, in not finding his old habits more corrected than they are." Despite George's persistent indolence and mischievous behavior, Andrew maintained, "His heart is in the right place and his morality and faith untainted."[48]

Perhaps George had grown uneasy under the pressure of familial and social expectations. The shifting social and economic changes that forced his father to curtail planting and prompted other family members to leave Virginia had to have left an impression him. He probably worried about his own place in society. The army provided him with something his loving family could not: a sense of belonging and place. Despite his numerous demerits and questionable academic performance, Pickett stopped short of expulsion. Failure most assuredly would have brought humiliation to himself and his family.[49] Once he successfully graduated and became an officer, this sense of identity and place within the army only grew stronger.

Pickett was not alone in making the army his foster home and family. The military's all-male subculture redefined each cadet's identity, refashioning his sense of self in American society. The academy's location in upstate New York was removed from civilian, and especially female, contact and added to the academy's isolation. West Point sought to reshape cadets by replacing their prior habits with new behavior based on strict discipline and rigid conformity. Living quarters were sparse, food bland, and regulations strict. By the fourth year, this unique milieu and "monastic isolation" created a shared, even elitist, "mystique" among cadets. Men from diverse regional and social backgrounds found prior allegiances weakened and former identities recast. Cadets felt primary loyalty to the academy, to the army, and to each other.[50]

In such an environment George Pickett did not lose his old habits and ways; if anything, they became more apparent. But the military's structure gave Pickett the equilibrium he so sorely lacked. The army tempered but did not entirely extinguish his tendency toward excess or display. He had clearer boundaries for behavior and a sense of place, developing an allegiance to the army seemingly stronger than the one to his family. Increasingly, his inner sense of self appeared to come from the outer workings of the U.S. Army.[51]

Developing new concepts of identity and purpose were West Point's most important lessons for Pickett. Even if he had concentrated on his studies, he would have learned little about the realities of soldiering at West Point. In fact, the academy failed to give cadets much practical or relevant training as officers. West Point's curriculum emphasized engineering and mathematics with little time spent on ethics, history, international law, or government. Faculty ignored purely military subjects and gave scant attention to the type of warfare most officers would soon face: fighting Native Americans. Raw experience would prove a better teacher than four years at the Point.[52]

As graduation loomed, cadets anticipated their appointments to the army's various branches. Individuals could express a preference, but the more prestigious branches of engineering, ordinance, and artillery were reserved for higher ranking candidates. Pickett's poor standing reduced his choices to three: mounted riflemen, infantry, or dragoons. He opted for the dragoons or mounted riflemen. A fellow West Pointer remarked of the dragoons: "A good square seat in the saddle was deemed of more importance than brains." Perhaps for Pickett the image of the mounted soldier had more appeal than the unglamorous infantryman.[53]

Pickett decided to test his limits. Although he seemed to resent continual family pressures, he turned to a family member for help. Just two weeks before his graduation, Elizabeth Symington wrote directly to the Secretary of War on her nephew's behalf. She notified the secretary that

Pickett's low "standing in class" would place him "either in the infantry or dragoons." She stressed that he preferred the dragoons or the mounted riflemen. Elizabeth hastened to add that, "from his active enterprising character" and his skilled horsemanship, "I question not he would prove useful in that situation."[54] The letter made no difference. George Edward Pickett was destined for the infantry.

CHAPTER 2

Mexico, 1846–1848
Streams of Heroes

As George Pickett neared the end of his West Point experience, war was on the horizon in Mexico. During the spring of 1846, President James K. Polk ordered Brig. Gen. Zachary Taylor and an "Army of Occupation" north of the Rio Grande River into land claimed by both countries. Pursuing a policy of overt expansionism, Polk sought a confrontation and hoped Mexico would respond belligerently to the presence of armed American troops. Clandestine attempts at negotiating had already failed, and the Mexicans refused to sell large tracts of territory to the land-hungry Americans. Polk only awaited an excuse to declare war formally on the Mexicans.

As the crisis unfolded, Pickett and his classmates feared they would miss out on this grand opportunity to prove themselves as officers and as men. By graduation in June, Taylor's army had already fought and won the battles of Palo Alto and Resaca de la Palma. The victorious U.S. troops despised their foes as both Roman Catholics and ethnic inferiors. It seemed divinely ordered that the superior Americans would win—but what if that happened before the USMA class of 1846 even arrived on the scene?[1]

After graduation, Pickett left the academy and headed home to Virginia for summer furlough, hoping soon to receive his wartime assignment. By late July 1846, however, his furlough was winding down and he had yet to hear from the War Department. When he received a copy of the *Washington Union* containing notice of his assignment to the 8th U.S. Infantry, his worry turned to panic. Without written orders directly from the government, he did not know where to go or what to do. On July 31, Pickett anxiously notified Washington, asking if his "orders might have been forwarded to Illinois from which state I received my appointment as a cadet," rather than to his residence in Virginia. He closed, "I shall be much obliged to learn from you, if it is so, in order that I may write on for them immediately and hand in my acceptance as quickly as possible."[2]

That same day, Pickett's uncle Andrew Johnston wrote to the War Department about receiving a package in Quincy addressed to his nephew. Johnston felt at liberty to open the package and quickly realized the importance of its contents. Inside were George's appointment, instructions for duty, and his official oath as an officer of the U.S. Army. Johnston explained to the secretary of war that his nephew "was appointed from this district but his parents reside in Richmond, Virginia, from which place all the reports from West Point have been sent where he is now on furlough as I understand from private letters."[3]

Somehow the confusion was resolved, Pickett took his oath, and proceeded to Matamoras, Mexico, where he was to join his regiment.[4] Bad luck, however, again intervened, and he did not arrive until November 9, 1846, a full two months late. Pickett's commanding officer, Col. J. D. Clark, was not pleased and demanded a written explanation for the young lieutenant's tardiness. Pickett submitted a rambling, defensive excuse, unwilling to accept any personal blame for his actions. He pointed to broken steamers, low water levels, and a variety of additional mishaps and obstacles. Pickett closed his convoluted narration with the "hope the above will prove satisfactory."[5] George Pickett's military career had begun, not with a dramatic bang but with a whimper. Despite his future wife LaSalle's later insistence, there were no early signs that Second Lieutenant Pickett was destined for military greatness.

While Pickett wandered southward, President Polk and his military advisers worked on a new strategy. Zachary Taylor's army had won another battle at Monterrey, but it was becoming obvious that his campaign in northern Mexico would not achieve a decisive victory. Beaten but not broken, the Mexicans refused to discuss peace. President Polk suggested attacking Mexico's chief seaport town of Vera Cruz and marching overland directly toward Mexico City. By October 1847, Maj. Gen. Winfield Scott had submitted an extensive plan for the amphibious expedition and the 270-mile inland march to the capital. Polk, the Democrat, distrusted the ambitions of Scott, the Whig. The president had no option but to give Scott, the ranking general in his army, authority to undertake the invasion. All that winter, Scott organized and concentrated men and supplies on the Island of Lobos. He hoped to open the campaign early in the new year.[6]

Meanwhile, Pickett had his first taste of army life outside the protective walls of the academy. As part of Scott's army, he and his fellow junior officers endured the monotony of drill and more drill. For many older officers, who had spent recent years at small posts on the frontier with no opportunity to train anything larger than a company, these exercises were important. To Pickett, fresh from West Point and much drill and ceremony, this was hardly the excitement he expected. Initially, he found military life dull and monotonous—little more than tiring marches and raw recruits. Still, an undeniable undercurrent of anticipation pervaded the daily routine. Men knew that the army was preparing for a large-scale campaign.[7]

In late January 1847, Pickett's division was en route to the Island of Lobos. He wrote a hasty letter to his aunt recounting his constant marching and drilling, and complained of "exaggerated reports" of enemy attacks. "We have the delectable pleasure," he observed sarcastically, "of drilling [fresh recruits] . . . four times a day besides a dress parade." He expressed the growing contempt regular officers felt toward volunteer officers, calling them "*mustang* generals" and asserting that even Mexicans "have the greatest dread and hatred for 'los voluntarios' who have been guilty of the most disgraceful conduct in the treatment of the inhabitants."[8]

Volunteer soldiers were, in fact, often undisciplined in camp, unreliable in battle, and especially ruthless toward Mexican and Indian civilians. Still, most Americans, including President Polk, held to the belief that the best soldier was an untrained civilian who would heroically fight for his country. Civilian distrust of professional soldiers and the reckless behavior of the volunteers strengthened the bond among career officers and provoked in them a sense of isolation from the rest of American society. Pickett and his West Point classmates saw themselves as a new generation of professionals, politically neutral, trained and disciplined in the science of war. Mexico was their opportunity to display their skills.[9]

Pickett probably also felt exhilaration at being stationed in a foreign land. He had traveled far from his native Virginia and the worried eyes of his family. The terrain of Mexico was rugged, barren, wild, tropical, and like nothing he had ever seen. As he journeyed deeper into the countryside, he found the inhabitants "more civilized" than he expected and the women "prettier, more of the Castillian blood."[10] This exotic setting, combined with the prospect of imminent combat, must have fueled his imagination and increased his nervous anticipation. To a romantic young man like Pickett, well versed in tales of chivalric knights, the war became a modern-day fairy tale. He and his comrades could play roles of gallant knights engaged in mortal combat for glory and honor.[11] The delay must have seemed unbearable as weeks turned to months.

While Pickett and his fellow soldiers longed for battle, logistical problems plagued the American high command, from the acquisition of wagons and food to the need to send home an excess of unprepared volunteers. Finally, on March 9, 1847, General Scott launched his invasion, and Americans splashed ashore to invest Vera Cruz. It was a beautiful springlike day, and army bands played "The Star Spangled Banner" as troops planted the American flag on the sandy dunes of Collado Beach, three miles below Vera Cruz. By 11:00 P.M., over 8,000 U.S. soldiers reached the beach with little or no opposition. For three days Scott's men worked their way northward through hills and forests to arrive on the inland side of Vera Cruz. Winfield Scott predicted, "The whole army is full of zeal and confidence, and cannot fail to acquire distinction in the impending operations."[12] American artillery pounded away at the seaport town, and the siege of Vera Cruz began. The city formally surrendered to Scott's invading army on March 29, 1847.[13]

George Pickett experienced his "baptism of fire" at Vera Cruz. His division, commanded by Brig. Gen. William J. Worth, was among the first arrivals at Collado Beach. Worth's was also the first division to march triumphantly into the fallen city of Vera Cruz on March 29. The siege produced few American casualties, and Pickett had not engaged in fierce combat. Yet, already a complete American victory seemed imminent.[14]

Scott chose the city of Jalapa as the next target for his advance inland toward the enemy's capital. Seventy-four miles long, the route from Vera Cruz to Jalapa promised food and forage for men and animals. The highway wound northwest from the coast through the Sierra Madres, far above yellow fever–infested lowlands.

Scott did not realize that Mexican general and president Antonio López de Santa Anna was quickly concentrating troops at Jalapa. Santa

Anna selected Cerro Gordo, a hilly position just off the road to Jalapa, as the place to meet the Americans. He arranged his 12,000 men and many guns along several rises below the village of Cerro Gordo. The Mexican leader confidently expected to halt and destroy the Americans in toto. The Mexican army, however, was hardly in the best condition to accomplish such a feat. Beset by sickness, disaffection, dehydration, and poor training, Santa Anna's forces threatened to crumble at the very hint of formidable opposition.[15]

Reconnaissance missions probed the fortified Mexican position at Cerro Gordo and engineer Capt. Robert E. Lee discovered a route around the enemy's left flank. By April 17, Scott had formulated a plan. Sending a division on the path Lee uncovered, Scott ordered coordinated assaults all along the enemy's works. Included in the attack was the steeply sloped El Telégrafo hill rising some 600 or 700 feet from ground level. If everything went as planned, Scott hoped to turn the Mexican lines by midmorning.[16]

Scott's battle plan for Cerro Gordo called for concentrated frontal attacks by the infantry on the Mexican entrenchments. The tactics and strategy used in the Mexican War revolved around infantrymen armed with muskets and bayonets advancing in close order on the enemy's position. Since muskets were unreliable, limited in range, and awkward to handle, it was important to concentrate infantry fire on a specific target. Intense and directed musket fire could be lethal.[17]

At Cerro Gordo, Scott's men marched column by column toward the Mexican works, firing in careful concentration. Troops quickly ascended the arduous El Telégrafo hill, only once stopping to catch their breath. Within a few yards of the Mexican guns, American soldiers fixed bayonets and charged. Hand-to-hand combat ensued, and the demoralized Mexicans retreated with little resistance. By 10:00 A.M., Santa Anna's defenses began shattering. By afternoon, his army no longer existed as an organized entity.[18]

Pickett was with Worth's division as it followed in close pursuit of the retreating foe.[19] His unit stopped twelve miles beyond Jalapa to take Fort San Carlos de Perote and the booty within. Inside the fortress, General Worth announced, were "the fruits of victory at Cerro Gordo," including American prisoners, munitions, and two Mexican generals.[20] Winfield Scott later wrote the secretary of war that the American success was so complete over the Mexicans that "we are quite embarrassed with the results of victory—prisoners of war, heavy ordinance, field batteries, small arms and accouterments."[21] Like Vera Cruz, Cerro Gordo was an overwhelming American victory with relatively few casualties.[22]

In May 1847, Worth's division moved on to Puebla, seventy-five miles from Mexico City. The rest of Scott's army soon arrived at the village to wait three long months for reinforcements. After the exciting victories at Vera Cruz and Cerro Gordo, daily military routines probably seemed especially tedious. Days were hot and long, and few officers had money for entertainment or diversions. West Point classmate William Gardner remembered meeting Pickett on the streets of Puebla one afternoon in May 1847. Combat had not diminished Pickett's love of a good time and a stiff drink. He revealed a fifty-cent piece and invited Gardner to join him for a mint julep at a nearby bar. Thirsty and empty-handed officers quickly surrounded the two men when they entered the bar. Gardner admitted that he felt guilty realizing that juleps cost twenty-five cents each. In a moment that recalled his days on the Quincy stage, Pickett rapped for attention and loudly announced, "Fellows, I have asked Gardner to take a drink, and I am simply bound to have one myself. . . . Now if anyone can squeeze any more liquor out of that coin," he declared, throwing the fifty-cent piece on the table, "let him step up and imbibe." The two men drank unmolested by the crowd of onlookers.[23]

Notwithstanding the months of relative inactivity, Pickett discovered military life to be pleasant and his relationship with fellow officers gratifying. West Point initiated his exposure to the military subculture, and Mexico solidified it. He strengthened friendships and began to feel he had a place in the army. There was ample time for socializing and entertainment without the rigid regulations of the academy. Just when Pickett probably felt especially comfortable among the men and officers of the 8th U.S. Infantry, however, in July 1847, he received a transfer to the 7th U.S. Infantry. Perhaps the thought of going into battle with strangers troubled him. He and classmate Samuel B. Maxey, who was transferred from the 7th to the 8th U.S. Infantry, protested the move. They maintained their desire "to remain in the Regiments with which we have been serving." The army granted the junior officers' requests.[24]

In August 1847, long-awaited reinforcements arrived and Scott's army resumed its march toward Mexico City. Facing formidable marshes, lakes, and volcanic rock formations, the Americans sought to find an accessible route to the well-fortified capital. On August 19, at the battle of Contreras, Mexicans attempted to halt Scott's efforts to open a road through a five-mile-wide rugged lava field known as the Pedregal. Darkness halted plans to turn the Mexican flank, but early the next day, Americans successfully attacked the enemy position, causing the Mexicans to retreat northward toward Churubusco. Scott followed in pursuit.[25]

Pickett participated little in the battle of Contreras, but from San Antonio, his brigade cut a tortuous path through the lava fields to stop the fleeing Mexicans. One officer described the landscape as "covered with fragments of volcanic rocks, so broken and so thick as to present nowhere a smooth or level surface, intersected at many points by deep chasms or ravines around some of which it was necessary to pass, owing to the impracticability of leaping them."[26]

At the village of Churubusco, Americans assailed a growing throng of retreating soldiers, animals, and civilians headed for Mexico City. Desperate Mexicans barricaded themselves in the village convent and grimly fought back with uncommon tenacity wave after wave of attacking Americans. Pickett's brigade maneuvered up the main road into the village, darting behind broken-down artillery wagons. Enemy fire from the *tête de pont*, a semi-rectangular earthwork guarding a bridge across the Churubusco River, forced the regiment into overgrown cornfields along the road. For three long hours, Americans attacked piecemeal, and casualties began to mount. When Mexican defenders showed signs of wavering, Americans amassed a final drive all along the enemy position. Pickett's 8th U.S. Infantry frantically reformed its confused ranks to support the 6th U.S. Infantry's attack on the *tête de pont*. With bayonets fixed, Pickett's regiment charged across a twenty-foot-wide, water-filled ditch to the fifteen-foot-high walls. Mexican artillery fired into the ranks with devastating effect. Pickett joined in leading the regiment out of the ditch onto the earthen walls. Lacking scaling ladders, the men desperately climbed out with their bare hands and hoisted themselves over the ramparts by standing on their comrades' shoulders. Through sheer will and determination, the Americans successfully stormed the enemy's well-fortified works. The 8th U.S. Infantry was the first to plant its regimental colors in the fallen fort.[27]

Col. Newman S. Clark and Maj. Carlos A. Waite both made special mention of 2d Lt. George Pickett in their official reports of Churubusco.

Clark recognized him "for having participated in the assault upon the fort."[28] Waite listed Pickett as one of the "officers who assisted in the attack on the fort, and whose conduct came under my personal observation." He added, "Lieutenants Snelling and Pickett were actively engaged during the action, and rendered important services."[29] Recognition from his commanding officers earned Pickett the honorary brevet rank of first lieutenant for his participation in the battle of Churubusco.[30]

Scott's hard-won victories at Contreras and Churubusco failed to bring peace. While Santa Anna stubbornly bolstered defenses of his capital, Scott's army formed an arc south of the city. By the first week of September, Scott commenced formulating final plans for his attack on Mexico City.

On the western edge of the capital lay El Molino del Rey, a cluster of stone buildings rumored to contain large supplies of cannon and artillery. The supposed foundry was some 1,000 feet east of the castle of Chapultepec, Scott's real target of attack. On September 8, 1847, Scott ordered Worth's entire division to take El Molino del Rey. During the dark morning hours of September 8, three columns of infantry quietly readied themselves for battle. A special force of 500 men under Maj. George Wright of the 8th U.S. Infantry spearheaded the offensive. Although George's widow, LaSalle Corbell Pickett, would later claim that her husband was part of this storming party, army records fail to support her. Instead, Pickett, with the Second Brigade, participated in the less dramatic, but no less dangerous, fight on the enemy's right.[31]

The resulting battle of El Molino del Rey was a blood bath. Brigadier General Worth seriously misjudged the enemy's artillery strength, and as Wright's column advanced toward the stone buildings, a withering cannon fire tore apart their ranks. American artillery could do little because their own infantry blocked their guns. The rest of Worth's division soon entered the fray, including George Pickett. His brigade commander, James S. McIntosh, later recalled: "When within one hundred yards of the enemy's first position, a very heavy and destructive fire was opened upon us, but we charged after delivering our first fire, and the enemy fell back upon his second, and more strongly fortified position."[32] It did not take long for the columns to break down, leaving men to fight in desperate pell-mell fashion. Mexican counterattacks from Chapultepec only worsened the American carnage. When Worth's troops could stand no more, they finally retreated, allowing their artillery to open upon the Mexican position. American gunners were more successful than the infantry. By 6:15 A.M., the enemy withdrew and, mercifully, the fight was over. Worth's division lost a fourth of its strength; Pickett's brigade lost nearly a third of its men and half of its officers. Americans found a few old cannon molds inside the abandoned buildings at El Molino del Rey, but no foundry.[33]

Pickett continued to gain recognition from his superiors. Brigadier General Worth himself included the first lieutenant's name in his list of officers "especially noticed by subordinate commanders" on September 8.[34] The drama and chaos of battle and gratifying praise from commanding officers, combined with the novelty of a foreign enemy and environment, made war an exciting and appealing experience to young West Pointers.[35] And George Pickett's most unforgettable day in Mexico was yet to come.

Just southwest of Mexico City, atop a formidable hill, sat a grouping of buildings, gardens, and groves called Chapultepec. A former Aztec palace and Mexican military college, the entire complex was surrounded by walls and gates, with artillery posted on all sides. Inside the enclosure were an estimated 1,000 Mexican soldiers and cadets. Overriding the protests of his other officers, Scott chose the site as the initial target of his assault on Mexico City.[36]

Five days after the battle of El Molino del Rey, an artillery bombardment signaled the beginning of Scott's final offensive at Chapultepec. On September 13, 1847, at 8:00 A.M., a group of regulars and volunteers with ladders and pick-axes, led the attack on the palace. The fighting soon turned fierce; it was difficult for individual soldiers to stay with their commands.[37] Winfield Scott watched from afar and later wrote:

There was death below, as well as from above the ground. At length the ditch and wall of the main work were reached, the scaling ladders brought up and planted by the storming parties; some of the daring spirits first in the assault were cast down—killed or wounded; but a lodgment was soon made; streams of heroes followed; all opposition was overcome, and several of the regimental colors flung out from the upper walls, admist long, continual shouts and cheers, which sent dismay into the capital. No scene could have been more animating or glorious.[38]

Lieutenant George E. Pickett
(Valentine Museum, Richmond, Va.)

George Pickett was one of those "streams of heroes." His unit had followed closely behind the storming party into the walled citadel. When James Longstreet, carrying the American flag, suddenly fell wounded, Pickett snatched up the colors. With one hand, he hoisted himself over the ramparts and shot his way toward the flagstaff. Pickett hurriedly tore down the Mexican flag and unfurled Old Glory.[39] The entire attack lasted little more than an hour, but he would remember that hour for the rest of his life. The very next day, Mexico City fell to the Americans.[40]

Winfield Scott later praised Pickett as one of the "most distinguished in those brilliant operations" at Chapultepec.[41] William Worth mentioned him as "distinguished for gallantry and zeal" during the battle.[42] Bvt. Maj. William R. Montgomery described his dramatic hoisting of the American flag and included him as one of the officers "conspicuous for their noble exertions and gallant conduct." Montgomery recommended: "All are entitled to, and are commended for, the most favorable notice of the proper authority."[43] Indeed, Pickett soon earned another honorary brevet for "gallant conduct" at the battle of Chapultepec.[44]

The American victory in Mexico had lasting meaning to both soldiers and civilians. Prevalent romanticism and ethnocentrism caused many Americans to view this war as a great "moral drama." Victory over the Mexicans reaffirmed the republic's vitality and eased fears of industrialism, expansion, and egalitarianism. But battles were costly and decidedly unromantic; the celebration of professional officers' exploits in Mexico was often overstated. Still, West Pointers felt undeniable pride in their institution and openly compared their war experiences to those of leaders in battles past.[45]

The war also offered tactical lessons for its officers. The battles of Contreras, Churubusco, and El Molino del Rey were confused and costly; whatever his genius as a strategist, Winfield Scott proved to be an uneven tactician. Nonetheless, American troops had been repeatedly victorious over a numerically superior foe.[46] Professional officers were learning that close formation fighting, frontal assaults, and bold flanking movements were effective, even against an entrenched enemy. These officers were part of Scott's daring foray into the Mexican interior, living off the land, and surviving far from their supply and communication base. Pickett's observation of and participation in battles like Cerro Gordo, Churubusco, El Molino del Rey, and Chapultepec taught him that charging forward with a spirited and determined force could eventually overtake any enemy.[47]

Pickett's Mexican War experience was all he could have hoped for.[48] Fighting a poorly trained and undersupplied though numerically superior foe, he and his comrades had prevailed. There had been fatigue, monotony, carnage, and suffering; he witnessed the killing and maiming of many friends, including the death of his classmate and fellow Virginian Thomas Easely at the battle of Churubusco. Expressing sympathy to Easely's relatives, Pickett praised him as "gallant and promising," a man with an "amiable disposition," universally liked by all who knew him. The loss was great, but Pickett assured the grieving family that their loved one had died in an act of "extreme bravery." He claimed to look forward to the day when "this disastrous and bloody war has closed."[49]

Yet for George Pickett, feelings of acceptance and the gratification of victory outweighed fear, repulsion, and boredom. Meeting his cousin Harry Heth soon after the war ended, he announced: "I am going into Jalapa as we pass by to have a good time; can't you come with me?" According to Heth, the two officers "painted the town red before leaving."[50] To young officers like Pickett, war in Mexico meant male companionship, conquering a dishonorable and inferior enemy, and gaining recognition from comrades and officers.[51] It meant frontal charges and flanking attacks that always succeeded, and daring feats that always brought glory. For George Pickett the Mexican War was raising that flag over Chapultepec. In the midst of death and suffering, he had found his life's calling.

CHAPTER 3

Texas, 1848–1855

The Buoyancy of Youth Is Past

George Pickett and his fellow Mexican War comrades returned home in 1848 hoping for a hero's welcome; instead they found a nation dramatically divided. News of high casualties and disagreement over the war's aims caused political and social discontent in and outside of Washington. The acquisition of nearly half a million square miles of new territory only added to the turmoil. In the halls of Congress, politicians hotly debated organizing the new land into territories. Increasingly, these debates revolved around the vexing issue of slavery and its future in the growing republic.

Antimilitarism also reemerged in the aftermath of war. Congress cut the army to numbers lower than they had been after the War of 1812. And the federal government was not willing to pay for manning adequately forts scattered through the expanded western territories. Professional soldiers returned to their previous unpopular social status.[1]

While government and public support of the military dwindled, demands on the regular army increased. Settlers spread across the country, requiring soldiers for protection from hostile natives. The army also mapped new travel routes, constructed internal improvements, and explored unfamiliar areas. Negative public sentiment toward the military forced the army to beg the government for funds. The result was a scattering of undermanned and isolated military posts spread across the western frontier.[2]

Notwithstanding lagging public and government support for the military, Pickett cast his lot with the regular army. His first peacetime assignment placed him at the school of infantry training at Jefferson Barracks in Missouri. He spent most of the summer and fall of 1848 at the barracks improving and expanding his skills as an infantry officer.[3]

Jefferson Barracks was close to St. Louis and a central spot for recruits and supplies. Single officers could find plenty in the way of diversions and nightly entertainment. Lt. Edmund Kirby Smith, stationed with Pickett in 1848, described the barracks: "We, some time since regularly entered upon the routine of garrison life—drills, guard and dress parade, the billiard room after breakfast and a visit to the ladies in the evening." Yet life had changed greatly from the heady days in Mexico. "Gracious!" Smith wrote. "What a contrast to the excitement and incidents of the past three years. . . . Now, automaton like we involuntarily glide through the same monotonous scene, needing only like the works of a watch to be wound up each twenty-four hours, when away we spin tickety tick till the stirring notes of reveille again winds up our rickety machines for a repetition of the same revolutions."[4] Pickett's West Point classmate Sam Maxey found the place so dull that he maneuvered to resign his commission a year early. Pickett remained to complete his assignment in Missouri. Perhaps he found reassurance in the daily and predictable routine of army existence. He apparently gave no thought to resigning his commission.[5]

In late 1848, orders came for the young lieutenant to leave Missouri for frontier duty in Texas. Ill health plagued Pickett his entire life, and just as he was to head west, he fell severely sick. His concerned father learned of his son's illness in November. He immediately wrote to the War Department with a special request to allow George to come home to Richmond and recuperate. Robert Pickett implored Adj. Gen. Roger Jones, "Can you as an old friend of the family procure him a furlough, if so you would confer a great favour [sic] on me." Robert added that he himself was suffering from a "paralytic attack" and "should very much like to see him [Pickett] again."[6] George Pickett was two months shy of his twenty-fourth birthday in November 1848; he had lived for six years away from home and experienced armed combat in a foreign country. Still, the protective and paternal Robert Pickett used whatever political influence he could to bring his son home again. On November 20, the adjutant general's office responded: "I regret to inform you that action in this matter rests entirely with the commanding General Western Division and not with the War Department."[7] Pickett's duty to the army had to take precedent over the desires and wants of his concerned family.

Pickett went to Texas to become part of the frontier army, responsible for mapping routes, constructing new posts, and escorting and protecting civilians traveling westward. Following the Mexican War the U.S. Army created a string of forts scattered across the Texas heartland. By 1852, two lines of forts dotted the landscape: one along Texas's international border, the other connecting San Antonio to El Paso.[8]

Ideally, these posts were to prevent Indian raids on white settlements. Officers soon learned that neither their West Point education, Jefferson Barracks instruction, nor Mexican War experience prepared them for Indian warfare. Indians refused to fight unless they believed their families directly threatened. Even then, their avoidance of close combat and use of guerrilla tactics made Native Americans a difficult and highly mobile foe. As in Mexico, Pickett would learn by raw experience.[9]

Throughout the 1850s, the army spread across Texas, attempting to contain the Indian threat. Pickett found himself moving from place to place, just as his father had feared. From Camp Worth he marched with the 8th U.S. Infantry to Fort Gates. Located on a small tributary of the Brazos River and tucked away in a range of mountains, Fort Gates was a full fifty miles from the white settlement of Austin. He later traveled to Forts Chadbourne, Clark, and Bliss, each one increasingly farther from the last. Pickett's West Point classmate D. H. Maury labeled one such Texas post "desolate and uncomfortable."[10] Another officer complained, "It is melancholy to think how I am spending my best days, in this out of the way place without society, amusement or improvement." As a young lieutenant writing from Fort Brown, Texas, asserted, "Military life in peace, made up as it is of routine and uninteresting little incidents, is weary at best."[11] Pickett himself wrote a cousin from Fort Chadbourne, Texas, in 1852: "We manage to exist, [but] it is scarcely more than an existence."[12]

Pickett was learning that a soldier's life on the frontier was not an easy one. These crude garrisons were self-contained and self-sufficient communities. Life followed a routine, only sporadically broken by skirmishes with Indians. Officers and men faced the harsh Texas terrain and climate, constant drilling, disease, and isolation. Food was bad, living conditions Spartan. Pay was notoriously low and hopes for promotion nonexistent. Soldiers drank, gambled, hunted, and smoked to break the monotony. Garrison life revolved around an unchanging routine of drill, target practice, guard and police duty, scouting, and escorting civilians. Opportunity for combat was limited, and officers had little chance to gain individual distinction on the frontier. Desertion was common, and many officers left the army to pursue civilian careers.[13]

Despite all of this, George Pickett remained in the army. The lack of comforts may have bothered him, but he had ample time to indulge in his favorite pastimes: socializing and hunting with fellow officers. Given his exploits in Mexico and West Point, it seems likely that he drank, gambled, and smoked. A civilian profession apparently did not concern him; he perhaps could not imagine himself succeeding in any other occupation and realized that the military offered him safe haven. Pickett had already been initiated into the army's subculture at West Point and Mexico. In Texas he had continued solidarity with fellow officers and achieved a definite sense of place, purpose, and identity. Early into his frontier existence, however, Pickett's loyalty to the army was shaken when he unexpectedly became a widower in November 1851.[14]

Existing records provide only sketchy details of Pickett's courtship and marriage to Sally Harrison Steward Minge. The Minges were slaveholders like the Picketts who traced their roots back to Virginia's finest families. It was the Minge family that sold the James River plantation "Sherwood Forest" to President John Tyler. Twenty-one-year-old Sally was the eldest daughter of Dr. John and Mary Minge of Petersburg. She probably seemed a good match for George given his social standing, and no doubt his family approved. Sally's parents may have been less enthusiastic when they realized that their daughter would live far from them on the western frontier. George was a decorated Mexican War veteran, but what could he offer Sally in the way of financial prospects and future stability?[15]

Sally Minge may have worried little about such concerns. Since his teens George had exuded a certain charm and charisma toward women. The officer corps conceived of itself in a "quasi-aristocratic" fashion that appealed to George and possibly to Sally as well. Young officers like him self-consciously created a martial image of themselves, rich in masculine bravado, independence, and recklessness. Despite (or because of) the conformity and hierarchy of the army, officers collectively embraced the ideal of the careless gentleman-soldier ready to defend his honor at the slightest insult. Lieutenant Pickett probably could captivate female listeners with stories of exotic Mexico and dangerous feats he and his fellow officers accomplished on the battlefield. To an elite young white southern woman like Sally, whose main purpose was to find a protective and manly mate, George probably seemed perfect. He appeared glamorous and honorable, his life on the frontier romantic and exciting.[16]

It is not known when their courtship began, but sometime in 1850 Sally and George set a wedding date for late January 1851. On December 22, 1850, George left Texas to begin a sixty-day furlough. Instead of going home to Virginia, he met his bride in Louisiana, where, on January 28, three days after his twenty-sixth birthday, the couple married. The wedding was held in the town of Franklin at St. Mary's Episcopal Church near the plantation of Sally's sister and brother-in-law, Richard and Margaret Wilkins. The Picketts honeymooned in New Orleans at the St. Charles Hotel.[17]

George and Sally may have chosen to marry in Louisiana rather than Virginia for fear that George would not have enough time to travel east before his furlough ended. In case her husband-to-be could not obtain the necessary extension to go home, Sally came west. By the time Sally arrived, he had successfully lengthened his initial month-long furlough to two months. Soon after their brief stay in New Orleans, he and his new bride set out for the long journey back to Virginia.[18]

By late February, they arrived in Richmond, and George quickly requested an extension of his furlough to six months so that he and Sally could enjoy a long honeymoon. By May 1 however, six weeks before his leave was up, George was ready to return west. He wrote the adjutant general's office: "Should a detachment of recruits be about to proceed to Texas at any time after the 20th of this month I wish to be considered ready to accompany them, should an officer be wanted for that purpose."[19] Perhaps George was eager to settle into his new life with Sally; or perhaps he realized how much he missed army life, despite its discomforts. He may have found himself reassuming the role of the restless son battling his protective family and yearned for his freedom. Most probably George's impatience was due to his growing concern for his wife, who was now pregnant. George no doubt wanted to return to his post before Sally's pregnancy interfered with her ability to travel. By July, they were back in Texas, and their baby was due at the end of the year.

If George's wife had any romantic notions about life on the frontier, reality quickly dispelled them. Life on these military posts could be difficult for officers and men, but for the few officers' wives who accompanied their husbands it could be devastating. Teresa Viele, who joined her officer husband at Ringgold Barracks in south Texas, had second thoughts soon after her arrival. As she described, "The vermin, the famine, the hot winds, and dry soil, which caused clouds of dust to fill the sultry air of July and August and lodge on everything made me begin to think . . . that it would be better to remain in New Orleans and keep a thread and needle store than go to Texas."[20]

Sally Minge Pickett's life changed drastically. Gone was the protective world in which she had grown up. She now faced sickness, hostile Indians, and an undeniable sense of isolation and loneliness. She was pregnant and suddenly very far from her friends and family in a strange and barren land. Her new home promised to be crude at best, perhaps a rat-infested cabin or simply a rustic hut or tent. She had few female companions; most of the other women at the post were lower-class white laundry women. She mainly interacted with men. It is not known if she brought any slaves with her.[21]

Sally's stay at Fort Gates was tragically short. On November 13, 1851, she died giving birth; the baby did not survive either. Possibly the delivery was an especially difficult one, or the new mother and baby fell victim to persistent fevers that plagued Fort Gates. In any event, both bodies were shipped back to Richmond for burial in the Pickett family cemetery.[22]

George immediately applied for a leave of absence. After a week of grieving in Texas, he returned to his post for three days before obtaining another furlough. George then left the army for five months, several weeks of it unauthorized. In a letter to the War Department, he referred to his loss as "my recent severe family afflictions." He journeyed home to Richmond to mourn his young wife and baby.[23]

Available records give few clues to Pickett's five-month limbo. He may have spent time lingering at his wife and child's grave or taking long, solitary walks. Sometime during his days of grief he apparently made an unexpected acquaintance. Wandering on the beaches of Old Point Comfort at Fort Monroe, Virginia, he met LaSalle Corbell.[24]

The Corbells were from Chuckatuck in nearby Nansemond County, Virginia. They were planters like the Picketts but with less pedigree and wealth. Sallie alleged that her parents so wanted their first born to be a boy that her "poor, disappointed, heart-broken mother turned her face to the wall" when she learned her baby's sex. David John Corbell greeted the news that he had a daughter rather than a son with similar disbelief and disappointment. "How did it happen?" he reportedly exclaimed.[25]

In 1852, John and Lizzie took their young family to the seaside for a holiday and to visit relatives. Sallie was a child but already precocious and inquisitive well beyond her years. One day she spotted "a solitary officer on the sands, reading, or looking at the ships as they came and went, or watching the waves as they dashed to sudden death against the shore." He seemed the perfect picture of a gallant soldier and ideal man. She noted his physical exterior, especially his hair, "which hung in shining waves almost to his shoulders," his neat attire, and erect gait. Learning that he was a Mexican War veteran, LaSalle remembered: "It seemed impossible to me. How could anyone so immaculate and so beautiful to look upon have really fought and killed people?" To Sallie he appeared the " 'Good Prince' in the fairy stories my grandmother told me."[26]

One warm afternoon as he sat reading under an umbrella, the girl approached the soldier. Sallie had whooping cough and wondered if George shared her ailment and thus had to stay away from any social interactions. George denied having the illness but explained that he had "something worse, a broken heart, and he did not like to make others sad with his sorrow." Sallie asked how he broke his heart. He answered, "God broke it when He took from him his loved ones and left him so lonely." She claimed that "in his solitude I felt that we were comrades in sad experience."[27]

"He drew me to him," LaSalle remembered, "telling me that he had lost his wife and little girl, and that he was very lonely. I asked him their names; they had both been called Sally.

" 'You can call me Sally,' I offered. 'I'll be your wife and little girl.'

" 'That's a promise,' he replied. 'You shall be named Sally and be my wife.' "[28]

The soldier and child spent the rest of the day playing games, building sand castles, and singing. They both felt a bond, LaSalle recalled. "In return for his confidence," she later wrote, "I promised to comfort him for his losses and to be his little girl now and his wife just as soon as I was grown up to be a lady." To symbolize their pledge, he gave her a ring and gold heart with the inscription "Sally" on it. "Then and to the end,"

LaSalle affirmed, "he was my soldier, and always when we were alone I called him 'Soldier.' "[29]

LaSalle would later mark the day she encountered Lt. George Pickett as her "point of beginning—a period back of which life to present consciousness, was not."[30] She insisted that she knew at that very moment that one day their fate would be joined.

The historical "facts" of this first meeting between LaSalle Corbell and George Pickett are hard to prove.[31] No other sources exist, besides La-Salle's published writings, to corroborate the account. Her tendency to fabricate and romanticize her past make using LaSalle's writings as reliable historical evidence difficult. Still, there are always significant meanings and elements of "truth" to the images she conveyed.

Much of what LaSalle wrote corresponds with George's frame of mind in 1852. She described him as sad and melancholy, taking walks alone and socializing little with fellow officers. He clearly continued mourning his wife and child. It seems entirely plausible that their meeting happened as LaSalle recorded it, although George probably thought little of this curious and persistent girl who thought he had whooping cough. If he did spend hours playing with her on the beach, she may have become a temporary substitute for his lost family. Friendship with a child may have been a form of escape for him; perhaps he felt more like the careless and playful youth he himself had once been. It seems unlikely that he considered her to be his future wife, as she insisted in hindsight.

Something or someone finally shook George Pickett from his deep depression, and he returned to the army in May 1852.[32] His regiment had already abandoned its post at Fort Gates, and by the time Pickett arrived in Texas, his unit had moved to Camp Johnston. Located on the south side of a fork of the Concho River, Camp Johnston was the regimental headquarters of the 8th U.S. Infantry. It was 150 miles from the closest white settlement, and soldiers and officers lived in canvas tents, instead of any permanent structures. Rattlesnakes, prairie dogs, and Indians were constant companions in what one army surgeon called "a wild country."[33] On November 18, five days after the anniversary of Sally's death, George and his regiment left Camp Johnston for Fort Chadbourne, thirty-five miles deeper into the Texas heartland.[34]

Soon after his arrival at Fort Chadbourne, George wrote a long letter to his cousin Lizzie Heth in Richmond. He continued to mourn his wife and child. He apologized for not writing sooner but explained that his prior letters were "too gloomy and melancholy" and he burned them. He admitted that the thought of his cousin Lizzie only reminded him painfully of Sally. He had difficulty not dwelling on her memory: "I wish constantly to speak of that dear being who is now an angel in heaven." George had grown morose and depressed, craving distraction from his daily routine "to divert my thoughts from their usual melancholy train." The careless and aimless young man who laughed, sang, and socialized with friends was gone. He seemed lost in his deep personal pain. "I know it and I feel it," he wrote Lizzie. "I am no longer the same person[;] the buoyancy of youth is past—I look forward to nothing with pleasure." He felt unworthy of consolation and guilty for being so concerned with himself. George asked: "Why should I wish to make others bear a portion of the burden which has been assigned to me[?]" He felt alone in the world, far from his family, far from Richmond, and "a long long way off from civilization—two hundred miles to the nearest settlement."[35]

Pickett stayed in the army despite his despair and depression. The monotony of drill and the hierarchy of command perhaps gave structure and meaning to his pained existence. He could rely on the army to guide him, even though he may have felt personally lost. Pickett's growing reliance on the army was not unusual; the officer corps offered better emotional and economic security than most civilian occupations. There is no evidence that Pickett had any interest in any other profession.[36]

In the meantime, friends and family maneuvered to obtain Pickett a promotion. If he were going to make the army his life, surely he could be something more than a lowly lieutenant. Pickett's father had neither stopped worrying about his son nor seeking help for him with his political connections. Since Sally's death, Pickett's family may have been even more concerned that he not lose himself in his melancholy. They still wanted him to have a successful and honorable career. In the fall of 1853, Pickett had himself requested consideration for captaincy. The War Department could only respond that his application "will be duly submitted to the Secretary of War, should the contingency contemplated by you occur."[37] In 1854, Congress uncharacteristically considered a request by Secretary of War Jefferson Davis to expand the army. To Pickett's family and friends, this seemed an opportune time to press for his promotion.[38]

Robert Pickett, apparently without his son's knowledge, began building his own case for George's promotion. In January 1854, Robert traveled to Washington to talk directly to Secretary of War Davis. He presented a letter of introduction from his friend and prominent Richmond lawyer James Lyons. Lyons's letter stated: "Understanding that there will probably be an increasing of the Army, Col. Pickett desires to obtain his son the appointment in one of the new Regiments." Lyons assessed Pickett as a "gentleman of the most estimable and unblemished character," adding that he believed the young officer entitled to promotion after having distinguished himself in Mexico.[39]

Robert also obtained from James Longstreet, George's West Point classmate and Chapultepec comrade, a glowing appraisal of his son's military service. Longstreet recounted Pickett's Mexican War experience, noting that at Churubusco "he was particularly distinguished as one of the most gallant soldiers on that field. I was near him through the day, and can safely say that more conduct and gallantry was not exhibited by an American officer during the Mexican War." Longstreet stated that, after the war, "your son has commanded a company on the Texas frontier, and has performed most important and arduous services." He praised his friend as "well worthy of command and position," and "always attentive and zealous in the discharge of his duties."[40] Armed with these letters from Longstreet and Lyons, Robert sought additional political support for his son's promotion.

South Carolinian Louis F. Robertson had served with Pickett in Mexico and willingly agreed to use his influence in his state. Robertson wrote Lawrence M. Keitt, a fiery young congressman from South Carolina, in mid-February 1854. Robertson described his "old friend and companion of arms" as "heroic" and "gallant." Informing the congressman of Pickett's Virginia roots, Robertson argued that southerners sacrificed more in the Mexican War than northerners. Thus, veterans like Pickett who remained in the service required a share of government patronage to compensate southerners "who bore the heat and burden" of the war. Robertson closed: "I would state that my friend is now out in the western wilds with his regiment and this is done for him without his knowledge. All that is done for him must be done by his friends and for that reason I would press his claim." Robert Pickett planned another visit to Washington to deliver this letter in person to Keitt.[41] Meanwhile, George

Pickett traveled over 200 miles farther west to Fort Bliss, Texas, near present-day El Paso. He stayed another year in Texas, perhaps unaware of the efforts his father was making to obtain him a promotion.[42]

In March 1855, Robert Pickett journeyed to Washington to push again for George's advancement. On March 3, Robert decided against trying to see Jefferson Davis personally and instead composed a letter to him to address his concerns. He wrote: "Knowing your time is fully occupied just at this close of Congress I deem it almost useless to try and see you in person. I have therefore thought it best to call your attention to the promotions about to be made in the new Regts. and would most humbly submit the name of my son Brevet-Capt. Geo. E. Pickett as an applicant for a captaincy in the Cavalry." To sustain his request he asked the secretary to refer to Lyons's letter from the year earlier.[43] About the same time, Davis received a signed petition with the signatures of several prominent congressmen asking that George Pickett be considered for promotion. The petition praised Pickett for being "well up in his Regt." and having "a high reputation for gallantry and soldierly bearing," referring to his Mexican War service as proof.[44] Three weeks later, Pickett received his promotion to captain in the reactivated 9th U.S. Infantry.[45] He was to leave Texas and report immediately to regimental headquarters at Fort Monroe, Virginia. George Pickett was coming home.

Pickett's family must have been pleased with his promotion and new assignment at Fort Monroe. He would be within a day's ride to Turkey Island and close to relatives in Norfolk. Since his teenage years, when his parents sent him to Quincy, Pickett had returned to Virginia only as a visitor. His years in Mexico and Texas had changed him: he was a grown man with new loyalties and concerns. The loss of his wife left painful emotional scars that still festered. It was unclear how long his stay at Fort Monroe would last, but even temporarily, Pickett would be in the South again.

By midsummer, however, he had not returned from the West. Robert began to worry. In July, he wrote the War Department: "You will confer me a great favor by informing me, if my son Capt. Geo. E. Pickett has been ordered in to join his new Regt." George had not informed his family of his new assignment, and Robert began to "feel under some apprehension about him."[46] His parents anxiously awaited the return of their son from the wilds of Texas. Adj. Gen. Samuel Cooper responded promptly to Robert's inquiry, assuring him, "I have the pleasure to inform you that a letter was yesterday received from your son Captain George E. Pickett dated at Fort Bliss June 5th accepting his appointment in the 9th U.S. Infantry. He is under orders to report to his colonel in person at Fort Monroe, but the time of his probable arrival in his quarters cannot be readily stated."[47] In August 1855, Pickett finally arrived at Fort Monroe.[48]

George Pickett closed a chapter in his life when he came home to Virginia in the summer of 1855. He never returned to the Texas frontier. His life was soon to take an unexpected turn, drawing him farther from his family, his native South, and for a time, Sallie Corbell.

CHAPTER 4

Washington Territory, 1855–1858
Farther Than the End of the World

George Pickett's tour of duty at Fort Monroe, Virginia, lasted less than six months. From August until December 1855, he and his fellow officers trained recruits for Indian fighting on the far western frontier. The 9th Infantry commander, Col. George Wright, hoped to have the new unit ready by year's end. Through the summer, fall, and early winter, 600 men learned infantry tactics, took target practice, and withstood "physical toughening" to prepare them for marches of twenty to thirty miles per day. Captain Pickett had command of his own company, some eighty green privates.[1]

On December 15, 1855, Pickett's regiment boarded two westbound steamers with orders to report to the Department of the Pacific. LaSalle Corbell later described the regiment's departure: "The first real sorrow of my life was when I watched the *St. Louis* go out to sea with my Soldier on board, bound around the Horn to Puget Sound, where he was stationed at Fort Bellingham, which I thought must be farther than the end of the world."[2]

George was not on the *St. Louis*, nor is it likely that LaSalle witnessed the ship's departure. However, after a four-month stint in Florida on detached service, George did travel far from his home, his family, and the eastern slaveholding society to join the 9th Regiment in Washington Territory. With orders to pacify "the hostile Indians on Puget Sound, Washington," George was about to have his first real encounter with Native Americans.[3] He probably had little idea what to expect.

Congress created Washington Territory in 1853, a vast segment of land that included present-day Washington State, northern Idaho, and western Montana. The region attracted large numbers of white settlers who came for the mild climate, rich soil, and promise of gold. By the fall of

1853, some 7,000 white emigrants poured into the Pacific Northwest, creating great apprehension among dwindling Native American tribes. Displacement and disease had taken a devastating toll on the region's indigenous population and stirred tensions. Isaac I. Stevens, the young and ambitious governor of the territory, visited tribes and drafted treaties offering compensation for land while proposing their removal to designated reservations.[4]

Army surgeon Rodney Glisan witnessed firsthand growing tensions between whites and Indians in the territory. He wrote: "The hostile feelings among the Indians is supposed to extend to several tribes. Proposals, it is said, have been made to all the Indians east of the Cascade range to unite in a general war of extermination against the whites." Army officers identified the Yakima Indians as the main culprits in stirring antiwhite sentiments in the territory.[5] It only seemed a matter of time before open fighting would break out.

The discovery of gold at Fort Colville, deep in the Washington Territory, was the spark that ignited the flame of war. Indians killed several whites who were on their way to the mines during the summer. In September, a group of angry Yakima Indians cut the throat of a government agent sent to investigate the murders. The army organized an expedition to retaliate in October, but a small band of regulars barely escaped with their lives. Hostilities spread to the coast, and during the fall and winter, tribes staged raids on white settlements all along Puget Sound. Rumors fanned the flames, and whites insisted that a general Indian uprising was under way.[6] The Yakima War had begun.

Pacific Northwest Indians were difficult foes for the U.S. Army to combat. Just before the 9th Regiment's arrival in the Washington Territory, Gen. John E. Wool described the state of Indian affairs in the Department of the Pacific to Adj. Gen. Samuel Cooper. Wool found that the Yakima, like Indians in Texas, "will not engage in a field fight with any considerable number of regulars. Their mode of carrying on war is not by regular engagements, but one of ambush and surprise." Wool proposed, "They can only be conquered and brought to terms, by occupying their country, and such position as would command their fisheries and valleys."[7]

Wool did not necessarily want to fight the natives. Under his direction, the regular army had tried to act as an intermediary between local tribes and angry whites. General Wool informed 9th Infantry commander George Wright in January 1856 that most white settlers "are for exterminating the Indians and accordingly do not discriminate between friends and foes." He noted that such an aggressive policy "only tended to increase our Indian enemies whilst it has subjected the regular service to great inconvenience and expense."[8] Wool wanted his officers to encourage Native Americans to surrender their arms in exchange for protection from the army.[9]

Despite Wool's efforts, war had escalated out of his control by January 1856. Volunteer units defied Wool's orders and engaged in aggressive campaigning, even in the bitter winter weather. While volunteers defiantly took to the field, regular army officers and men garrisoned themselves at forts, hoping for milder temperatures and reinforcements.[10]

In February 1856, two army expeditions set out to bring a decisive end to the war. Lt. Col. Silas Casey, commander of the 9th Infantry, marched into the White River valley to try to impose peace to Puget Sound, while another portion of troops occupied the Yakima and Walla Walla valleys. Over the next several months, volunteers, regulars, and natives clashed repeatedly, but only twice did whites and Indians fight battles of any significant scale. In almost every engagement, white troops were victorious, but both sides suffered losses. On March 1, Pickett, under Casey's command, saw action at Muckleshute Prairie on the White River. Casualties were light, and after a brief engagement, the Indians fled. Pickett and his company returned to Fort Steilacoom until late summer. In May, Casey reported that many Indians were either seeking peace or withdrawing beyond the mountains. Two months later, he announced that "war in this district has ceased." The American government made treaties with several tribes, and a shaky peace ensued.[11]

After the Yakima War ended, Pickett moved with Company D 100 miles north of Fort Steilacoom to stop hostilities in the vicinity of Bellingham Bay. Like the rest of the territory, friction between Indian and whites in the bay area deepened during the mid-1850s, resulting in raids, death, and destruction of property. By December 1855, the Washington territorial legislature had petitioned Congress three times for a military post on the bay. One year later, R. V. Peabody, a resident of Whatcom, warned that northern tribes had plans to "exterminate all the whites." "They say," Peabody wrote Governor Stevens, "that we are all girls and that they are coming to show us what men are, take what they want, kill where they can."[12] The small white community organized a militia, built a stockade and crude "Fort Defiance," and repeated their plea to Congress for army and navy protection. George Pickett arrived by ship on August 26, 1856, to find about thirty skittish settlers crowding into the stockades and blockhouses at night.[13]

Pickett and his men quickly set to work building a post on a site selected and surveyed by the army months before. Located on a bluff about eighty feet above the sea, Fort Bellingham eventually included two blockhouses, an officers' mess, a soldiers' barracks, a blacksmithy, a sutler's store, a hospital, laundress houses, and a garden. The men cleared a field for drilling and installed a seventy-foot flag mast. Pickett anticipated the wooden structures were "capable of lasting ten or fifteen years" with only occasional repairs. Soldiers also began cutting a road connecting Bellingham Bay with Fort Steilacoom and building a bridge over Whatcom Creek.[14]

Claiming "military necessity," Pickett seized over 300 acres of land from a white family living adjacent to the post. When Maria and Charles Roberts refused to vacate their property, Pickett had them forcibly removed. Soldiers disassembled the Robertses' cabin and rebuilt it on a beach below the bluff. Promising to reimburse the family for their land, Pickett had the property surveyed and a value placed on their claim. However, the army's bureaucracy slowed the process, and the Roberts never received any compensation. Pickett grew frustrated over the situation, and in August 1857, he complained to the War Department: "As a matter of justice to the Claimant, is it right and proper that we should deprive the citizen of his land for a whole year and not pay him what the law entitles him to viz.—the valuations of his improvements[?]" He admitted, "I shall be most truly grateful when I can settle the just claims of this citizen, remove him, and have undisputed *command* of this post."[15]

In theory, Captain Pickett had undisputed command of two lieutenants, about sixty enlisted men and a few civilian contract laborers. But as this letter attested, his new post brought challenges to both his authority and his patience. Desertion was a constant problem in the frontier army, but the allure of gold made desertion from places like Fort Bellingham especially acute. From August 1856 until December 1858, over fifty men deserted Company D. Although Pickett began to establish a reputation for harsh discipline, many privates were poorly trained and prone to drink and petty crimes. Out of necessity, they spent most of their day building the fort and cutting the road rather than practicing gun and bayonet exercises. Many soldiers, often Irish and German immigrants recruited in eastern cities and quickly shipped west to the frontier, were illiterate. Commissioned officers had little respect for such recruits, dismissing them as "worthless" and "unprincipled."[16]

Pickett had other things on his mind besides the headaches of company command and the disgruntled Roberts family. The Indian situation was a complex and pressing one, and he quickly set to work assessing the threat of attack from the feared northern tribes. He became adept at Chinook, the language used to converse with natives, and found himself, like many other officers, sensitive to the plight of the Native Americans.[17]

There were a number of reasons for this attitude. Army officers frequently believed that only they protected the "noble savage" from greedy and brutal white civilians. Traditional animosity of white civilians toward professional army officers increased officers' paternalism toward Indians, although they still retained the ethnocentrism of the larger Euro-American culture. Military men assumed that it was inevitable that the superior white Protestant republic should spread from coast to coast, but they believed that only they best understood the Native Americans' dilemma.[18]

In addition to sympathy there was resentment and embarrassment. George Pickett and other West Point–trained officers disliked having to fight Indians, an enemy they did not see as "civilized" or as a legitimate foe. Although much of what the antebellum army did was police and protect whites on the frontier, many officers considered their real mission as preparing for and fighting international wars. Army surgeon Glisan voiced common complaints against Indians, "whose home is in the forest and mountain strongholds; who subsists on the wild fruits and animals which he finds wherever he may roam, who fights only when the advantage of position or numbers is in his favor and vanishes when the fates are against him; who battles mostly under cover of rocks and trees, and with a deadliness of aim only to be acquired by constant practice in hunting and fighting."[19] In addition, the U.S. government's blatant exploitation of the natives embarrassed army officers. As men immersed in the military's subculture of honor and order, officers like Pickett believed that their government failed in its obligations to a weaker people.[20]

To be sure, some army officers did blame Indians for the wars and raids and felt only anger at their presence. Surgeon Glisan wrote in his diary that the white male settlers were moral family men harassed by a handful of Indians who were "reckless and bad men, who disregarding the restraints of their chiefs, are constantly stealing from and committing other lawless acts upon their white neighbors, who sometimes are forced, in self-defense, to put a stop to their aggressions, in other modes beside moral suasion." Glisan admitted that there were some "vagabond whites" but concluded, "Indians and whites are so diametrically antagonistic that it is simply impossible for them to live side by side for many years without contentions."[21]

Pickett's assessments of the Indian situation on Puget Sound revealed conflicting feelings of sympathy and fear, admiration and racism. In May 1857, he wrote departmental headquarters that the Lummi were "like all savages, indolent and full of ardent spirits of which unfortunately they get too much in spite of the strenuous efforts on the part of Col. Fitzhugh, the Indian agent, and myself to prevent it." Pickett predicted no trouble with tribes on the bay unless the "inferior class of settlers" instigated it with liquor or "ill wage."[22] Later that year, Pickett assisted Lt. Col. Thompson Morris of the 4th Infantry in judging Indian-white relations on Puget Sound. Morris, relying on Pickett's opinion of and interaction with nearby tribes, complained that the government failed to recognize most treaties made by whites with local tribes, especially peaceful ones. "Whites are gradually encroaching upon their country," Morris wrote, and "they are justly afraid they will lose their country altogether, and can put no faith in what is told them by the Agents of the Government." Morris urged: "At any rate some immediate steps should be taken to show the Indians that it is not the intention of the government to take their lands without giving them a fair valuation for them." The two officers agreed that if these steps were not taken, wars would flare, which would require more money and troops to quell.[23]

Pickett felt especially sympathetic to Bellingham Bay's Nooksack Indians, whom he judged "superior to the tribes on the Sound." He related their predicament to Morris, who summarized the captain's remarks in his own report to departmental headquarters:

They are mountain Indians, subsisting by the chase, and different altogether from those who live by fishing. Last summer a party of white men commenced cutting a road into their country, which caused a great deal of bad feeling among the Indians, and there is no doubt but what the Indians have commenced hostilities, if the whites had not been induced to desist making the road by the influence of Col. Fitzhugh, the agent at Bellingham Bay. Capt. Pickett also says that these Indians say that they never made a treaty with the whites, that a few of their men were at the treaty when it was made but that they were not authorized by their nation to make any such terms as were made, and that if the treaty were to be ratified they would object to going on the reserve which is the large island near Bellingham Bay called "Lummi Island." This objection of theirs arises from their mode of life, as they have always been accustomed to live by the chase, they cannot now make up their minds to go on a small (in comparison) island, where game is scarce and depend mostly for subsistence upon fishing.[24]

After a particularly brutal massacre of a white settler on nearby Whidbey Island, Pickett remained supportive of the Indians. Although recommending punishing the guilty tribe, he noted that among Puget Sound Indians "great dissatisfaction is rising from the fact that their land is being continually occupied by the whites and no remuneration, or attempt at it." He criticized the "insincerity of white settlers of the Sound" toward any "in roads" made by northern tribes.[25] Some Whatcom residents accused him of overstepping his bounds by using soldiers to police civilians and by attempting to shield Indians from what he deemed as white exploitation.[26]

Yet Pickett's main mission was to protect whites, no matter how unappreciative and insincere he found them. He recognized that the danger was real but felt severely undermanned and overwhelmed. Vowing to do "all in my power to protect the citizens," he believed that, without additional troops, "a war disastrous to the inhabitants of the Territory and one which can not redound to the honor of the U.S. troops will and must be the consequences."[27] Pickett saw only one solution: ban belligerent northern tribes from the region. He proposed chasing them out of the Sound with an armed steamer and additional troops.[28]

Indian agent E. C. Fitzhugh offered a decidedly different picture of the situation at Fort Bellingham. In April 1857, Fitzhugh published a letter to the governor in an Olympia newspaper, maintaining that both bellicose tribes and local whites derided Pickett's post. "It is most unpleasant, as well as dangerous, to remain here—The citizens are all wrangling amongst themselves & there is so much ill feeling existing that many intend leaving." Fitzhugh concluded: "We might all be killed, as we expect no assistance from the military post, they having as much as they can do to protect their perimeter, their pickets not being furnished, and many of the soldiers being in irons in the guardhouse."[29]

But all was not bleak for George Pickett during his first few years at Fort Bellingham. While he tried to keep the peace among displaced natives, resentful whites, and unruly soldiers, he enjoyed camaraderie with American and British officers stationed nearby. He still had a reckless streak, especially if liquor was involved. One particular afternoon he allegedly commandeered a whaling boat to take him, a lieutenant, and an orderly sergeant across the bay to Vancouver Island. The three officers later returned, each bearing five gallons of port and brandy.[30]

George also fell in love, if local legend is to be believed. But, like much of his life, Pickett's relationship with an Indian woman is a bewildering mix of fact and fiction. Several versions exist attesting to how the couple met, their alleged marriage, their son, and their Bellingham home. Bellingham historian Lelah Edson claims that George met the beautiful Indian princess when her father came to Fort Bellingham to discuss peace with the army.[31] National Park ranger Michael Vouri maintains that George spotted her while touring Indian villages on the international border at Semiahmoo.[32] Fiction writer and native Washingtonian Archie Binns offers a more dramatic story. In his historical novel *The Laurels Are Cut Down*, Binns writes that it was during an attack on her village that Pickett first saw "Morning Mist." Binns describes:

> He had rushed the village with his full force and taken them by surprise. Squaws and children had screamed and run for shelter while the men debated the use of bows and flintlocks against the heavily-armed force. Morning Mist was coming from the spring with water, not knowing the village had been invaded. Voices called to her to drop the jar and hide. The expression of her child-like face didn't change to betray the moment she realized what had happened. But in that hidden moment she decided it was already too late. She walked past the

line of rifles and the glittering company with the air of being utterly alone and untroubled. She didn't ignore the soldiers. They didn't exist.[33]

The sight of the young woman defiantly carrying water through the midst of a battle instantly captivated the captain, Binns continues. George called out to her in Chinook to wait. She was startled by him and stared in wonder as the white officer approached, ceremoniously unsheathed his sword, bowed, and reached for the water jar. Morning Mist explained that she was carrying the water to her father, who had hidden in a plank house. George, himself suddenly oblivious to the fighting raging around him, offered to carry the water for her. He accompanied her to the house and asked for a truce from her father. George then asked for Morning Mist's hand in marriage.

While the novelized treatment of the story obviously cannot be credited, all popular versions of the story agree that George wed his Indian princess "according to the rites of her tribe and it is said, by white rites also."[34] George and his bride lived quietly in a modest two-story wooden house (now known as the Pickett House) a few miles from the fort. His devotion and love for Morning Mist, local legend insists, was remarkable.[35]

Unfortunately, little corroborating evidence exists to verify these stories about George, Morning Mist, and their brief life together. As Whatcom County historian P. R. Jeffcott states, "Much has been said and quite considerable has been written [about Pickett], but much controversy remains as to the truth of some statements." "Local tradition unsubstantiated by facts," Jeffcott notes, "is often misleading."[36] County records fail to authenticate the marriage, and they do not confirm George as the original owner of the Pickett House. A 1926 history of Bellingham denies that George ever lived in the home.[37] Although Binns offers the most detailed version of George and his Indian lover's story, his is also the most suspect. A literary critic observes that whenever anyone questioned the novelist's "occasional carelessness with facts," Binns "would retort that he was a creative writer, not a historian."[38]

It is not clear to what tribe Morning Mist belonged. Most accounts allege that she was one of the Haida Indians, a northern tribe that inhabited Queen Charlotte Island, just north of Bellingham Bay. Skilled fishermen, traders, and warriors, the Haidas excelled in carving elaborate canoes and totem poles. Although classified by anthropologists as hunters and gatherers, these Indians lived in permanent villages in a complex and hierarchical society. They lacked a formal and unified political organization, but chiefs wielded considerable power through hereditary claims and the ceremonial exchange of gifts. Elite members of the tribe maintained their wealth and status by conducting extensive raids on Indian and white settlements on Puget Sound, capturing material goods and slaves. It was because of Haida aggression and brutality that whites petitioned Congress for protection; it was why Pickett had come to Bellingham Bay.[39]

If Morning Mist was a member of the Haida elite, she would have distinctive markings on her body: tattoos and a labret, or lip plug. Women of any status played an important role in Haida culture as perpetrators of lineage and status. The ideal Haida female was submissive, modest, industrious, enduring, and sexually aggressive.[40] George's alliance with a Haida princess could have done two things: stabilized Indian-white relations and provided him the female companionship he had so sorely missed since he lost Sally.

The birth of James Tilton Pickett in December 1857 is perhaps the only undeniable proof that George had an intimate relationship with a Native American woman. No birth records exist, but in 1888, James gave a sworn deposition to his right as George's legitimate heir and son. Census records and obituaries also confirm James's Indian blood.[41]

The question of whether Pickett legally married a native woman is more difficult to answer. White officers and soldiers frequently had sexual relationships with Indian women on the frontier; and married officers sometimes lived with native women while they were far from their own families. The same feelings of racial superiority and class consciousness that gave white slaveholders license to sexually exploit black women similarly encouraged white officers to take Indian mistresses. But racism and elitism also brought social ostracism when an officer actually married a native, no matter what her status was. Sometimes "wife" meant nothing more than concubine. Still, it was entirely possible and not unprecedented for an officer and white southerner, like George Pickett, to marry an Indian woman. Jefferson Davis's nephew, Robert, who served under George at Fort Bellingham, wed an Indian princess. Native Virginian, Whatcom County judge, and Indian agent Edmund C. Fitzhugh also had an Indian wife and family.[42]

James Tilton Pickett, circa 1860
(Whatcom Museum of History and Art, Bellingham, Wash.)

Married or not, George's relationship with his son's mother proved tragically short: she died soon after giving birth. George left no record of his grief, but his actions lend some insight into his feelings. He apparently could find no solace in the visible reminders left behind, his infant son or their alleged house, for he abandoned both. He sent James to live with a white family in another county and rarely saw him again. Until his death in 1889, James's greatest possession would be a red trunk belonging to his mother and a Bible inscribed by his father.[43]

George seemed to have the same desire to escape as he did when Sally died years earlier. In June 1858, he took a sixty-day furlough and went east. During his three-year absence, his father, Robert, had died and his mother's health was weakening. It is unclear how much, if any, time George spent in Richmond.[44] On July 21, 1858, he wrote the War Department from the Metropolitan Hotel in New York City to request an extension of his furlough an additional six months. Hostilities with Indians had resumed in the territory, but Pickett did not want the army to think that he was ignoring his duty. He explained, "There are two officers present with my company, which is stationed on Bellingham Bay, and I was informed by the General Comdg the Dept. that no troops could be taken from the Sound to the present scene of war east of the Cascade Mountains, otherwise I should not make this application." Secretary of War John B. Floyd granted the captain's request.[45]

LaSalle claimed that she saw George twice between 1855 and 1861 and that one of those times was at White Sulphur Springs, Greenbrier County. She may have seen him during his furlough in the summer of 1858, but she did not date either of their alleged meetings. According to LaSalle, he preferred her company to "the belles nearer his age." It certainly would be significant if he rekindled his attachment to this teenage girl in the aftermath of his Indian lover's death. But there is no way to know for sure.[46]

When LaSalle later looked back on George's life in the Washington Territory, she made no public mention of a second wife nor his son James. In 1908, she referred to her husband's good relations with the natives of the Washington Territory: "He made them his friends, learned their languages, built school-houses for them and taught them, and they called him Nesika Tyee—Our Chief. One old Indian chief insisted upon making him a present of one of his children." Even she may not have known the whole truth.[47]

CHAPTER 5

San Juan and Southern Secession, 1859–1861
The Most Trying Circumstances

George Pickett returned to Fort Bellingham in the winter of 1858–59 and soon had an opportunity to regain the military glory he had once enjoyed on the battlefields of Mexico. It could not have come at a better time. In July 1859, Pickett received orders to build a post on San Juan Island, located just across the bay from Bellingham, at the entrance of Puget Sound. The U.S. and British governments had quarreled over ownership of the San Juan Islands for several years. The 1846 Treaty of Washington had not clearly established the boundary between British and American claims. The treaty, meant to decide ownership of the scattering of islands on Puget Sound, instead caused more problems by using unclear language and referring ambiguously to "the channel which separates the continent from Vancouver's Island."[1] There were two channels, and the United States chose the Canal de Haro Strait, the British chose the Rosario Strait. Americans settled on the island's southern end, while the British Hudson Bay Company claimed ownership of the entire island. Constant concern for Indian raids further strained relations among white inhabitants. In 1855, Secretary of State William L. Marcy predicted that "a collision may take place between our citizens and British subjects" somewhere along the disputed boundary.[2]

Tempers flared to a new pitch during the summer of 1859. Members of the Hudson Bay Company allowed their hogs and cattle to run free on the island. One morning in June, American settler Lyman Cutler spotted a boar tearing up his potato patch. After a brief chase, he shot the pig dead. Charles Griffin, the pig's British owner, refused Cutler's offer of money to pay for the animal, especially when Cutler angrily announced he would rather shoot his neighbor Griffin than the pig. Griffin filed an official complaint, demanding that the British government seize and try the American for criminal behavior. Cutler denied that he had killed the animal on British soil. The "Pig War" then threatened to escalate.[3]

In mid-July 1859, Gen. William S. Harney, commander of the Department of Oregon, decided that American inhabitants on San Juan required military protection. Without the knowledge of the War Department, Harney ordered George Pickett and a company of regulars to abandon Fort Bellingham and erect a post on the island. Pickett's mission was twofold: to safeguard American settlers and to secure the interest of the United States on the island. Harney's acting adjutant general, Capt. Alfred Pleasonton, relayed to Pickett the "serious and important duty [that] will devolve upon you in the occupation of San Juan Island, arising from conflicting interests of the American citizens and the Hudson Bay Company establishment at that point." Pleasonton explained, "The duty is to afford adequate protection to the American citizens in their rights as such and to resist all attempts at interference by the British authorities residing on Vancouver Island, by intimidation or force, in the controversies of the above mentioned parties." Pleasonton closed his letter by assuring Pickett of Harney's confidence in him: "The General commanding is fully satisfied from the varied experience and judgment displayed by you in your present command that your selection to the duties with which you are now charged will advance to the interest of the service, and that your disposition of the subjects coming within your supervision and action will enhance your reputation as a commander."[4]

Harney had handed Pickett independent command. Certainly this was more autonomy than most captains enjoyed in any assignment. Harney sent Pickett's regimental commander, Lt. Col. Silas Casey, to Fort Steilacoom, leaving Pickett responsible for the entire upper Puget Sound. As Harney implied, this assignment could bring not only recognition and commendation but also promotion. Not since Mexico had he had such an opportunity, and he did not want to let this chance pass him by.[5]

Pickett arrived at San Juan on July 27, 1859, and quickly issued a proclamation: "This being United States Territory, no laws other than those of the United States, nor courts, except such as are held by virtue of said laws will be recognized or allowed on this Island." To assert his control, he ordered all inhabitants of the island to report to him "in case of any incursion of the Northern Indians." He then set his men to work on "Camp Pickett" on the gravel beach off Griffin Bay. That evening, he invited the island custom's inspector, Paul K. Hubbs, to a celebratory glass of brandy. Pickett appeared wholly confident that the War Department had sanctioned his presence and purpose on the island.[6]

British response was immediate and explosive. The same day Pickett issued his proclamation, a British justice of the peace visited the American encampment and questioned the presence of the troops on the island. On July 30, 1859, Hudson Bay Company agent Charles John Griffin reaffirmed the British claim to San Juan. Also on July 30, two British war steamers moved threateningly close to the island. A few days later James Douglas, governor of the British colony at Vancouver Island, declared San Juan British territory and angrily protested the presence of American troops.[7]

Pickett stood his ground. He refused to recognize the magistrate's, the governor's, the company agent's, or anyone's right to question his presence. "I am here," Pickett responded, "by virtue of an order from my government and shall remain till recalled by the same authority."[8]

Yet, beneath this bombast, Pickett worried. Hour by hour, the stress increased, and he felt isolated and vulnerable. He characterized the atmosphere on the island as "Dog eat dog" and complained to Harney's chief of staff, Alfred Pleasonton, of the "very great want of courtesy exhibited toward us by these 'Bulls.'" "You know I am a peaceable man," Pickett wrote Pleasonton, "but we cannot stand everything."[9]

Soon after his arrival, Pickett dispatched an urgent letter to Colonel Casey, asking that the armed vessel promised him be sent immediately. Pickett admitted: "I do not know that any actual collision will take place, but it is not comfortable to be lying within the range of a couple of war steamers. The *Tribune*, a thirty-gun frigate is lying broadside to our camp, and from present indications, everything leads me to suppose that they will attempt to prevent my carrying out my instructions."[10] Casey believed that the British were "trying to bluff a little" and did not "apprehend anything serious."[11] Still, Casey warned Harney that if the British chose to they could easily blockade the island and destroy the small American force.[12]

Pickett seemed to take the entire matter personally. Harney had put great trust in him as a soldier and officer, but Pickett felt uncomfortable with any threat to his authority. He assured Pleasonton that "everything

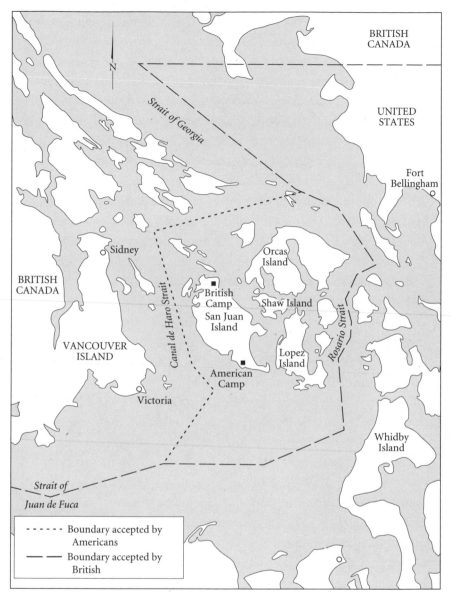

San Juan Island, Washington Territory

will be conducted properly—or I will go under," but he worried when the crew of a British ship failed to notify him of their arrival and fire the ceremonial gun salute. "Please my dear amigo mio," he begged Pleasonton, "tell me anything—entre nous—that you think ought to be done."[13]

On August 3, Capt. Geoffrey Phipps Hornby of the H.M.S. *Tribune* requested a meeting between officers to discuss peaceful negotiations on the island. Pickett agreed, and by midafternoon, three British captains arrived at the American camp. Hornby openly challenged Harney's authority to place troops on the island, contending that military occupation by the United States warranted the same action by the British. Since evacuation of American troops did not seem a possibility, Hornby argued for joint occupation until civilian authorities could resolve the boundary question. Pickett flatly refused to consider Hornby's plan. He maintained that if British forces came ashore, his orders from Harney to "resist all attempts at interference by the British authorities . . . by intimidation or force" compelled him to fight. Hornby closed the tense meeting, expressing his regret that the American captain was unwilling to cooperate. He later reiterated his position in a letter to Pickett, stating: "The responsibility of any such catastrophe does not, I feel, rest on me or on her majesty's representatives at Vancouver Island."[14]

In a note written that night, Pickett restated his stand to Hornby and shifted the blame back on the British. He could not allow joint occupation without approval from Harney, and he refused to make diplomatic decisions himself. Pickett used all the self-discipline the army had installed in him and tried to be courteous but firm. He closed the letter by stating, "I hope, most sincerely Sir, you will reflect on this and hope you may coincide with me in my conclusion." If a confrontation occurred, Pickett would put the responsibility on the British: "Should you see fit to act otherwise you will then be the person who will bring on a most unfortunate and disastrous difficulty and not the U.S. Officials."[15]

That evening, Pickett notified Harney of the day's events. Excitement was growing, and he estimated some 500 people had visited him since his arrival. "I have had to use a great deal of my *peace-making* disposition," Pickett maintained, "in order to restrain the sovereigns." He recounted his refusal to allow joint occupation, emphasizing that he had been cordial and courteous to the British captains but that at anytime they could defy him and land anywhere on the island. So far Pickett felt that he had control of the situation, but time was running out: "I must respectfully ask that an express be sent to me immediately for my future guidance. I do not think there are any moments to waste."[16]

Pickett did not trust the British. He angrily condemned the "miserable subterfuge of Governor Douglas" and insisted that they had every intention to "intimidate" innocent American civilians on the island, including Lyman Cutler. He predicted that if he and his company had not come to the island, the Hudson Bay Company would have seized Cutler and thrown him into a Victoria jail. Perhaps to quell his anxiety and distrust, he asserted unquestioning belief in the mission: "We are right," he announced to Pleasonton on August 3, "tho' we all knew it before."[17]

A week later, August 10, 1859, Harney sent Col. Silas Casey with several companies to reinforce the American camp on San Juan Island. Maneuvering through fog and past the two British frigates, Casey skillfully landed troops and artillery without detection. With these arrivals, the American land force numbered about 450 men and a dozen guns. When the fog lifted and the British became aware of the additional American troops, one of their armed ships moved closer to the island. Pickett, believing that an attack was imminent, suggested hastily putting up a brief fight, then spiking the guns and scattering into the woods. Casey, the senior and more experienced officer now in command, hesitated: "Not having time to form any well considered plan of my own with regard to the state of affairs, I did not countermand the directions that Captain Pickett had given." Rather than preparing for battle, Casey moved the American camp to a safer location behind sand hills and suggested a meeting with the British. Casey recalled: "Seeing the dangers of a collision at any moment which would inevitably lead to war between two mighty nations connected by *so many* common bonds . . . I resolved to make an attempt to prevent so great a calamity."[18]

On Casey's behest, the two American officers went to Victoria to try negotiations with British officers again. Casey requested to talk with Adm. R. Lambart Baynes, commander of the British fleet, to urge patience and to quiet "the rising excitement on both sides among the people and to give time for the intentions of the Home Governments to be made known in regard to the matter." Baynes, however, refused to meet Casey on an American ship, instead preferring to confront Casey aboard the British *Ganges*. Casey lost patience. "I have traveled 25 miles," he protested, "to see a gentleman who is disinclined to come 100 yards to see me!" No meeting occurred.[19]

The British were averse to take any real action. The last thing the British government needed at this time was an armed conflict with the

United States. Napoleon III's war in Italy threatened European stability, and British officials at Vancouver were hearing disturbing, often contradictory reports from the island. They were more interested in reaching an agreement than provoking a war.[20]

Throughout the crisis, Harney dutifully sent detailed reports and copies of correspondence to Washington. Referring to the "wanton and insulting conduct of the British authorities," Harney claimed that British officials threatened the rights and security of American citizens on the island.[21] He recounted the pig episode as justification for ordering the military post on the island. He also accused the British Hudson Bay Company of stirring up northern tribes and bearing responsibility for Indian raids.[22]

President James Buchanan and the War Department did not receive Harney's reports written in mid-August until September. Buchanan was astonished to learn that Harney had pushed his country to the brink of war. Acting Secretary of War W. R. Drinkard wrote Harney, "The President was not prepared to learn that you had ordered military possession to be taken of the island of San Juan."[23] Buchanan hastily contacted the British government to assure them that Harney acted without his knowledge or support, and he promptly dispatched Winfield Scott to Washington Territory to assess the damage. Scott arrived at Fort Vancouver on October 20, 1859. His main object was to keep the peace.[24]

By the time Scott arrived, tensions had cooled on the island. With only one British ship remaining off shore, everything seemed quiet at San Juan. Scott immediately agreed to joint occupation and removed all American troops from the island except one company of infantry. Calls for military action ceased, and in early December Pickett found himself back at Fort Bellingham.[25]

By the spring of 1860, the defiant Harney overturned Scott's orders. With Scott safely gone, Harney returned Pickett to San Juan, rejecting joint occupation as formally authorized by the army. He instructed Pickett to declare publicly that the island was now entirely part of Whatcom County, Washington Territory. Harney added that if Captain Bazelgette, commander of British troops on the island, ignored this proclamation, there would be "deplorable results out of his power to prevent or to control." Pickett followed Harney's orders without question but did not press the issue of jurisdiction. The British were shocked but no more willing to fight than they had been weeks earlier.[26]

Harney was notoriously impulsive and bad-tempered and his personality had much to do with creating and prolonging the crisis at San Juan. The general had had a successful career as an Indian fighter but earned Scott's disfavor during the Mexican War. Like Pickett, Harney craved military glory, and San Juan offered him an excellent opportunity. He nearly single-handedly blew the pig incident out of proportion and entangled the United States in an unnecessary war with Britain.[27]

George Pickett's behavior and personality also contributed to the crisis. He initially respected the British, who, unlike Indians or even Mexicans, were an honorable foe. Still, open questioning of his authority troubled him. He tried to follow his orders literally, his seeming insecurities preventing him from making decisions for himself. Some scholars have suggested that Pickett's narrow reading of his orders, his stubborn refusal to make decisions without Harney, and his determination to hold his ground actually stabilized the situation. In fact, it was more a combination of British indecision, hasty American diplomacy, and pure luck that prevented war. Pickett did all he could to bring war on.[28]

Despite his insistence that he was a "peaceable man," Pickett no doubt would have welcomed war.[29] Harney's prediction that the mission would bring recognition and promotion probably played constantly on his mind. More than ten years had passed since his heady days in Mexico, where he won commendation and brevets. Since that time, Pickett had suffered great personal pain and loss, and he seemed to look to the army as his surrogate family. To professional officers like Pickett, war was their reason for being, and foreign war was the "pinnacle of their professional lives."[30] As a young man he had experienced one war; now he was ready for another.

If he did not have the opportunity to fight, Pickett at least expected praise for his obedience to orders. He was hurt and shocked to receive censure instead. Local newspapers alleged that he was "obnoxious" to British authorities, and Scott condemned him as proud, jealous, and "extremely offensive" in his dealings with British authorities. The general in chief quickly removed Pickett from command and replaced him with a man Scott believed more courteous and trustworthy.[31] Pickett bristled at the thought that fellow officers condemned his actions, especially superior officers he admired, like Winfield Scott. In February 1860, he brooded to fellow West Pointer George Cullum, "The question arises why am I punished without even knowing what has been my fault?" Why was General Scott casting an "implicit censure upon me for obeying orders[?]"[32]

Others did praise him, and Pickett relished their approval. General Harney applauded his "cool judgment, ability and gallantry" and recommended that President Buchanan reward him with a brevet.[33] Colonel Casey stated that he was as "impressed as the general with the gallant behavior displayed by him during the late difficulties on the island."[34] When the legislature of the Washington Territory passed a joint resolution officially thanking Pickett for "the gallant and firm discharge of his duties under the most trying circumstances," he called that day "one of the proudest days of my life."[35]

For William Harney, censure far outweighed praise, and in June 1860, the U.S. government relieved him of command and ordered him back to Washington, D.C. The administration adopted Scott's proposal for joint occupation, and the crisis abated. Both sides awaited the decision of a neutral third party as final arbitrator of the boundary dispute.[36]

With Harney gone, Pickett's belligerence cooled. He maintained civil relations with British officials and civilians and tried to enforce strict regulations in the small town of San Juan. Prostitution and illegal liquor trafficking ran rampant, and excessive drinking was a constant problem among soldiers, settlers, and Indians. As he had in Bellingham, Pickett acted more as a constable than a soldier, although he felt severely ill-equipped to keep the peace. "My hands, my hands are tied," he complained in April 1860, demanding help from civil authorities.[37] Two months later he described "perfect bedlam day and night" and declared the island "a depot for murderers, robbers, whiskey sellers—in a word for all refugees from justice." Bemoaning the lack of "good citizens and farmers" on the island, he recommended banning all northern Indians, especially females, and liquor vendors from San Juan.[38] When a white man killed a northern Indian outside a whorehouse, Pickett acted decisively. Paying restitution to the Indian family, he quickly quelled any potential for avenging raids. Despite Pickett's many complaints, he managed to continue his active social life, entertaining American and British officers and attending dinners and dances. On July 18, 1860, Pickett reported that everything was relatively quiet on San Juan Island.[39]

LaSalle Corbell Pickett later alleged that her husband and General

Harney purposefully stirred hostilities on the island to start a foreign war and thus prevent civil war. According to her, these men had an "ulterior purpose" greater and more important than the "mere saving of a fragment of earth." She explained that the two officers "had seen the 'little cloud, no bigger than a man's hand,' drifting along the southern horizon, and had read its threatening import." To prevent disunion, they "were ready to risk their lives at the mouths of British guns."[40]

William Harney and George Pickett clearly welcomed war. Perhaps it is true that, given a choice, they would have opted for one with Britain. Leading men in battle would be a far more glamorous job than policing lawless whites and "savage" Indians. In the postwar years, George expressed hope that a foreign war would occur to reunite the country and distract it from the divisive racial issues of Reconstruction. Perhaps, in retrospect, he would tell LaSalle how he wished a war with Britain had occurred in 1860 and thus prevented the failures, disillusionment, and fears he endured in the Civil War.[41]

In the summer and fall of 1860, George Pickett was far from southern slaveholding society and secession. Fellow officer and southerner Edward Porter Alexander would later look back and assert that "there was generally little active interest taken by army officers in political questions, but with few exceptions, the creed was held that, as a matter of course, in case war should result from secession, each officer would go with his state."[42] Professional army officers like Pickett had prided themselves on their political neutrality during the explosive years preceding the Civil War. All through "secession winter," as seven southern states left the Union, Pickett waited and watched, and probably worried about what to do.

Pickett was a native southerner, but since the age of fifteen, he had lived far from Virginia and his family. Both of his parents were dead, laid to rest next to his first wife, Sally, and their child. His brother Charles had grown up and was a student at the University of Virginia; his sister, Jenny, had married a respectable doctor and moved to Williamsburg. His aunts and his uncle Andrew lived on, and thoughts of them may have fueled an old familiar desire to return home. LaSalle Corbell also waited anxiously for his return. He had responsibilities in Washington Territory, however: to the army and to his son. Would he leave his beloved army and his motherless son to fight in a war for southern independence? Could he fight his former comrades and classmates? These could not have been easy questions for George Pickett to answer as he waited news from the East.

During that long winter, Pickett wrote fellow army officer Benjamin Alvord for advice. This is the only original letter yet uncovered that provides insight into Pickett's views on secession and civil war. By February 1861, he knew professional officers would play an active role in war if it did come. He worried about mundane details of leaving his post, like appropriating public property and funds and paying the troops. Personally he seemed torn: "I myself come from a Union loving state," but he argued that Virginia and other "outer border states . . . cannot make their voices heard." He condemned "the Republicans [who] in their pride and flush of victory will not listen to the terms proposed by the conservative element, from those good and true states." However, he was equally critical of the fire-eaters: "I do not like to be bullied nor dragged out of the Union by the precipitatory and indecent haste of South Carolina."[43]

In the meantime, Pickett kept his post at San Juan. Perhaps Scott's censure embarrassed him; he now bent over backward to maintain good relations with the British. On January 24, 1861, British captain John D. S. Spencer indicated to Col. George Wright his satisfaction with the current situation at San Juan Island: "I must Sir . . . take this opportunity to express what pleasure I have derived from the very cordial and friendly feeling which had existed between the troops of the two governments during the time of joint occupation, and I have on all occasions received from Captain Bazalgette the assurance of having always experienced the utmost courtesy and friendliness on the part of Captain Pickett."[44] In February, Bvt. Brig. Gen. Albert Sidney Johnston, recently appointed commander of the Department of the Pacific, hoped that "this cordial and friendly feeling may continue to the end."[45] On February 22, 1861, Johnston's assistant adjutant general wrote Pickett that Johnston was "pleased to learn from Captain Spencer that between the forces occupying the island harmony prevails. He is anxious that this continue, and if possible to be avoided, no question for discussion may be raised."[46]

The United States had avoided foreign war; but civil war was about to erupt. On April 12, 1861, Confederate batteries fired on the U.S. garrison at Fort Sumter in Charleston Harbor, South Carolina. President Abraham Lincoln called for 75,000 volunteers to suppress the rebellion. As a consequence, another four states seceded, refusing to arm themselves against their southern sister states. On April 17, 1861, Virginia cast her lot with the southern Confederacy.

News traveled slowly from East to West in 1861. Pickett's West Point classmate and fellow Virginian D. H. Maury, who was stationed in New Mexico, recalled the "suspense and anxiety which we suffered as the days dragged their slow lengths along from the arrival of one mail to the next."[47] Pickett was at an especially remote spot on San Juan Island. Weeks passed, and wild rumors circulated about the events occurring 3,000 miles away. In March, he had written his uncle Andrew that he was trying to obtain leave. But if Virginia seceded, Andrew attested, "*He will come.*" His uncle estimated that it took six to eight weeks for mail to travel across the continent and did not expect Pickett to return South until the summer.[48]

In southern California, the army feared a Confederate outbreak. In June 1861, Brig. Gen. Edward V. Sumner, newly appointed commander of the Department of the Pacific, withdrew a considerable part of the forces from Oregon and Washington Territory to reinforce troops in California and Nevada Territory. On June 11, 1861, Special Orders Number 9 ordered the abandonment of Camp Pickett on San Juan Island.[49]

Two weeks later, Pickett resigned his commission from the U.S. Army. Virginia had already seceded in April, but he delayed resigning for several weeks. Despite his uncle Andrew's prediction, Pickett may have had second thoughts and considered remaining in his adopted home, Washington Territory. When it became clear that he would have to fight for the United States against secession in California, he acted. Still, he refused to abandon his post until the War Department formally accepted his resignation.[50]

As Pickett made plans to leave, the army reconsidered keeping the post at San Juan. There was concern over the resulting defenseless condition of the northwestern coast, and fear of Indian raids persisted. The governor of the territory urged the retention of a military post on the island. Colonel Wright also protested against abandoning the camp, convincing Sumner that San Juan Island had national importance, especially during these times of disunion and crisis. Pickett, too, argued that it was unwise to leave the island unprotected. Special Orders Number 13 sent Pickett and his company back to San Juan. Four days later, Pickett formally resigned, and by late July, he began his long journey home.[51]

Pickett left Washington Territory without his son. Since his mother's death, James had lived with a white family named Collins in Mason

County. His namesake, James Tilton, acted as overseer, consulting the Collinses periodically to see how he fared. It is unclear how much, if any, interaction actually occurred between father and son between 1858 and 1861. In early July 1861, Pickett expressed his desire that Tilton and the Collinses continue to act as guardians to young James. He sent Tilton $100 and expressed his gratitude that "Tilton has been kind enough to look after the welfare of my little boy, and will during my absence continue to take care of him."[52]

Why did Pickett leave his child behind? Perhaps his family in Virginia did not yet know of his second marriage, nor that he had a son. Perhaps Pickett had every intention of returning to the West once the crisis passed in the East. Perhaps he realized that there was no place for a child of mixed race in southern slaveholding society.

Since the death of his mother, James had rarely seen his father. Pickett provided money for his son's upkeep but little, if any, emotional support. When Pickett left, he did not even say good-bye. Tilton relayed Pickett's emotionless apology to Mrs. Collins: "He bid me say good-bye to Mr. Collins, yourself, and the boy. He regrets much that he could not take time to come down, but he was on a 30 day leave and had to reach Washington City in that time, so he went through via St. Louis and Sacramento and Portland, overland." Tilton added, "He hopes some other time to come out here again and promises to write to me as soon as he can." Pickett left his Bible and records of his army commission and leave of absence so that the boy "might know who his father was." Should the captain die, Tilton assured the Collinses, one of Pickett's aunts would care for the boy. James Tilton Pickett never saw his father again.[53]

Details of Pickett's trip east are unclear. Tilton stated that Pickett planned to travel across the continent, rushing to arrive in Washington, D.C., within thirty days, but changed his plans and took a steamer from San Francisco to New York. According to LaSalle, Union officials followed him at every turn, forcing Pickett to travel with a companion, disguised, and under an assumed name. She traced his convoluted route, along the Panama Railroad and Panamanian Isthmus, up the Atlantic Coast, and through New York City and Canada. Eventually, she explained, he turned south again, trekking across one of the midwestern states before entering neutral Kentucky, passing through Tennessee, and finally arriving in Virginia. LaSalle's story of spies and intrigue is probably pure fiction; many army officers resigned and accepted Confederate commissions with no harassment from the U.S. government.[54]

Either way, George Pickett was not headed for Washington, D.C., but the new Confederate capital in Richmond. He had never shown a particularly strong allegiance to his native South nor slaveholding society. In fact, his greatest loyalty seemed to be to the U.S. Army itself. But remaining in the Federal uniform would prove embarrassing and awkward, especially when close army friends and male family members joined the Confederate war effort. Pickett no doubt looked forward to the chance to prove himself in battle, and perhaps he thought the new southern nation offered him his best opportunity for professional advancement. Joining the Confederacy also marked a fresh personal beginning. In abandoning the U.S. Army, his life on the frontier, and his son, he was abandoning his past. In many ways, George Pickett was starting again.

Virginia, 1861–1862

War Meant Something More

George Pickett arrived in Richmond in September 1861 and immediately applied for an officer's commission in the Confederate army. As a professional soldier and decorated veteran with fifteen years experience, he knew that his services were in great demand. George could at least expect to receive rank equivalent to what he had had in the U.S. Army, if not one significantly higher. Affairs at the Confederate adjutant and inspector general's office moved slowly in 1861, and for several days Pickett heard no news of his rank and assignment. On September 14, he received an appointment as major in the artillery, but six days later his rank changed to captain of infantry in the provisional army. On September 23, he received orders to take command of the Lower Rappahannock River along with an immediate promotion to colonel. In about a week, he had made the transition from captain, to major, to captain again, then to colonel. For a man who spent nine years as a second lieutenant and six as a captain, this must have seemed like an excellent omen of what was to come.[1]

While Pickett's experiences in San Juan had attracted some attention in newspapers, and his family name probably still commanded respect in certain social circles, he returned to Virginia essentially unknown. When James J. Archer's brother found himself in Pickett's district, Archer wrote, "He will be a strict disciplinarian but most kind to you."[2] In the prewar army, many fellow officers showed real affection and high regard for George Pickett, and there is evidence that he took good care of his men.[3] Still, his promotion to captain was essentially due to his father's persistence and family political connections, and his service in the Washington Territory was not free from controversy. The Confederate army offered Pickett a fresh start to prove himself, not only as an officer but as

Early wartime photograph of George E. Pickett with an unusually full beard
(The Library of Virginia, Richmond, Va.)

a loyal and honorable white southern male. He had spent years crossing and challenging the social boundaries of southern white slaveholding culture; now he found himself defending them in armed conflict.

His first assignment placed him in charge of the far right flank of Confederate forces in northern Virginia. Pickett established his head-quarters at Tappahannock, guarding a section of the Rappahannock River that seemed a likely target for a northern amphibious attack. Any Federal force that landed successfully on the Lower Rappahannock would be closer to Richmond than the main Confederate army defending the city. Throughout the fall and early winter, Pickett anxiously watched closely for any sign of enemy concentration on the river.[4]

Soon after his arrival, Pickett received a serious scare. In late October, Secretary of War Judah P. Benjamin acquired seemingly reliable information that a Federal fleet was about to assault Pickett's position. Secretary Benjamin ignored regular military channels and hastily telegraphed him directly to "call out all the forces you can collect in the country, to be armed with such weapons as they can bring, to repel the invasion."[5] Pickett begged the War Department for more men and weapons. No reinforcements came, and neither did any Federal fleet. Fortunately, this incident proved to be a false alarm.[6]

This false alarm exposed the reality of Pickett's tenuous command. If an actual attack occurred, he had few reliable troops at his disposal. Several of the counties in his district were essentially undefended: only the skeleton of a militia existed in the region after most able-bodied men had received commissions as officers or had enlisted in state regiments. Worse, signs of Unionism emerged among the remaining population.[7]

Pickett was not alone in his concern. On October 21, 1861, a group of citizens from Lancaster and Northumberland Counties met to discuss their vulnerable position. As taxpayers who had "unlimited confidence" in the Confederate government, they felt that their homes were dangerously unprotected.[8] One month later, Maj. R. L. T. Beale, a resident of the region who had joined the 9th Virginia Cavalry, expressed his own uneasy feeling that there existed a certain amount of "disaffection in this section."[9] Poor whites close to enemy lines in the region were disgruntled, complaining bitterly that this was a war fought for the rich. Pickett's immediate superior, Maj. Gen. Theophilus H. Holmes, heard frequent reports of such sentiments, and he, too, felt "apprehensive of danger in that quarter."[10] In December, Pickett traveled to Westmoreland County and met with Major Beale. On December 10, he submitted a report strongly urging that "some strenuous and immediate measures should be taken to avoid, if possible[,] the contamination which might ensue."[11]

The reports George Pickett submitted during the Civil War offer insights into his state of mind throughout the conflict. This December 10 report from the war's early months, in which Pickett described what he believed to be a crisis brewing on the Rappahannock, is one of the most revealing. "A greater portion of our loyal men," he wrote, "the chivalry and high-toned gentlemen of the country[,] have volunteered and are far from their homes. There is a strong element among those who are left either to be non-combatants or to fall back under the old flag." Pickett added: "I do not consider we have any time to lose." He proposed that the government immediately organize the ineffective militia units, send them somewhere else, and replace them with a regiment of well-armed and better-disciplined men. It was a prudent and not unreasonable recommendation, if only Richmond authorities could find such a regiment. His report closed with a candid personal admission:

> I cannot close this communication to the general commanding without saying that many more complaints are made by a certain class of population[12] than are warranted. We have to fear them most. All during a war like this must suffer, but for the good of the general service it will not do to yield to those persons who have refused to volunteer, while the proprietors of the country are actually in the field, and who plead poverty and would join the enemy should an occasion occur. It will be a mistaken leniency and would only lead to further trouble.[13]

Pickett obviously counted himself in the ranks of the "loyal men, the chivalry and high-toned gentlemen of the country" who sacrificed for the new nation. It was his duty as an officer and a gentleman to protect the women and children of white men who had gone to the battlefront. "As commanding officer of that part of the country," he maintained, "the inhabitants looked to me for protection." Conscious of power relations and threats to his authority, Pickett dreaded being "placed in a false position." There were even rumors that the Confederacy might abandon the Northern Neck, leaving families "who are supporting this war" at "the mercy of the Northern marauders."[14] Pickett was learning that civil war blurred accepted demarcations separating aggressor and victim, friend and foe. He found himself fighting his own former comrades, army, and countrymen. Southerners who refused to support the Confederacy were in some ways more dangerous than Union armies.

The situation on the Rappahannock had striking similarities to Pickett's experiences in Washington Territory. At Fort Bellingham and San Juan, Pickett tried to protect civilians and calm their fears with what he deemed insufficient troops and unsettling challenges to his command. Like civil war, the frontier had confused lines between friend and foe, Indian and white man. At Bellingham and the Northern Neck, Pickett distinguished two types of white civilians: those worthy of protection and the "inferior class," whom he blamed for instigating trouble with the enemy.[15]

And as in San Juan, Pickett's patience was wearing thin. Unaware that Holmes had forwarded his report to the War Department with a strong endorsement, he took matters into his own hands. Without authorization, Pickett left his command on the Rappahannock and went directly to Richmond to see Samuel Cooper, the adjutant and inspector general, personally. Pickett was convinced that somebody in the chain of command was not telling him everything he should know. He urgently requested that Cooper do something immediately "to prevent the possibility of the disaffected element from gaining the ascendancy."[16]

Rather than improving his control of the situation, Pickett's efforts to protect the Northern Neck cost him his command. Shortly after his visit to Richmond, the secretary of war approved Pickett's original proposal and ordered a Virginia regiment to the district.[17] On December 24, Col. John M. Brockenbrough and his 40th Virginia Infantry arrived on the river. Brockenbrough's initial instructions were to cooperate with Pickett in protecting the district.[18] However, the two officers quickly discovered that, by date of commission, Brockenbrough outranked Pickett. In fact, Pickett himself was junior to all other colonels stationed up and down the river. Maj. Gen. Holmes relieved Pickett from command, feeling that two colonels posted so close to each other "would have produced a conflict of authority." Holmes did commend Pickett for his managing the command "admirably well" and for his organizing and distributing "the small force at his disposal in the most judicious and effective manner."[19] Even Pickett admitted that he could "not see the necessity of two colonels to command less than a regiment" and asked to be relieved. His zealousness had undercut his own authority, and he anxiously hoped he would receive a new, perhaps even better, assignment.[20]

Military and government officials were working on obtaining for Pickett not only reassignment but promotion. On January 6, 1862, Maj. William N. Ward submitted Pickett's name for promotion to brevet brigadier general. Four days later, Adjutant and Inspector General

Cooper recommended him for full rank as brigadier general. The same day, Judah P. Benjamin formally submitted Pickett's promotion to President Jefferson Davis.[21]

What caused George Pickett to receive such powerful support for promotion this early in the war? Ward's recommendation may have carried more weight than one would expect. Although only a major, Ward was a noted friend of President Davis and General Lee, with apparent political connections. In addition, Ward was a resident of the Northern Neck, and his family, including twelve children, was caught behind Union lines.[22] Still, Pickett's commanding officer, Theophilus Holmes, had not recommended him for promotion. Despite one historian's contention that Pickett had earned the general's "warm good will," Holmes's commendation of Pickett was rather noncommittal. Holmes described him as someone who "managed his command . . . admirably well," but he neither recommended Pickett for promotion nor fought to keep him.[23]

Pickett may have simply benefited from being at the right place at the right time. He was an unattached colonel with formal military education and real, if limited, combat experience. Johnston's main army at Centreville suffered from chronic shortages of general officers to command brigades, one of which was composed entirely of Virginia troops. President Davis normally insisted that brigadier generals be from the same state as the men. Pickett's visit to Richmond may have brought his name to the forefront and highlighted his availability at the most opportune time.[24]

And his tenacity probably helped. Although officers all across the South constantly begged for reinforcements, his personal visit to Richmond may have convinced the Confederate War Office that he was an officer with some initiative and ardor. He sought formal recognition and promotion, just as any professional army officer would. Only George Pickett did not intend to stand by and allow an opportunity to pass him by.

Despite Pickett's impatience, an entire month passed without word of his promotion or even reassignment. But he did not remain idle. In mid-February he accompanied presidential aide Col. G. W. C. Lee on a tour of the defenses of the Rappahannock and continued to stress the area's vulnerability to attack. He complained, "I have waited for some time past in anxious expectation of some definite instructions from Richmond but

George E. Pickett, circa 1862
(Library of Congress)

receive nothing."[25] He heard rumors of his promotion but nothing definite until February 13, when he received his official appointment to brigadier general.[26]

Pickett's orders were to report without delay to Joseph Johnston's army in Centreville.[27] Although he was clearly eager to acquire a new assignment, Pickett was late in reaching Centreville. On February 15, 1862, Johnston impatiently wired the adjutant general's office: "General Pickett's appointment has been sent to me. Where is he? Order him here."[28] Ten more days passed, and Pickett had still not arrived. Johnston complained to the War Department that his "army is crippled and its discipline greatly impaired by the want of general officers; . . . a division and five brigades are without generals."[29] Pickett arrived finally on February 28 and took over the brigade in the army corps commanded by James Longstreet, who was now a major general.[30]

George Pickett and James Longstreet had been friends and comrades for many years, but the Civil War strengthened their relationship. There is an often repeated anecdote that George handled funeral arrangements for three of the Longstreet children who died suddenly in February 1862. James and his wife, Louise, the story claims, were too distraught to do it themselves, and George intervened and comforted the grieving parents. Since the only source for this account is a letter LaSalle Pickett wrote Longstreet's second wife, Helen, in 1903, there is a strong possibility that this is yet another one of her postwar fabrications. Nonetheless, the two men were close, and after the war, Longstreet became one of Pickett's greatest public defenders, surpassed only by LaSalle in his loyalty and devotion.[31]

George's relationship with LaSalle Corbell was also apparently intensifying in 1862. During the second year of war, LaSalle was continuing her studies at Lynchburg Female Seminary in Lynchburg, Virginia. As the eldest daughter of a large tidewater planter, Sallie was learning how to be a cultivated southern lady. At the seminary, she studied Latin, French, music, and literature. There were daily walks, Bible study, dinners, and dances to augment more or less academic classes. LaSalle later claimed that her education prepared her "to be a soldier's wife."[32] Indeed, believing that cultivated elite women made better mates, southern slaveholding society viewed such schooling as excellent training for marriage and motherhood.[33]

LaSalle later recalled that by 1862 war had shattered her peaceful and predictable existence at the academy. Her published memoirs recount her and her classmates excitedly clustered in their school rooms, believing "that we knew something of war." During the war's early months, she and her classmates cheered at the sight of the First National Flag and felt confident that their brothers, fathers, uncles, and male friends would come home safe and soon from the battlefront. They held a festival to raise money for knapsacks to equip a local rifle company. LaSalle later admitted to her postwar readers that she, like so many other white southerners, believed the conflict would be relatively bloodless and quick. "We saw then," she remembered, "only the bonfires of joy and heard the paeans of victory." LaSalle's impression changed when she met a man wounded in battle: "I began to feel that war meant something more than the thrill of martial music and shouts of victory." In retrospect, she remembered, "Not only soldiers in the field had obstacles to encounter; they loomed in the pathway of the school-girl."[34]

Although military historians rarely acknowledge it, war has always affected women. America's armed conflicts have had a seductive appeal not only to men but also to women, heightening as well as challenging traditional gender roles. While young males felt compelled to prove themselves as men at the battlefront, females clamored to prove that they were women, actively playing the part of dependent wife, daughter, sister, or mother. War's message to women was a conflicting one: on the home front a war demanded women to be self-sacrificing and stalwart, but the very nature of combat stressed female dependence and helplessness.[35]

Men like George had a purpose and mission in war, and LaSalle was determined to have one too. Her marriage to a general would allow her to share more directly in the war effort; until then she was not content to sit by and watch. LaSalle Pickett's published memoirs recount her doing what other elite white women did early in the conflict: applauding marching soldiers, waving flags, and selling her jewelry for the sake of "the cause."[36] But her books show her doing and wanting more. Throughout her recollections she combined traditional female repulsion to war with a decidedly masculine fascination with battle. She often depicted herself at the forefront of battle, oblivious to the danger surrounding her. At times it seemed that she could not pull herself away.[37]

In March 1862, as George readied himself for his new field command, LaSalle, too, was anxious for action. LaSalle later recalled visiting her uncle Col. J. J. Phillips in camp on the day of the famed naval battle between the *Virginia* and the *Monitor*. When her uncle prepared a dinghy to join in the action, LaSalle pleaded to join him. "No, No!" he reportedly shouted. "Go Back." Unshaken by his refusal, LaSalle took a seat in his small vessel while he turned his back. When her uncle realized that LaSalle had defied him, "a look of horrified amazement" came over his face. She described him declaring: "You needn't think I am going to try to keep you out of danger, you disobedient, incorrigible little minx. . . . It would serve you right if you were shot." LaSalle explained that she had little thought of the hazards, only wanting to get a good view of the sea battle. When she asked for her uncle's field glasses, he cautioned her not to lose her balance and fall overboard, "though," according to LaSalle, he said, "I reckon it would be a good thing if you did. Teach you better than to put yourself where you have no business."[38] LaSalle's postwar recollections of the war put her, whether in fantasy or reality, where she had "no business."

LaSalle's courtship and marriage to George seemed a foil and justification for her intense interest in war. Although she insisted that the seeds of their love affair sprouted earlier, their romance probably actually began to blossom in the winter of 1861–62. George apparently found her wildly distracting, and she may have been the reason he was so tardy in reaching Centreville. By 1862, LaSalle had matured into an attractive young woman with dark hair and eyes. Although he was thirty-seven years old, George still had a boyish quality to him. He continued to wear his hair long, and he took great pains in his dress and appearance. Nevertheless, the years had taken a toll on him: wartime photographs reveal a swollen face and deep rings outlining his eyes. A weakness for liquor, probably dating from his frontier days, and weight gain aged him. To Sallie, he was and would remain her handsome and gallant soldier. It is no wonder that George sought her company. Around her he could no doubt feel young again, manly and powerful, and through her eyes, he could be the man he wanted to be.

George would, in fact, find himself relying more and more on LaSalle as he faced the responsibilities of his new command. At San Juan his largest command had been a single company of sixty-odd men. Now he had forty times that many, men who had been together and fought a major battle months before Pickett even joined the Confederate army. The former captain suddenly found himself responsible for more than 2,500 men. His brigade consisted of five units recruited from all over Virginia: four infantry regiments and one battery of artillery.[39]

Pickett had much to learn about this level of command. Even discounting the question of whether or not he could successfully maneuver such a large body of men on the battlefield, the new brigadier had to deal with the administrative problems of keeping his men fit to fight. He was responsible for their food, quarters, medical care, and training. Providing for a brigade was a constant struggle in the Confederate army, which rarely had enough supplies of anything. Worse, his men could not necessarily be depended upon to take care of themselves. That March, a fellow officer explained, "It is astonishing how hard it is to keep a body of men in good health; they are just like children—in Summer they eat green fruit and green corn, and in winter take colds and pneumonia and expose themselves."[40]

Fortunately, Pickett inherited a battle-tested group of men, ably led by officers who were, for the most part, trained soldiers. During the battle of Manassas, the brigade had "seen the elephant" when it participated in the successful defense of Henry's Hill. Unlike other Manassas brigades, this one remained relatively intact in the months following the battle. Eppa Hunton, the colonel with the least military experience led the 8th Virginia. A lawyer and militia officer before the war, Hunton proved to be a talented, natural leader. He later earned promotion to brigadier general. The rest of Pickett's regimental commanders had professional training. Twenty-nine-year-old Virginia Military Institute graduate Henry A. Carrington commanded the 18th Virginia. Both the 19th Virginia's Col. John B. Strange and the 28th Virginia's Robert C. Allen were also VMI graduates. Capt. James Dearing, former member of the West Point class of 1862, commanded the artillery battery.[41]

Less than a week after Pickett assumed command of the Third Brigade, orders arrived to withdraw from winter quarters at Centreville. General Johnston feared interruption of his line of communications by amphibious assault and therefore decided to abandon the position his army had occupied since his victory the previous summer. From March 9 to March 11, 1862, the Confederate Army of the Potomac conducted a torturously slow march southward to a more defensible line behind the Rappahannock River.[42]

The weather in northern Virginia was abominable that early spring of 1862. Rain fell incessantly, and roads were nearly impassable. Johnston reported to the War Department that a well-mounted horseman could travel just twelve miles in six and a half hours.[43] Major General Longstreet recalled that "with the beginning of the new year, winter set in with rain and snow, alternate freezing and thawing, until the roads and fields became seas of red mud."[44]

It was a miserable march. Maj. E. P. Alexander remembered: "The whole soil of that section seemed to have no bottom and no supporting power."[45] To make matters worse, men lacked adequate food and many were sick. No doubt, as his brigade skirted swollen streams and waded down flooded roads, Pickett felt as Maj. Gen. G. W. Smith did when he reported that he was "fairly launched in a sea of mud. . . . At any rate can't turn back now even if I wished to."[46] After three days of struggling through the mire, Pickett's brigade crossed the Rappahannock River on a plank-covered railroad bridge, reached the vicinity of Culpeper Court-house, and halted.[47]

Not quite a week passed before events justified Johnston's caution in ordering the retreat. On March 17, 1862, Union major general George B. McClellan began sending his Army of the Potomac by water to the tip of the York-James Peninsula. Federal troops landed at Pickett's old post, Fort Monroe, held by the Union since the beginning of the war. A Union offensive up the peninsula toward Richmond seemed imminent. Almost immediately after Johnston encamped his army at its new position, Gen. Robert E. Lee, overseeing operations at Richmond, began ordering away brigades and divisions as reinforcements for Confederate defenses on the peninsula. During the next month, nearly half of Johnston's army joined Maj. Gen. John B. Magruder's forces manning entrenchments at York-town. General Johnston purposely retained under his own control what he considered to be his two best divisions, those of Generals Longstreet and G. W. Smith. Pickett and his brigade remained near Culpeper Court-house.[48]

While awaiting additional orders, Pickett's men became better acquainted with their new commander. Pvt. R. A. Shotwell's published diary offers a rare look at Brigadier General Pickett that early spring of 1862. One day in April, Pickett personally inspected his regiments. Shotwell described him as "an old West-Pointer . . . [who] conducted himself accordingly." To Shotwell's horror, Pickett singled out the young soldier, took up his gun, gingerly ran a white gloved finger along the barrel, "and lo!" found "a rusty streak on the glove." To add insult to injury, Shotwell's colonel rushed over to introduce the private to the displeased commander. "General," Colonel Hunton announced, "this young man left college at the North to come South and fight with us." Pickett took out a handkerchief, blew his nose, and turned away without speaking a word. Shotwell recalled, "It was a little mortifying to be pointed out as 'this young man,' and stared at without even a nod of recognition; but alas! all the patriotism in the world wouldn't count in the scale of a West-Pointer with one or two degrees of higher rank; however the great equality in all other respects!"[49]

Meanwhile, Johnston and his two divisional generals met personally with President Davis, newly appointed secretary of war George W. Randolph, and General Lee. When Longstreet returned to his division, the day after a marathon conference, he brought new orders: his entire division would rejoin the rest of the army at Yorktown.[50]

The march ran within a few miles of George's birthplace and the former plantation of his first wife, Sally Minge. He and his brigade would halt only a short distance from the fort where he began his slow recovery from his deep depression after Sally's death. He passed close by the beach where he may have met LaSalle Corbell at Old Point Comfort. The fortunes of civil war had brought him back to his family home, assigned him to participate in its defense, and made former classmates and comrades the hated enemy.

By April 18, Pickett's brigade was in position at the center of the Confederate line at Yorktown. McClellan's siege of Yorktown had already commenced; he was slowly bringing up so many cannon in front of the rebel army that when he opened fire he expected to pound it into submission in a few hours. Pickett and his brigade remained on the Yorktown line for about two weeks.[51]

The siege of Yorktown was a miserable affair for the Confederates, who lacked strength to do much more than wait. E. P. Alexander later concluded that "in the whole course of the war little service was as trying as that in the Yorktown lines."[52] The men, while cramped in poorly drained dirt trenches, daily had to endure rain showers and enemy sniper fire. Brig. Gen. Robert A. Toombs bitterly commented that soldiers were "kept in the trenches, often times a foot deep in water for eighteen days, without necessity or object I could [learn, except] the stupidity and cowardice of our officers."[53]

During one of these skirmishes in the trenches, Pickett gave additional evidence of his hot temper. In a nighttime attack, a small group of Yankees successfully seized a Confederate redoubt with little opposition.

Confederate batteries posted near the redoubt failed to fire on the attackers, allowing the Yankees to escape without harm. Pickett was livid. He, accompanied by artillery captain James Dearing, confronted the gunners who had stood idly by while their comrades were killed or captured. The battery officers defended themselves by stating that they had had no orders from their colonel to fire. Dearing wrote, "Pickett is not noted for keeping his temper, so he ripped out with a whole handful of pretty strong words & told them that he ranked Col. Brown & was in command down here just then & if they didn't fire they had better leave." Division commander James Longstreet also appeared on the scene to support Pickett's angry avowal, and Dearing soon relieved the gunners from their position.[54]

As the siege continued, Johnston suspected that McClellan was about to open his cannonade, a bombardment that would quickly bleed the southern army of 55,000 men to death. There was no stopping McClellan's deliberate advance of 100,000 men this close to the coast, where they had full support of the Union navy. Johnston determined to find a better position to confront the enemy. He began withdrawing his men up the peninsula toward the Confederate capital.[55]

On May 3, after two confused days of orders and counterorders, Johnston started his move up the peninsula. McClellan, discovering the abandonment of Yorktown defenses, sent troops to close upon retreating Confederates. J. E. B. Stuart's cavalry clashed with pursuing Federals near the old colonial town of Williamsburg. Johnston ordered a rearguard defense to shield his army, first sending troops commanded by Maj. Gen. Lafayette McLaws, then replacing them with Longstreet's division.[56]

Longstreet ordered his whole division to unite two miles outside Williamsburg and confront the enemy. During the rainy night of May 4, his men positioned themselves along a line of earthworks built by Magruder in anticipation of the necessity of such action. Orders went out immediately to Pickett to bring his brigade up to the central redoubt, Fort Magruder.[57] Pickett's brigade had already lost over 1,000 men to sickness and details before the retreat from Yorktown; he had only about 1,500 effectives with which to fight. Early on May 5, just as his men fell into line to continue their march, Pickett received Longstreet's orders to turn back.[58]

Initially held in reserve, Pickett's brigade stood ready to move onto the field and reinforce the heavily pressed South Carolinians of Brig. Gen. Richard H. Anderson. They did not have to wait long, however, before Anderson's courier came to Pickett and instructed him to move rapidly forward. Federals brought up more troops and widened their attack. Soon Pickett's Virginians became hotly engaged. Pickett recalled that his regiments "sturdily . . . maintained their ground returning the fire with the most telling effect."[59] As the day wore on, more reinforcements came up to support each side, and there followed a series of attacks and counterattacks. By late afternoon, the ground before Pickett was "literally covered with dead."[60] Nightfall brought an end to the fighting, and Longstreet, determining that he had bought enough time for the main army, withdrew his division to rejoin Johnston's move up the peninsula. The battle of Williamsburg was over.[61]

Pickett felt his brigade had performed well, though he described his losses as "quite severe." He counted a total of 26 dead and 138 wounded, casualties amounting to slightly more than 10 percent of the men he had carried into battle. He believed that "the gallantry and energy exhibited by both officers and men cannot be too much praised. After hard night marches, drenching rains, and but scanty rations, they met an enemy well-fed, superior in numbers, better armed and equipped, and well posted, and drove them a mile during the engagement." He concluded, "It is with pleasure that I state that their confidence in their own ability and cause is redoubled since their action."[62]

Pickett's report also spoke for himself. The battle tested his ability as a brigadier general and officer, and he passed with flying colors. Longstreet praised his friend in his official report: "Brig. Gen. George E. Pickett, greatly distinguished in other fields, used his forces with great effect, ability, and his usual gallantry."[63] Such warm recognition of Pickett's past services, notably his days in Mexico, had to have bolstered his confidence.

The battle of Williamsburg was small compared to future fights, but Pickett expressed alarm regarding the nature of this civil war. The enemy seemed unwilling to follow the "rules of war" that he and other southern professional officers, he fervently believed, followed. Pickett described how he had watched with disgust when Yankees coldly shot a Confederate colonel after the officer had halted a charge at the sight of a white flag. He was shocked: "I must mention also the dastardly subterfuges of an enemy pretending to surrender in order to stop our fire to allow their reinforcements to come up and enable them to pour in a deadly volley upon an honorable and too unsuspecting foe."[64]

Chilling rains fell as Johnston's army trudged toward Richmond. McClellan was not far behind. Again Pickett passed near his family home at Turkey Island. This time he was leaving it to the enemy, adversaries he saw more and more as contemptible barbarians.

CHAPTER 7

Virginia, 1862

Shaking with the Thunders of the Battle

Two weeks after the battle of Williamsburg, rival armies camped less than ten miles from Richmond. Union soldiers recalled that they were near enough to the Confederate capital to tell time by city church chimes. Close as he was to Richmond, Federal commander George B. McClellan was not positioned at the most favorable location. His 105,000-man Army of the Potomac awkwardly straddled the swollen Chickahominy River. A lack of serviceable bridges made it doubtful that his army's two wings could support each other if the Confederates threatened. As the weather turned even more violent, Johnston decided to take advantage of McClellan's vulnerable position.[1]

After the stormy night of May 30, Johnston ordered an early morning, three-pronged attack on the Federal left wing. When James Longstreet marched his division down the wrong road, he created so much confusion that several hours passed before any fighting broke out.[2] Pickett and his brigade took no part in the disjointed attacks on May 31. All day, he and his men waited impatiently in reserve as the battle raged before them. They may or may not have known that General Johnston had been seriously wounded, only adding to the battle's chaos.[3]

Johnston's replacement, G. W. Smith, determined to renew a coordinated assault the next morning. On the evening of May 31, Pickett received orders to march toward Seven Pines and report to Maj. Gen. D. H. Hill, located just below (or southeast of) Fair Oaks Station near the Richmond and York River Railroad. Hill, unaware of Smith's plans, was hesitant to stage a large advance on the enemy's left. Although Longstreet had essentially turned over tactical command of his brigades to him, Hill worried over the losses suffered by his men the day before. Besides, no one seemed entirely sure just where the Federals were along the railroad.[4]

Pickett set out with two of his staff members through wild "under-growth and thickets" to find the enemy. Scanning dark woods before him, Pickett strained for signs of movement. Visibility was poor, and there had been no reconnaissance of the area by cavalry. "In fact," he recalled, "I had no definite idea, where [the enemy was], as I saw no one and had not had time to examine the nature of (the) ground or position."[5] Suddenly, a stream of brightly colored Confederate Zouaves rushed out of the woods. They belonged to the 1st Louisiana Battalion, which had actually been a part of Pickett's brigade at Manassas. Grabbing hold of one Zouave on muleback, Pickett demanded an explanation for their flight. The terrified Louisianian shouted at Pickett, "The enemy were within a few yards of us and entreated me to let him save himself."[6] An officer in the 18th Virginia remembered, "A perfect mob of men rushed from that wood without semblance of organization, each men [sic] running for his life."[7] The sight of these fleeing soldiers disgusted Pickett.[8]

Pickett returned to Hill and hastily reported his findings. "He ordered me to attack," Pickett recalled, "and I supposed [the] same order was given to other brigade commanders." He supposed wrongly. Hill apparently only sought a limited but intense assault by Pickett's brigade, not a large-scale attack. George Pickett, however, believed he was part of a massive deployment to turn the tide of battle. As his regiments fell into a line and began advancing, Pickett followed on foot. He later praised his men for "moving on beautifully and carrying everything before them."[9] For a short time the very audacity of the advance paid off, and it seemed to be a success. Abruptly, an accompanying brigade broke and fled. Before he knew it, Pickett and his men were alone on the field. In reality, Pickett's men had not pushed back a sizable force of Federals; they had wandered at an inverted angle into an area between two Union brigades. "Instead of driving a defeated foe," as one historian of the battle observes, "Pickett had accidentally stumbled into the clutches of two brigades that had not seen any action."[10] Hurriedly riding to Hill's headquarters, Pickett pleaded for help. Hill sent two brigades, but Federal attackers easily outnumbered southerners. Later, Pickett attested that if only Hill had sent sufficient reinforcements, "we would [have] drive[n] the enemy across the Chickahominy."[11]

Pickett's fighting blood was up nonetheless, and even when no support came and Confederate fire slackened because of casualties and lack of ammunition, he refused to withdraw. He reported that "a most perfect apathy seemed to prevail" among his superiors, while enemy fire poured into his lone brigade.[12] In the midst of the fight, Pickett witnessed a memorable exchange between his men and the enemy. When a line of Federals came threateningly close, a Union officer stopped his men from firing and asked what troops they faced. Pickett's men shouted, "Virginians." According to Pickett, the Federal officer called back to his own men, "Don't fire; they'll surrender; we'll capture all these d—d Virginians." "Scarcely were the words uttered," Pickett reported, "when the Nineteenth and the left of the Eighteenth rose up in the abatis and fired a withering volley into them, killing the commanding officer and literally mowing down the ranks."[13] After clinging to the abatis for nearly an hour, Pickett returned his men 400 yards to the rear. Two other Confederate brigades moved to cover his flanks, and he and his men stubbornly held their own for the remainder of the day.[14]

On June 2, Confederate forces left the field at Seven Pines and Pickett's men covered the withdrawal. That evening, just after midnight, Pickett and his brigade "leisurely moved off, not a Yankee in sight or even a puff of smoke." His brigade lost over 350 men, killed and wounded.[15] A colonel in the brigade concluded, "I have always thought, and still believe the second day's fight at Seven Pines was the most useless sacrifice of life I have ever known. There seemed to be no plan, no object, no purpose in anything that was done."[16]

Historian Douglas Southall Freeman stated that the only tangible results of the battle of Seven Pines "were more casualties, confusion, recrimination, and a gallant, futile fight in which Brig. Gen. George E. Pickett increased the reputation he had gained at Williamsburg."[17] To his superiors, Pickett was proving an aggressive and zealous brigadier general. Johnston noted: "On the morning of June 1 the enemy attacked the brigade of General Pickett supported by that of General Pryor. The attack was vigorously repelled by these brigades, the brunt of the action falling on General Pickett."[18] Longstreet, too, made special mention of "Pickett's brigade bearing the brunt of the attack and repulsing it." He declared Pickett's performance at Seven Pines that of a "true soldier" and praised him for his "usual gallantry and ability."[19] Later in June he would recommend his good friend for promotion.[20] As D. H. Hill reported, "A furious attack was made upon Generals Armistead, Mahone, Pickett, Pryor, and Wilcox. . . . Armistead's men fled early in the action. . . . Mahone withdrew his brigade without any orders. I sent up Colston's to replace him, but he did not engage the Yankees, as I expected him to do. Pickett, Pryor and Wilcox received their orders to fall back. . . . Wilcox and Pryor withdrew, but Pickett held his ground against the odds of ten to one for several hours longer, and only retired when the Yankees ceased to annoy him."[21] It is no wonder that, after Seven Pines, Pickett's men earned the name "Gamecock Brigade."[22]

For LaSalle Corbell, the battle of Seven Pines "brought the war closer to me than any other had yet done."[23] In 1862, she recalled coming to Richmond to spend her summer vacation, unable to visit her tidewater home caught behind Federal lines. Although her writings romanticized and glorified her husband's military career, her recollections realistically captured the raw fear of war. Her description of Richmond during the battle of Seven Pines is especially striking. "If I could lay before you the picture of the Richmond of those battle-days," she told her readers in 1914, "you would say that I had written the most powerful peace argument ever penned." Emphasizing horrific sights and sounds Richmonders witnessed, she described the Confederate capital "shaking with the thunders of the battle while the death-sounds thrilled through our agonized souls."[24] Carts loaded with wounded and dead crowded the streets, and LaSalle alleged that few residences were not open to the injured. Women and children found that the horror of war had come directly into their homes: "Women, girls, and children stood before the doors with wine and food for the wounded as they passed."[25] Soldiers and civilians formed a desperate mix in Capitol Square, anxiously awaiting news of loved ones. Black crepe began to appear on doorways and windows. Recalling a mother who lost her son at Seven Pines, LaSalle declared, "Sometimes the Richmond of those days comes back to me now, and I shudder anew with terror."[26]

Robert E. Lee replaced the wounded Joseph E. Johnston on June 1. For a solid month, Lee prepared his newly styled "Army of Northern Virginia," for an offensive against McClellan. Lee drew Maj. Gen. Thomas J. "Stonewall" Jackson's Army of the Shenandoah Valley and assorted brigades from the Atlantic Coast to reinforce the army around Richmond.[27]

On June 26, 1862, Lee tried to crush the Federal V Corps under Maj.

Gen. Fitz-John Porter encamped in an isolated position north of the Chickahominy River. The new army commander devised a complicated assault on the Union right flank at Beaver Dam Creek, but like Johnston's at Seven Pines, his plans went awry. On paper the plan called for Jackson's Army of the Shenandoah Valley to advance on the enemy's rear and flank. Once Jackson's attack was in motion, the divisions of A. P. Hill, D. H. Hill, and James Longstreet were to assail the Federal front; another portion of Lee's army waited to follow the expected rout. Jackson failed to arrive on time, and A. P. Hill, impatient to attack, sent his men forward anyway. The resulting battle of Mechanicsville was little more than a fiasco. Porter's men fell back to formidable entrenchments along Beaver Dam Creek, well protected from the Confederate's disjointed and costly attacks. D. H. Hill recalled, "Our engineers seem to have had little knowledge of the country and none of the fortifications of the country, and none of the fortifications of the creek."[28] Pickett's brigade, part of Longstreet's unused division, found itself again waiting and watching this indecisive and bloody engagement.[29]

During the night of June 26, Fitz-John Porter pulled his corps back about a mile and a half, where, with reinforcements from the other side of the river, he set up a new position. Lee, undaunted by his setback, followed close behind, determined to renew the attack on the Federal right flank near New Cold Harbor. The impetuous A. P. Hill was the first to discover Porter's location; the Union general had arranged his troops in a semicircular entrenchment behind a boggy swamp. Hill's men set out across the marsh in a series of piecemeal, futile attacks. Lee waited and watched, continuing to hope that he could pull off a large-scale offensive.[30]

As the day wore on, it must have seemed to Pickett and his men that circumstance had relegated them to the status of spectators. Finally, around 4:00 P.M., Lee called on Longstreet to make a demonstration on the Union left to relieve pressure against Hill's weakening right flank. Pickett's brigade quickly moved onto the field toward the sound of intense firing. Col. John B. Strange of the 19th Virginia recalled: "Passing through woods we soon reached a large, open, undulating field, with heavy timber on all sides, where we formed in line of battle and awaited a few minutes the approach of the enemy, which was momentarily expected, as they were exactly in our front." Pickett's troops had become separated from the rest of the division in their passage through the woods. He did not yet know that his right flank was dangerously exposed to Union artillery in place atop the hills on the opposite side of the Chickahominy.[31]

Pickett hurriedly deployed his men forward toward the brow of a hill. Almost immediately, the enemy barrage grew fierce from both Porter's troops in front and cannon across the river. Staff officer Harrison remembered: "The fire from the enemy's batteries and small arms was now terrific. I have never seen such a storm of projectiles of every description and at short range, concentrated upon so narrow a field of battle."[32] Soldiers instinctively threw themselves to the ground, loading and firing their rifles as they lay on their stomachs. Harrison wrote, "The effect upon our ranks was terrific, but the brave brigade pushed on. The men fell around us like leaves in autumn."[33] Colonel R. E. Withers, of the 18th Virginia, estimated that, within a span of fifteen minutes, his regiment lost over 200 men and officers, killed or wounded.[34]

Existing battle reports from Gaines's Mill make it difficult to reconstruct accurately the movements of Pickett and his brigade that day in June. Men guessed distance and time in the heat of battle, units became separated, and friendly forces sometimes fired into each other. "The roar of musketry was so terrific," one soldier recalled, "that it was impossible to hear anything else."[35] Pickett's inspector general agreed: "It was almost impossible to see or hear anything distinctly, such was the continual rush of the shot and shell."[36] Most senior officers had never seen a map of the battlefield; neither Lee nor Longstreet probably ever knew for certain just where Pickett's brigade was. Before nightfall, when the last Confederate lunge broke the exhausted Federal line, Pickett's brigade had sustained over 400 casualties. This number included their commander.[37]

Roughly a quarter of a mile from the Union line, while leading his brigade toward the clearing, Pickett abruptly fell from his horse. Some ten paces behind him, staff officer Walter Harrison remembered, "I did not perceive his fall until he said to me in very expressive terms that—*somebody*—had hit him. I immediately dismounted, examined his wound and found the *hole* of a minie ball in his shoulder." Harrison had no time to linger, pressing on with the rest of the brigade into the fight.[38]

LaSalle Corbell Pickett naturally painted a more melodramatic portrait of her husband's wounding. LaSalle described George being shot

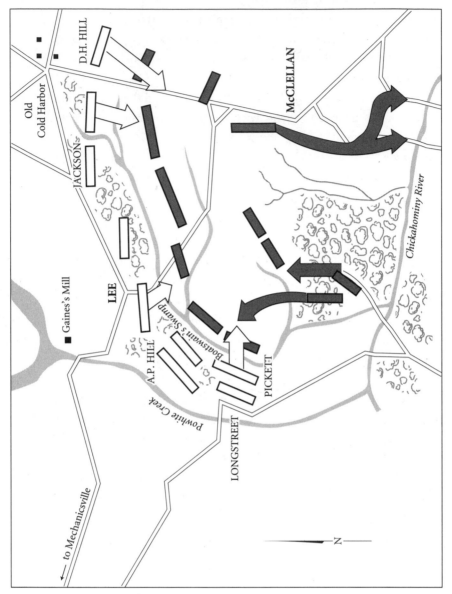

The Battle of Gaines's Mill, Virginia, June 27, 1862

suddenly from his horse while he was leading and cheering his men forward. He struggled to go on, "waving his cap and cheering his men, his arm hanging limp and helpless at his side."[39] A doctor rushed to the injured general's side and ordered him carried from the field. According to LaSalle, George refused to go: " 'My men need me,' replied my Soldier, 'Take the bullet out here and fix me up quick, doctor, I must go back—see they need me.' " The doctor obediently attended to the injured shoulder, while George continued to give orders until the loss of blood and pain overcame him and he was carried to a field hospital.[40]

Maj. John Cheves Haskell related a very different story. Haskell came across the injured brigadier a few moments after the bullet struck him. Haskell recalled passing by Pickett, "who was standing by his horse in a deep small hollow, almost like a well, bewailing himself. He called to me to send a litter as he was mortally wounded. I had none and was too busy with my men. He was very slightly wounded and perfectly able to take care of himself."[41]

LaSalle's version of George's wounding is consistent with her postwar efforts to present her husband in the most favorable public light, and thus hers is probably factually inaccurate. Haskell's account, written no closer to the time of the battle than LaSalle's, may be closer to the "truth," but it is impossible to know for sure. The contrast between these two versions is worth noting. The George Pickett in Haskell's account is cowardly, unmanly, and weak. In LaSalle's, he is brave, selfless, and heroic. Haskell's scathing criticism of Pickett at Gaines's Mill is representative of wartime and postwar attacks on George's cowardice in battle.[42]

George's injury did prove serious enough to keep him out of action for several months. While Lee's army fought in the important and costly battles of Second Manassas and Antietam, George convalesced in Richmond. Sallie Corbell was allegedly constantly at his side, nursing him back to health. She told her postwar readers that she was on summer vacation from school and had plenty of time to spend with her soldier. During their many hours together, LaSalle recalled playing the role of nurturer, comforter, and protector, roles she assumed throughout their relationship, and roles upon which he increasingly depended. LaSalle's postwar writings described President Davis and Stonewall Jackson personally visiting George's bedside. Davis, whom LaSalle resented for taking up precious time with her lover, supposedly urged George's quick recovery with the plea, "We need you in the field."[43]

LaSalle's published accounts described George's restlessness and impatience during his convalescence. He spoke repeatedly, she attested, of his desire to return to the front and to his men. Such an attitude was only appropriate for a courageous officer, loyal Confederate, and strong white southern male. It was probably the way George felt in 1862: Much of his identity remained undeniably tied to the military and battlefield glory, and his injury kept him out of major campaigning in the late summer and early fall of 1862. But George may have begun to feel something less manly and less acceptable during wartime: fear of his own death.[44]

Whatever George's true feelings about returning to the front, by September 1862 he had recovered enough strength to rejoin his men at Martinsburg, Virginia. Lee's army was falling back to Winchester, bruised and bloodied by hard summer campaigning in Virginia and Maryland. After the indecisive battle of Antietam, weary troops on both sides licked their wounds. The autumn of 1862 proved militarily uneventful, as the war dragged on into its second winter. A Virginia private wrote home: "Our Army seems to be in very good spirits though they never seem to be so merry as when they are about to march into a fight."[45]

Although the men remained idle through the fall, activity was going on inside Lee's chain of command. On September 18, 1862, the Confederate Congress approved creation of army corps within the South's field armies. Lee divided his forces in two and labeled them the First and Second Corps. James Longstreet and Stonewall Jackson each earned promotion to the newly created grade of lieutenant general.[46]

These command changes shuffled the army's organization, leaving several vacancies open, including command of Longstreet's old division. Recently recovered Brigadier General Pickett became a viable choice. He was Longstreet's senior brigade commander, and Longstreet may have exerted considerable influence in persuading Lee to submit Pickett's name as major general on October 27, 1862.

As in the past, a combination of personal connections, good fortune, and circumstance seemed again to push Pickett's military career forward. In reality, he lacked demonstrated experience to warrant such a promotion. At Williamsburg and Seven Pines he took no part in the main action, and his wounding at Gaines's Mill prevented him from participating in major engagements that summer. Existing documents fail to explain Lee's decision, but he apparently had enough faith in Pickett to overlook inexperience. As was the case with so many wartime promotions, there were no real reasons to doubt Pickett's potential as a competent division commander. On November 6, George E. Pickett became a major general in the Army of Northern Virginia.[47]

One can only guess Pickett's reaction to his meteoric rise to major general. He must have been very pleased. To his staff officers, for whom he hoped to obtain promotions, Pickett humbly stated that their "promotion was the only good he knew his promotion would do him."[48] In a published letter LaSalle heavily edited, if not entirely wrote herself, George referred to division command in a brief postscript.[49]

Pickett had little time to savor his promotion. After four idle months, he commanded 15,000 battle-worn veterans. His salary increased to $328 per month in inflated Confederate dollars, but this hardly represented an adequate compensation for his greatly increased responsibilities as a division commander. His division included his former brigade of infantry, three more also composed of Virginians, and one consisting completely of South Carolinians. Attached to this group was an artillery battalion of three batteries. Following him, upon some twenty-five horses was a host of staff officers, necessary to help in administering command. Included in this entourage were three aides-de-camp, one assistant adjutant general, one inspector general, one division surgeon, one quartermaster, one ordnance officer, and four couriers.[50]

By early December 1862, Pickett and his division were encamped on the banks of the Rappahannock River. One year earlier, he had been little more than a frustrated colonel, lacking any real troops to command. Now, twelve months later, he led an entire division of men, positioned high above the banks of the river to combat the Union's Army of the Potomac. Aide-de-camp Ed Baird believed the two "armies are nearer each other than I have ever seen before." It seemed clear that a great, possibly final, battle was imminent.[51]

On the foggy winter morning of December 13, Federals assembled troops for a massed assault on heights located just behind the small town of Fredericksburg, Virginia. Longstreet's well-entrenched corps easily mowed down a succession of futile charges up the bare slopes in front of his lines. The resulting battle of Fredericksburg was a Federal debacle. Lee reportedly remarked, "It is well this is so terrible! We should grow too fond of it."[52] Assistant adjutant general of the First Corps, Maj.

Osmun Latrobe, rode across the red-stained field and recorded in his diary macabre satisfaction with the day's killing: "The sight of a Hundred Dead Yankees. Saw Much of the Work I Had Done in the Way of Several Limbs, Decapitated Bodies, and Mutilated Remains of All Kinds. Doing My Soul Good. Would That The Whole Northern Army Were As Such, And I Had Had My Hand In It."[53]

Pickett's men had no hand in the killings of December 13.[54] His division did little more than watch the enemy's suicidal advances across the open field below. It was unusual for reserve troops to have such a panoramic view of the action, and these men reacted differently. A soldier in the 11th Virginia saw blue tides of Yankees and heard booming cannon and roaring musketry, and believed "all nature was in convulsion."[55] A member of the 18th Virginia wrote his wife, "We could see both sides charging on each other all day yesterday and expected to be sent in every minute but thank God we were not needed."[56] Staff officer Walter Harrison was bitterly disappointed: "We were scarcely allowed or required to take any part." Harrison likened the feelings of Pickett's men to those of "impatient 'dogs of war' in leash, anxious to rush to the destruction of the foe who was not permitted to reach him."[57] Col. Eppa Hunton agreed: "I never was so anxious in my life to be attacked."[58]

Pickett was not content simply to watch and wait. Instructions from Longstreet required Pickett's men to "hold their ground, simply in defense, unless an opportunity should occur to pitch into the enemy while he was engaged with A. P. Hill on the right."[59] At one point during the day, Pickett thought he spotted an opening on the enemy's flank. Willing to enter the battle without consulting Longstreet, he quickly rushed to entreat Maj. Gen. John B. Hood, whose division also sat in reserve, to join him. Hood hesitated to enter the fray without checking with their corps commander. They lost precious time locating Longstreet, and Pickett could only shake his head in angry frustration as the opportunity to attack slipped by. Harrison, no doubt echoing his commander's sentiments, mused: "It has been said that if Burnside had succeeded in getting deeper into the 'toils' set for him by Gen. Lee on this field, it would have resulted in the total destruction of his army."[60]

Longstreet tried to make amends to Pickett and two other generals who remained in reserve during the battle by praising them in his official report. "Major Generals Anderson, Pickett, and Hood, with their gallant divisions," Longstreet wrote, "were deprived of their opportunity by the unexpected and hasty retreat of the enemy."[61] This was cold comfort to Pickett, who desperately sought a chance to prove himself as a division commander in a large-scale battle.

The year 1862 closed with Pickett's hopes partially unfulfilled. The year had brought him two significant promotions and marked recognition as a commander, but, as always, he seemed to crave more. At Seven Pines and Fredericksburg he firmly believed that others overlooked him and his abilities. At Seven Pines he vowed that, with support, he could have easily pushed the Federals across the Chickahominy River; at Fredericksburg he could have inflicted additional damage upon a defeated enemy. Like so many professional soldiers during war, Pickett sought outside assurances, specifically success on the battlefield, to affirm his own sense of worth as a man and as an officer. Perhaps 1863 would offer renewed opportunities to display his neglected talents and quiet any hints of uncertainty about his courage and competence in combat.

LaSalle, meanwhile, supposedly continued her studies in Lynchburg, "sheltered by academic walls, absorbed in our own budding ambitions." She anxiously awaited another vacation and another chance, she claimed, to see her soldier. She recalled that the winter of 1862–63 was "unusually rough, cold and stormy."[62] This was a fine metaphor for the months that were to follow.

CHAPTER 8

Virginia, 1863

Carpet-Knight Doings on the Field

In January 1863, Pickett and his division camped in the rear of Lee's army, below Fredericksburg on the Rappahannock River. Except for Ambrose Burnside's halfhearted attempt to cross the river in January, the only battles fought were spirited snowball melees between friendly forces. Soldiers built winter huts and cabins, expecting to be idle until the spring.[1]

In mid-February, Richmonders received a scare when Union forces seemed to be readying for another campaign up the York-James Peninsula. Responding to reports of enemy concentration at Fort Monroe and Newport News, Lee chose two of Longstreet's divisions, Pickett's and Hood's, to meet the Federal threat. Pickett's instructions were rather vague: "Take position on the South Side of the James River in immediate vicinity of Drewry's Bluff and there await further orders." He was to keep himself "advised and ready to move if necessary to repel advances from Blackwater [River] and to defend the City of Petersburg."[2]

Lee appeared hesitant to give Pickett the freedom and discretionary authority that he had given other officers. Major Generals D. H. Hill and G. W. Smith had both received broad discretionary authority when they commanded troops in this region. Pickett, however, was to be "ready to move if necessary," which, Pickett learned in the course of his correspondence with Adjutant and Inspector General Cooper and Secretary of War Seddon, meant that Confederate authorities in Richmond, not Pickett, would decide when he should move and where.[3] In addition, instead of placing the division in Richmond, which in fact would have made Pickett commander of the Department of Richmond, Lee sent him outside the city and put him under the authority of Secretary of War Seddon.[4] Pickett found himself in a position he most disliked: essentially powerless, with little idea of what was expected of him.

Fortunately, this situation did not last long. On February 18, Lee sent Longstreet to take charge of his detached divisions.[5] Three days later, Pickett received orders to "report without delay" to his trusted friend and corps commander.[6] Maj. Moxley Sorrel, Longstreet's assistant adjutant general, remembered the unique relationship the two men shared, almost that of a father and son: "Taking Longstreet's orders in emergencies, I could always see how he [Longstreet] looked after Pickett, and made us give him things very fully; indeed, sometimes stay with him to make sure he did not get astray."[7] Sorrel recognized the long history these two men shared, dating to their days in Mexico, remarking that Longstreet "was exceedingly fond" of Pickett.[8]

Pickett's men broke camp in mid-February for their fifty-mile march from the Rappahannock through Richmond, south to Petersburg. These soldiers had not been through the Confederate capital in several months, and as they passed through the city, crowds lined the streets to greet the veterans. As a Virginia sergeant described, "The sidewalks were filled with ladies and many highly palatable gifts were distributed by them to the men."[9] Secretary Seddon watched Pickett's and Hood's divisions file before him and commented that "their general appearance, spirit and cheerfulness afforded great satisfaction."[10] Despite the soldiers' good cheer, the winter march was a difficult one, and many of Pickett's men lacked shoes, blankets, or heavy coats. Some recalled the trek through "half frozen slushy roads" as the hardest of the war.[11]

LaSalle's postwar recollections described the scene, stressing a gap between the home front and battlefront, a gulf separating men in the field from women at home. She wrote, "The wives, mothers, sisters and friends of Pickett's men could scarcely have recognized these bedraggled, muddy, ragged men the trim, dainty soldier-boys whom they had sent out from their homes to win fame and glory two years before." Gone were the new uniforms and equipment, well-filled knapsacks and haversacks. Bystanders cheered them all the same, and "tramp, tramp, tramp, they marched away once again from home and friends."[12]

The Civil War heightened separations between civilian and soldier, home and battlefront, male and female, yet also blurred those same distinctions. Richmonders had experienced war firsthand during the intense and bloody Seven Days campaign the summer before, and they continued to feel its disturbing effects. Enemy raids, food shortages, separations, and continued death and destruction spread the consequences of armed conflict on a massive scale. The war seemed to take on a life of its own, feeding on death, suffering, and loss. Veterans on both sides had difficulty aligning their original expectations of battle with the realities of war. Soldiers hated and admired the enemy, loathed and welcomed battle, resented and longed for family. George Pickett, a man who tried and tested boundaries all his life, began to lose his ability to make crucial distinctions between enemy and ally, right and wrong, courage and cowardice.[13] There were signs of his inner turmoil earlier, but during the late winter and spring of 1863 that struggle became disturbingly apparent. Evidence of his troubled frame of mind surfaced just as his romance with LaSalle came to fruition.

In March 1863, the southern high command, fearing Union troops on the peninsula and desperately needing food, dispatched Longstreet on a foraging expedition into southeastern Virginia and eastern North Carolina. As commander of the Department of Virginia and North Carolina, Longstreet also sought to attack the Federals who held Suffolk. The resulting siege of Suffolk placed George and his division in close proximity to LaSalle's Nansemond County home and family. By April, his headquarters were on the Confederate right, along the Dismal Swamp, not far from Chuckatuck.[14]

LaSalle claimed that George saw her nightly during the siege of Suffolk when she went to stay with her aunt at Barber's Cross Roads, ten miles from the city. "Here when all was quiet along the lines," LaSalle attested, "my Soldier would ride in from his headquarters almost every night between the hours of sunset and sunrise to see me—a ride of about thirty miles."[15] Two officers corroborated LaSalle's assertions. Col. William Dabney Stuart of the 56th Virginia complained to his wife that his division commander was "continually riding off to pay court to his young love, leaving the division details to his staff."[16] Maj. G. Moxley Sorrel criticized George's "frequent applications to be absent" to see his lover. These nightly rides were long, and the major general did not return to his command until early the next morning. Sorrel sensed Longstreet's growing irritation with Pickett's constant requests to leave camp, and recounted that once Pickett asked Sorrel for permission instead. Sorrel declined, feeling he could not justifiably take responsibility for the major general's absence should the division move or be attacked. "Pickett went all the same," Sorrel wrote, "nothing could hold him back from that pursuit." He concluded, "I don't think his division benefited from such carpet-knight doings on the field."[17] In her 1913 book, *The Bugles of Gettysburg*, LaSalle acknowledged Longstreet's annoyance with George's constant nightly visits to see her. In her narrative, Longstreet ridiculed his friend for traveling so far "just for a look and a word and come dashing back to the field with the first glint of morning." George responded: "A look and a word? But they are worth the hardest ride that ever a soldier took."[18] Underscoring the danger and risk of these nightly visits, LaSalle alleged that Union troops set fire to her aunt's home.[19]

A lieutenant in the 9th Virginia Infantry noted that many soldiers in his unit came from that same area of Nansemond County. John H. Lewis recalled that the temptation to visit friends and family seriously "tested the manhood of our boys." But he insisted that there were no desertions and that when the unit withdrew in May, "the honor of each man had been tested, and each had proved his manhood."[20] But George Pickett openly defied regulations that his own men had to follow in order to satisfy his desires and see Sallie.

Other military contemporaries offered additional, unflattering glimpses of the general in the spring of 1863. Col. T. G. Barham of the 24th Virginia Cavalry described his first meeting Pickett during the Suffolk campaign. One day while Barham was resting on a fence, a rail broke and he fell upon a sleeping George Pickett covered by oilcloth. Barham wrote: "His waking was unceremonious and cuss words filled the air." The officer added, "Pickett was then about 35 or 36 years old, short and fat, with a red face, mustache and imperial. He was a free liver but never drank to excess when on duty."[21] When Pickett and his staff visited Ivor Station one day in March, a soldier observed, "Whiskey market buoyant with a decided upward tendency of course."[22] These descriptions show George's continued struggle to control his weakness for liquor and his hot temper.

Col. Eppa Hunton's postwar autobiography included an account of George Pickett at Suffolk that more directly censured the general's personal conduct and character. Hunton remembered: "In riding with Pickett along his lines with his staff, we came to an exposed position, and to my surprise General Pickett and his staff laid flat down on their horses necks." Hunton was shocked and angry and felt this was a poor example for the men in the ranks. The disgusted colonel "rode with him [Pickett] bolt upright in my saddle."[23]

Hunton sensed that Pickett's focus was no longer on his military responsibilities as a commander. He claimed that Pickett was "a gallant man," but his courtship and eventual marriage to LaSalle Corbell somehow changed him. "Up to the time he was married," Hunton maintained, "I had the utmost confidence in his gallantry, but I believe that no man who married during the war was as good a soldier after, as before marriage." Hunton believed that marriage during war "seemed to demoralize" men.[24]

Hunton was right: George Pickett was losing his stomach for war. His all-consuming love affair with LaSalle Corbell had changed him and his relationship with the army. Before the Civil War, the regular army had served as a surrogate family for George, giving him direction and identity, reaffirming his masculinity, especially during times of trouble and pain. The Civil War changed the rules and rearranged the players, and George had to look elsewhere for certainty and comfort. By the spring of 1863, LaSalle was replacing the army, reassuring her troubled soldier that he was a strong, heroic man even when others said he was not.

The controversial George Pickett missives LaSalle published after the war best illustrate this change. Although LaSalle's writings were often more fiction than fact, they frequently contained accurate insight into her husband's inner turmoil. Whether heavily edited or entirely created by LaSalle, these published letters portrayed dramatic contradictions in George's character: readers see a soldier bold in battle but personally peace-loving, a man duty-bound to the Confederacy but utterly and at times obsessively devoted to a woman. In one letter, he mused: "Oh, my darling, war and its results did not seem so awful till the love for you came. Now—now I want to love and bless and help everything, and there are no foes—no enemies—just love and longing for you."[25]

Some historians have turned away in disgust at such sappy and romantic sentiments expressed by a professional soldier. Scholars argue that such a romantic tone betrays a woman's authorship.[26] However, Karen Lystra's study of Victorian courtship and marriage illustrates that men expressed exaggerated sentimentality in private correspondence to sweethearts and wives, sentimentality culturally banned from their public behavior. Love letters allowed Victorians, male and female, to share great intimacy and reveal their essence, or ideal "romantic self," to one person. Thus, romantic love was an exercise in individual identity. Lystra concludes, "Contrary to the stereotype of the emotionally constricted Victorian male, the evidence indicates that middle- to upper-class masculine role performance did not require men to be emotionally controlled and constricted at all times. In the protected romantic sphere, men led richly emotional lives." Thus, an emotional and sentimental George Pickett may have indeed poured out his heart to Sallie, believing that to her he could express his deepest fears and intimate wants.[27]

George Pickett's crime, then and now, was his inability to maintain balance between his individual desires and his military duty, between perceived manly strength and feminine weakness. Although the southern cult of chivalry gave a man an outlet for romanticism, and even femininity, southern honor and military duty demanded that he be always conscious of his public reputation and self-restraint. His whole life Pickett had struggled to check his passions; the Civil War and his new love unleashed them once gain. By war's end, little of his self-control would remain.[28]

In early April, a transfer nearly interrupted George and LaSalle's arduous courtship, and, at least according to Eppa Hunton, would have "saved" Pickett as a gallant general. Secretary of War Seddon proposed sending Pickett's division to join Braxton Bragg's Army of Tennessee. Lee protested, maintaining that if Longstreet lost this division while engaged at Suffolk, "I fear he will be unable to obtain the supplies we hoped to draw from the eastern portion of the department, which as far as I am able to judge, are essential for the support of the troops."[29] One month later, after the Suffolk campaign ended, Seddon had another possible destination in mind for Pickett. When the secretary suggested transporting Pickett and his division to aid Lt. Gen. John C. Pemberton's defense of Vicksburg, Mississippi, Lee again argued against such a plan. He stated, "If you determine to send Pickett's division to General Pemberton, I presume it could not reach him until the last of this month. If anything is done in that quarter, it will be over by that time, as the climate in June will force the enemy to retire. The uncertainty of its application causes me to doubt the policy of sending it." Lee added, "Its removal from the army will be sensibly felt."[30]

Pickett probably knew nothing of this correspondence but would not have been happy with the prospect of leaving Virginia. In the past he had welcomed the opportunity to move whenever and wherever the army sent him. This war had changed all that. Now he had a reason to stay. Besides, Pickett was already annoyed with the War Department for detaching two of his five brigades to D. H. Hill's operations in North Carolina.[31] A member of one of these detached units wrote his wife: "I understand that Genl. Pickett was very much fretted when we were taken from him and sent south and that he said 'if they took away (us) his old Brigade—the rest of his Division might go to hell.'" The soldier added, "He had five Brigades and we were the first and gained him all his credit as a general."[32] In Pickett's mind, Richmond was purposefully undercutting his command and, again, overlooking his military talent.

By late April 1863, the Federal army's crossing of the Rappahannock River brought an end to the siege of Suffolk. On April 29, Lee instructed: "All available troops had better be sent forward as rapidly as possible by rail and otherwise."[33] Longstreet had not succeeded in regaining Suffolk for the Confederacy, but he had acquired badly needed supplies and had protected Richmond, two of the four tasks with which he had been entrusted. His final goal, to reinforce Lee when needed, now came to pass. On May 1, Longstreet's corps began their withdrawal, but they arrived too late to take part in the grand Confederate victory at the battle of Chancellorsville.[34]

Pickett and his division did not immediately unite with Lee's army on the Rappahannock. On May 4, 1863, Pickett received orders to proceed as rapidly as possible to Richmond to await further instructions.[35] For the next month, he moved to various key positions protecting critical lines of communication into Richmond. Lee, who planned a major offensive northward, continued to watch for enemy attacks on the Confederate capital.

On May 16, the division again marched through the capital. J. B. Jones, a clerk in the War Department, recorded in his diary how he watched the long gray columns march through town. "Gen. Pickett himself," he wrote, "with his long, black ringlets, accompanied his division, his troops looking like fighting veterans, as they are."[36]

Pickett and his men were eager to fight again. After playing spectators at Fredericksburg, they had then missed the dramatic victory at Chancellorsville. Unlike John Bell Hood's men, who immediately rejoined the main army, Pickett's division spent more than a month shifting from place to place, not staying very long before picking up to move again. One of Pickett's men complained to his sister, "The division which I am in is pulled and hauled about more than any other."[37] On June 2, Pickett and his troops waited at Hanover Junction with orders "to move at a moment's notice with three day's rations; no route indicated."[38]

As spring turned to summer, George had more reason to feel torn between his obedience to the army and his devotion to LaSalle. In particular, his relationship with Lee showed signs of serious strain. On June 2, Lee instructed Pickett to send wagons to a town he identified as "Newton." When Pickett could not find such a place on his maps, he twice telegraphed back for clarification. Pickett revealed just how sensitive he had become to his treatment by Lee when he wrote to Brig. Gen. Arnold Elzey that he had "telegraphed immediately to find out what place was meant. As usual from those headquarters, received no reply."[39]

Pickett also protested against a special restriction prohibiting soldiers and officers from riding trains into Richmond. Pickett took the order personally, perhaps realizing that his romantic midnight journeys to see LaSalle had caught up with him. He angrily complained that "this circumstance and its great detriment to the facilities of expediting military movements of importance I have reported three times to General Lee's headquarters (first communication two weeks since) but cannot obtain even the scratch of a pen in reply." Pickett asked that he might take a train into the city and meet personally with General Elzey to discuss his grievances. Elzey was ill, and it is not clear whether the meeting ever occurred, but Pickett resented his movement being restricted by seemingly arbitrary orders.[40]

As portions of his army moved northward, Lee was careful to leave troops on the Rappahannock, in case the Federals resumed an offensive across the river. A. P. Hill's Third Corps guarded Fredericksburg, while Pickett's and James Johnston Pettigrew's divisions were at Hanover Junction, safeguarding Richmond. On June 3, Pickett received word of a "marauding expedition" close to his position. Lee instructed him: "If you learn that the enemy has retired and is beyond your grasp, I desire you to return to your position. If they come within your reach, and you can do so with advantage, strike at them."[41] Two days later, Lee advised Hill to call on Pickett and Pettigrew if a large-scale Federal attack materialized on the river. Lee urged Hill to "deceive the enemy and keep him in ignorance of any change in the disposition of the army." If the enemy evacuated, Hill was to pursue, "inflicting all the damage you can upon his rear."[42] Lee preferred his commanders to act aggressively against movement on the river, especially as he readied his army for his invasion north.[43]

Also on June 5, President Davis ordered Pettigrew to send a courier to Pickett notifying him of the raiders in King William County, with instructions to "move or send a force rapidly" and "do the business" of capturing or destroying the enemy outright.[44] The next day, Pettigrew assured Lee that he reiterated these directions to Pickett but admitted: "He [Pickett] was here an hour ago, but I believe has gone to Richmond."[45] Lee could well have wondered if Pickett had slipped away again, perhaps to see his lover, ignoring specific restrictions against riding the trains.

Pickett was on the scene in time to attack the Federals, but, left to his own discretion, he faltered. Lee felt disgusted enough to criticize openly the major general's conduct to Lt. Gen. A. P. Hill. Lee wrote: "I feel Pickett did not go far enough. . . . I have telegraphed him that he must drive them back."[46] The initiative lost, the Union raiding party withdrew unmolested.

Lee soon determined that the Federals were not planning an attack on the Rappahannock and planned to unite his entire army for his campaign into Pennsylvania. But in the midst of this bold movement northward, George Pickett continued to believe that the Confederate high command discriminated unfairly against him. He received orders to leave behind two of his five brigades, making his the smallest division in the army.[47] Describing the condition of his troops as "very much weakened," Pickett complained to Lee's assistant adjutant general on June 21: "I beg that another brigade be sent to this division ere we commence the campaign." "I ask this in no spirit of complaint," he hastened to add, "but merely as an act of justice to my division and myself, for it is well-known that a small division will be expected to do the same amount of hard service as a larger one, and as the army is now divided, my division, I think, decidedly the weakest."[48] His efforts produced no results, and he had to make do without these additional brigades.[49]

There were a lot of things on George Pickett's mind as he crossed the

Potomac: his passionate feelings toward LaSalle, the weakened state of his division, and his deteriorating relationship with Lee. He must have sensed the scorn officers and men had felt toward his behavior in Suffolk. Still, he probably looked forward to battle: in his experience, most battles were simple, the large-scale violence somehow reassuring and gratifying, especially if he were given the chance to lead a charge or direct a successful offense.

As her lover marched northward, LaSalle returned to complete her studies at Lynchburg Female Seminary. After graduation, she recalled her eagerness to marry her soldier. "Cupid does not readily give way to Mars," she stated, "and in our Southern country a lull between bugle calls was likely to be filled with the music of wedding bells."[50] Included in the published Pickett letters is one from George en route to Gettysburg. He wrote LaSalle: "Oh, my darling, love me, pray for me, hold me in your thoughts, keep me in your heart." Whether LaSalle's or George's actual words, they were timeless lovers' sentiments during wartime.[51]

CHAPTER 9

Pennsylvania, 1863
With All This Much to Lose

LaSalle Pickett looked back on June 1863 as a time of bright and cheerful optimism. She recalled graduating from Lynchburg Female Seminary and going home to eastern Virginia. En route she stopped in Richmond, where, she claimed, several letters reached her from George. Each message she received, she alleged, was "breathing the same spirit of confidence and hope—hope and trust, always hope and trust."[1]

In the early summer of 1863, George Pickett was no doubt hopeful that he would play a conspicuous part in the coming campaign. He probably was confident that he would prove real and imagined naysayers wrong and show his talent as an officer. And he may have trusted that LaSalle would greet him with a hero's welcome when he returned. Yet underneath his usual bravado was a man increasingly distressed and distracted.

George Pickett was thirty-eight years old in the summer of 1863, and by then, he had made quite an impression on his military contemporaries. Many of them commented on his hair, his dress, his arrogance, his temper, and his drinking. To white southern men, Pickett seemed a strange mix of femininity and masculinity, a dandy in uniform. Staff officer Moxley Sorrel offered a typical description: "A medium-sized, well-built man, straight, erect, and in well-fitting uniform, an elegant riding whip in his hand, his appearance was distinguished." But, Sorrel added, it was Pickett's hair that made him memorable. "Long ringlets flowed loosely over his shoulders," Sorrel wrote, "trimmed and highly perfumed; his beard likewise was curling and giving out the scents of Araby."[2] Another member of Longstreet's staff, Raphael J. Moses, recalled Pickett as "dashing" yet "foppish in his dress," a man who "wore his hair in long ringlets."[3] Sir Arthur J. Lyon Fremantle, an English visitor with Lee's army, similarly observed: "He wears his hair in long ringlets and is altogether a desperate looking character."[4]

Although it was not uncommon for soldiers in the Civil War to wear their hair long, Pickett's hair became a favorite topic.[5] Frank Dawson recalled that along the march to Pennsylvania women stopped Robert E. Lee to request a lock of his hair. Dawson wrote: "General Lee said that he really had none to spare, and he was quite sure, besides, that they would prefer such a souvenir from one of the younger officers, and that he was confident that General Pickett would be pleased to give them one of his curls." According to Dawson, "General Pickett did not enjoy the joke, for he was known everywhere by his corkscrew ringlets, which were not particularly becoming when the rain made them lank in such weather as we then had."[6]

Perhaps one of the most dramatic descriptions of George Pickett on the eve of Gettysburg came from Yankee prisoner Bernhard Domschcke, who spotted the general on the morning of July 3:

> The archetype of a Virginia slave-baron strutted briskly, proud in bearing, head lifted in arrogance. On horseback he looked like the ruler of a continent. Obviously he took pains with his appearance— riding boots aglitter, near-shoulder length hair tonsorially styled—but the color of his nose and upper cheeks betrayed that he pandered the inner man. Pleasures of the bottle left indelible tracks. Indeed, the coarse plebeian features in no way matched the efforts at aristocratic airs. He galloped proudly that morning from his tent to the front.[7]

Inherent in these various wartime portraits of George Pickett were attacks on his personal courage, military ability, and, ultimately, his masculinity. Some of these descriptions dated from the war itself, and others were penned years later; some, like Domschcke's, were tinged by personal dislike for Pickett. Yet, there remained a consistent strain of doubt over whether Pickett was manly enough to be a competent Confederate general. There were lingering questions about his self-control and self-discipline. And the emphasis on feminine traits was dramatic. Even Pickett's admirers noted the paradox. Staff member Ed Baird praised his commander as "brilliant in his strategy, he had the courage of a man with the tenderness of a woman."[8] His brother Charles remembered: "He was tender, as he was brave."[9] LaSalle Pickett celebrated George as an ideal warrior-lover. In her 1913 book, *The Bugles of Gettysburg*, she wrote: "He sat on his horse with the grace of one who rides to win a guerdon from the hand of beauty rather than to meet the foe in deadly conflict. His face was almost womanly fair and his soft dark hair swept backward in the morning wind." She asked rhetorically: "Were ever grace and delicacy so opposed to the rude idea of war as in his person and life history?"[10]

George Pickett was a man of contrasts. As an adolescent he had exhibited discomfort with his family's and slaveholding society's expectations of him. He escaped to the all-male subculture of the professional army corps, seeming to find that through battle and frontier army life he could reaffirm his masculinity and quiet troubling insecurities that had plagued him as a teen. Rather than opposing "the rude idea of war," Pickett no doubt enjoyed the large-scale violence of combat. He apparently valued racial superiority and military aggressiveness over "savage" Mexicans and Indians, while he simultaneously respected Native American culture. The Civil War appears to have reopened old wounds and old questions and deepened contradictions in his character and in his life. His insecurities about rank and authority were likely to make him arrogant and short-tempered. His excessive concern with his physical appearance also became more obvious. In American and European eighteenth- and nineteenth-century societies, a dandy was often a male member of the elite whose public ostentatious, rowdy, arrogant, and irresponsible behavior derided republican ideals of equality, humility, and hard work. Dandyism was a form of reactionary rebellion that justified stratified society.[11] When the Civil War blurred traditional social, racial, and gender boundaries, a dandified George Pickett appeared to hold them up. Ironically, these were the same boundaries he himself had challenged as a young man.

To be an honorable and respected professional officer, Pickett had to control such "manly passions" as drinking, swearing, and sexual desire. Frequent references to his obsession with LaSalle, rumors of his cowardice in battle, his excessive drinking, and his explosive temper showed that he was losing that control.[12] Ensuing events would do nothing to reverse this impression among his male contemporaries.

By June 30, 1863, Pickett and his men had reached the vicinity of Chambersburg, Pennsylvania. Over the next three days, his soldiers set to work destroying the town's rail facilities, workshops, and public machinery, careful not to disturb private property. The remainder of Lee's army moved farther northward toward Harrisburg. Pickett's soldiers knew that a fight was imminent but were unsure what role they would play. During their march northward, religious revivalism swept through much of the division. Surely, God would not allow them to be left behind and miss out again from another grand battle.[13]

Initially, it appeared that circumstances might again make Pickett and his troops mere onlookers to the main action. On July 1, 1863, portions of the Army of the Potomac and Army of Northern Virginia collided in and around Gettysburg. By nightfall, Confederate forces had driven Federals to a defensive position southeast of town. Although Lee had not planned to fight at Gettysburg, that evening he determined to gather all of his army together to continue battle the next day. Not realizing the strength of the Federals, Lee sought a decisive victory, one that might seriously weaken the Army of the Potomac. To achieve such a goal, he knew he needed all of his army, particularly Pickett's fresh division of Virginians.[14]

During the dark morning hours of July 2, Pickett received word that Lee needed him at the front. He and his men fell into line, marching twenty-five miles in the hot summer sun. It was a twelve-hour journey, but Pickett's troops stepped at a steady pace without complaint. The prospect of battle cheered the ranks. One soldier later recalled, "Officers and men were alike inspired with the greatest confidence in our ability to defeat the enemy."[15]

Three miles outside of Gettysburg, his division halted to rest from the excessive heat and dust. Pickett sent aides ahead to consult with Generals Longstreet and Lee, reporting to both commanders that after a short respite his division could enter the battle at any location so desired. Lee sent back a message: "Tell General Pickett I shall not want him this evening, let his men rest and I will send him word when I want them." Longstreet likewise assured Pickett's courier, "I will have work for him tomorrow."[16]

On July 2, intense fighting raged all along the Union lines, with the Confederates on the attack. By nightfall, Lee had assailed both enemy flanks as well as the Union center. None of these attacks yielded decisive results for the Confederates, although casualties on both sides were severe. While Union general George G. Meade dug in to brace for another day of battle, Lee laid plans to strike again and gain a decisive victory.[17]

On the morning of July 3, a renewed Confederate attack on the Federal right at Culp's Hill faltered after several hours of fierce fighting and heavy losses. Lee then determined, against the strong disapproval of Longstreet, that Pickett's division, combined with portions of other units from General A. P. Hill's Third Corps, would strike forcefully at the Union center along the softly rolling ridge opposite the Confederate line. An artillery barrage would precede the charge to prepare the way for the 13,500 infantrymen and officers. By 9:00 A.M., Pickett's three brigades arrived on the battlefield and rested on their arms beneath a brightening sun, anxiously awaiting orders. A group of them playfully pelted each other with green apples.[18] A soldier scribbled into his diary, "It is impossible for us to be any otherwise than victorious."[19]

Pickett could hardly contain his excitement. Corps commander James Longstreet later remembered hearing that his friend Pickett had "felt hurt at being left at Chambersburg whilst the balance of the army was expecting to enter battle."[20] Any such feelings quickly vanished. Indeed, here, finally, was the climactic thrill of Chapultepec, combined with the important responsibility of the San Juan confrontation. It was a chance for Pickett to prove himself as a heroic general and courageous man, perhaps even to win the war.

LaSalle would later claim that her husband's entire life had prepared him for this moment. She portrayed him as ready to do his duty but cognizant of the blood and destruction the charge would produce. Her soldier, on the morning of the battle, was a man fighting a gnawing sense of pending doom. She summed up the events that brought him to Cemetery Ridge:

> Born of a race of warriors, schooled in military art, trained in camp and barracks and on the field, a boy soldier in the land of the Montezumas, catching the flag from the hand of his fallen friend, Captain Longstreet, and carrying it to the height of Chapultepec, a determined man, barring with slender force the gate of the West to a foreign foe, he looked not like one to revel in martial deeds, because of the wide and deep and high humanity dominating all smaller attributes as the spirit of God rules supreme over the world.[21]

George, she claimed, once remarked to her that at Gettysburg there was not "a man in his dear old division who did not know, when he heard the order, that in obeying it he was marching to death, yet every man of them marched forward unfaltingly."[22] In retrospect, she depicted him and his troops as tragic heroes about to meet their destiny.

George knew something dramatic was about to happen, but it was unlikely that he had any idea of the fate that awaited him. In fact, it appeared that he believed wholeheartedly that he and his men were about to participate in a great victory. Several individuals gave evidence of Pickett's optimistic state of mind the morning of July 3. A staff officer recalled overhearing Pickett chatting with Col. G. T. Gordon, formerly of the British army, who had served on the opposing side during the San Juan crisis. Gordon brought disturbing news that his regiment would refuse to participate in the charge, but Pickett took a moment to share with Gordon pleasant memories of his days in the Northwest.[23] Pickett also talked of the Mexican War during the hours before the charge. Col. Birkett Davenport Fry, from Pettigrew's division, visited Pickett to discuss coordination between units once the charge began. Fry wrote, "He appeared to be in excellent spirits, and after a cordial greeting and a pleasant reference to our having been in work of that kind at Chapultepec, expressed great confidence in the ability of our troops to drive the enemy."[24] Cavalry officer Fitzhugh Lee recollected an exuberant Pickett riding past him toward the front at Gettysburg, yelling: "Come on, Fitz, and go with us; we shall have lots of fun there presently."[25] Yankee prisoner Bernhard Domschcke thought he detected signs of inebriation in Pickett's high color that morning.[26] Although he was known to drink, Pickett's ruddiness that day probably resulted from his excited state; Pickett's fighting blood was up, and the prospect of battle reinvigorated him.

James Longstreet, could not share in his subordinate's eagerness for battle. As the moment grew near for the charge, Longstreet became more and more depressed. He later recalled himself telling Lee, "I have been a soldier, I may say, from the ranks up to the position I now hold. I have been in pretty much all kinds of skirmishes, from those of two or three soldiers up to those of any army corps, and I think I can safely say there never was a body of fifteen thousand men who could make that attack successfully."[27] Lee was unshaken. Longstreet then tried to shift some of the responsibility by sending ambiguous instructions to artillery colonel E. P. Alexander. Around noon, Longstreet wrote Alexander: "If the artillery fire does not have the effect to drive off the enemy or greatly demoralize him, so as to make our effort pretty certain, I would prefer that you should not advise General Pickett to make the charge."[28] Alexander, unsure of Longstreet's intentions by such a statement, predicted that even if both the artillery barrage and Pickett's charge succeeded, "it can only be so at a very bloody cost."[29] He suggested to Longstreet that if there were other options, he should carefully consider them. This shook Longstreet from his hesitation, and he quickly reasserted Lee's original plan. He ordered Alexander to begin the bombardment until the enemy appeared weakened or demoralized. "When that moment arrives," Longstreet wrote, "advise General Pickett and of course advance such artillery as you can use in aiding the attack."[30]

Pickett knew nothing of this exchange. As Union cannon fire loudly answered the roaring guns of the Confederates, he continued to feel confident and sure of victory. At one point Alexander went to see Pickett to feel "his pulse, as it were, about the assault." Alexander later recorded, "He was in excellent spirits and sanguine of success."[31]

Around 1:30 P.M., it appeared that Union gunfire had measurably slackened. Alexander even spied Federals wheeling guns to the rear.[32] He immediately dispatched to Pickett, "If you are to advance at all you must come at once, or we will not be able to support you as we ought."[33] For a passing moment, Pickett's feelings of confidence left him and the old uncertainties reappeared. Using precious time, he rode with Alexander's note to Longstreet. His friend and commander read the note without a word. Pickett scanned Longstreet's face, looking for signs of encouragement or reassurance. Seconds ticked by. Pickett asked, "General, shall I advance?" Longstreet could not speak. He nodded and turned his head so as to avoid Pickett's eyes. Pickett stiffly straightened and saluted, "I am going to move forward Sir." The veil of pride and cockiness returned.[34] Pickett mounted his horse and rode toward his division. A few minutes later, another note came from Alexander: "For God's sake, come quick, or we cannot support you. Ammunition nearly out."[35]

In retelling and embellishing the chain of events that led to the charge, LaSalle inserted herself into the narrative. Merely by making herself her husband's official biographer, she put herself at the battlefront rather than the home front, where women were traditionally relegated.[36] While recounting the charge at Gettysburg, she used any opportunity she could to emphasize Pickett's masculinity, pacifism, self-control, courageous leadership, and utter devotion to her. In a published letter that LaSalle claims Pickett wrote but she herself probably penned, there is a passage supposedly written a few days before the battle where George described his encounter with a defiant young girl in Pennsylvania. When the girl taunted his soldiers by wearing a U.S. flag as an apron, George, the sensitive and exemplary commander, bowed and saluted the flag, "fearing lest some [of his men] might forget their manhood." His obedient troops followed suit.[37] During the battle, when George received E. P. Alexander's frantic messages to advance, LaSalle maintained that George stopped to pencil her a brief letter of good-bye and God bless.[38] She also answered charges that her husband was drinking during the battle. When Brig. Gen. Cadmus Wilcox rode up to her soldier and offered him a drink, LaSalle alleged that George sternly refused, explaining: "I promised the little girl who is waiting and praying for me down in Virginia that I would keep fresh upon my lips until we should meet again the breath of the violets she gave me when we parted. Whatever my fate, Wilcox, I shall try to do my duty like a man, and I hope that, by that little girl's prayers, I shall to-day reach either glory or glory."[39] In each of these instances, LaSalle rewrote the historical record to present George as the model male, officer, and lover.

George had little time, or inclination, to make such dramatic declarations or romantic gestures. Instead, as soon as he consulted with Longstreet, he quickly rode his horse along his lines, passing orders to each of his brigadiers. As the men fell into line, Pickett stood straight up on his horse, waved his cap, and strained his voice to address the division. He shouted to the men as much to himself: "Up men, to your posts. Don't forget that you are from old Virginia." He then sang out, "Forward!" The command echoed through the ranks, passing from brigade to regiment to company commanders. Within moments, the division moved forward. It was approximately 3:00 p.m.[40]

Pickett's division began marching to the left oblique, while James Johnston Pettigrew's division set out at the opposite angle, 1,000 feet away. The two divisions fell into alignment some 1,400 feet from the enemy position. Here the brigades paused and dressed ranks. Then, in paradelike precision, three tightly formed columns of gray swept across the open field. Union artillery fired into the lines of oncoming men unmercifully.[41] Union infantryman watched in disbelief.[42]

Twenty-one-year-old Andrew Cowan, commander of the 1st New

York Artillery of the Union VI Corps, had a perfect view of the advance. He recalled, "They dressed their lines before advancing and from there they came on steadily in three lines at brigade front. . . . As gaps opened in their lines, where men fell under our cannon fire, they closed to their left and kept a splendid front."[43] The men marched slowly at first, picking up speed as they moved across the open field. By the time rifle bullets mixed with exploding artillery shells, charging Confederates broke into a run and rushed wildly forward. All semblance of alignment vanished. It was every man for himself.[44]

Pickett had ridden at the head of his division, halting some 400 yards from the main Union line.[45] Here he remained to watch and ascertain the needs of his men. Controversy has erupted over Pickett's whereabouts over the next few hours, much of the criticism again directly attacking his personal courage.[46] Participants asserted that Pickett was negligent in his duty by failing to lead his division directly into the battle. Others claimed that he hid inside a barn to escape the din and clamor of battle that raged across the open field.[47] One such story comes from Clayton Coleman, a member of Kemper's medical staff who attested to seeing Pickett "standing behind a large oak tree, holding his horse by the bridle, while his chief of staff, Major Harrison, was similarly situated a few steps distant." When an artillery shell burst over their heads, Coleman stated that Pickett and Harrison "rode rapidly to the rear."[48] Staff officer Moxley Sorrel maintained that he never saw Pickett on the battlefield once the action began.[49]

While contempt for Pickett continued to grow after Gettysburg, a survey of eyewitness accounts and postwar recollections appears to show that, at least initially, Pickett did not fail in his duty as major general. He led his men some distance and ordered his division to double-quick time with a rallying, "Boys, give them a cheer."[50] Then, as a division commander should, Pickett remained in the rear so as to assess the progress of the advance.[51] He sent aides and couriers to other commanders, rallied broken ranks, and kept his eye on a weakening left flank.[52] Had Pickett led his division into combat, there is little doubt that he would have suffered severe wounds, if not death. Col. Rawley Martin defended him: "I am sure he [Pickett] was where his duty called him throughout the engagement. He was too fine a soldier, and had fought too many battles not to be where he was most needed on that supreme occasion of his military life."[53]

It was indeed a supreme occasion, and Pickett desperately tried to turn the tide of the battle when things started to go wrong. He sent aide Robert Bright to General Longstreet, asking for support to help break the Union line. Although Longstreet had already declared the charge hopeless, he instructed Captain Bright to order troops under General Wilcox forward. Pickett anxiously sent three aides in rapid succession to Wilcox to hurry supporting infantry brigades on Pickett's weakening right flank. Minutes later, Bright returned to Pickett to warn of an enemy flanking movement on the left. Bright advised a withdrawal before the Yankees "sweep around our flank and shut us up." According to Bright, Pickett responded calmly that he had watched the left, expecting trouble. "Ride to Dearing's Battalion," he told Bright. "They have orders to follow up the charge and keep their caissons filled; order them to open with every gun and break that column and keep it broken."[54] He also sent another staff member to Longstreet to urge "vigorous and immediate support."[55] Pickett believed, quite understandably, that his men would not fight alone, that artillery and infantry support must come quickly to the rescue. Precious time passed with no support and both flanks exposed.[56]

Major Dearing responded to Pickett's plea for artillery support, but only with a disappointing three rounds of solid shot before his guns fell silent.[57] Confederate cannon had exhausted all available artillery supplies during the barrage earlier that day.[58] General Wilcox finally moved forward but failed to advance toward Pickett's right. Consequently, Wilcox received enemy artillery and musketry fire from two sides. After taking heavy losses, he soon retreated to his own lines.[59]

In the end, a combination of failed coordination between units, lack of specific instructions to others, exposed flanks, Lee's overconfidence, and Longstreet's hesitancy produced a fiasco.[60] Had southern artillery managed to provide adequate support to the infantry, and had additional infantry quickly and effectively moved to support the flanks, the charge might have succeeded.[61] But these failings left Pickett's division, in addition to the commands of Pettigrew and Trimble, open to slaughter. A small number of southerners did manage to break the enemy line, but Federals quickly had them surrounded and heavily outgunned. Unwounded Confederates either ran in panicked retreat or threw down their arms to the victorious enemy.

Pickett remained near the Codori barn helplessly watching the horrifying events unfolding before him. Several Confederates gave accounts of Pickett's dramatic change in demeanor as failure became obvious. Staff officer Frank Dawson credited himself with being the first to encounter Pickett after the repulse. Dawson recollected Pickett asking despondently, "Why did you not halt my men here? Great God, Where, Oh! Where is my Division?"[62] Artillery officer William Poague saw General Pickett gazing intently at the front. Poague rode toward him and said, "General, my orders are that as soon as our troops get the hill I am to move as rapidly as possible to their support. But I don't like the looks of things up there." Pickett, without turning his head, continued to stare at the field of battle "with an expression of sadness and pain." Poague persisted: "What do you think I ought to do under the circumstances[?] Our men are leaving the hill." Pickett responded, "I think you had better save your guns," and rode away.[63]

Historian George Stewart argues convincingly that Pickett then became "wholly useless" as a division commander. "At this point, honor and military procedures both demanded that he should gallop forward, join his troops and either inspire them to advance, or give them orders suitable to the emergency."[64] Instead, Pickett stood transfixed in horror and disbelief as his Virginian division crumbled before his tear-filled eyes.[65] In his self-absorbed despair, he failed to answer to the needs of his battered troops, and he again exhibited a loss of control.[66]

Courier William Youngblood overheard Pickett's desperate pleas to Longstreet. "General," Pickett cried, "I am ruined, my division is gone— it is destroyed." Youngblood listened as Longstreet tried to console Pickett and assure him that, with time, all would be right again.[67] Twenty years of friendship and camaraderie meant little that afternoon. Longstreet could not bolster Pickett's fallen spirit.

General Lee soon arrived on the scene to witness the sad conclusion to his grandiose plan for a decisive victory. He rode to Pickett and ordered him to regather his men in case of an enemy counterattack. Pickett, with his head slumped to his chest, bitterly sobbed, "General Lee, I have no division now, Armistead is down, Garnett is down, and Kemper is mortally wounded." Lee looked directly at the forlorn figure and sharply stated, "Come General Pickett, this has been my fight and upon my shoulders rest the blame."[68]

Even LaSalle admitted that a disturbing change occurred in her hus-

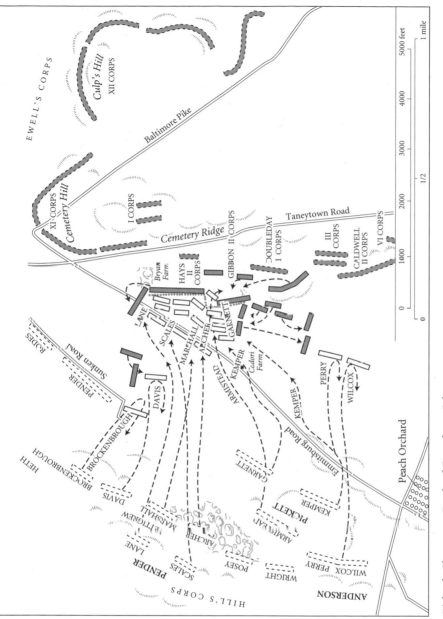

Pickett's Charge, The Battle of Gettysburg, July 3, 1863

band's demeanor that day in July. Fifty years after the battle, she wrote that his countenance became transformed: "The battle ardor had died out and left it pale with the sorrow of a great loss,—perhaps the greatest loss that had ever come to man since the first battle for supremacy was fought in a wildly ambitious world." The sight of so much senseless death and suffering stunned the lifelong soldier: "The tiger-eyes that had flamed with the fire of the coming conflict were softened in a gray tender light sadder than tears."[69] Still, LaSalle clung to her heroic portrait, replacing his despair and shock with coolness and courage. In her writings of the battle, a fellow Confederate officer marveled at Pickett's "motionless, erect figure under the falling shot and bursting shells." She maintained that Federal soldiers took aim at Pickett but changed their minds, exclaiming: "We can't kill a man as brave as that."[70]

Darkness mercifully brought an end to the killing. Next morning, both armies expected a renewal of battle, but Lee decided it was time to return to Virginia. Torrential rain fell during the afternoon of July 4. Trudging through washed-out roads and swollen streams, Lee's badly bloodied army began its retreat over the Potomac, through Maryland, toward Virginia.[71]

John W. Daniel aptly described Pickett's division and its commander immediately after the charge: "From the height of enjoyment, and anticipation, they had suddenly been plunged into the depths of pain and disappointment."[72] Pickett's men suffered staggering casualties, estimated to be 2,560.[73] The broken and battered division assumed the lowly job of guarding enemy prisoners captured during the battle. To men and officers alike, this seemed a humiliating task after the suffering they had just endured.[74] Pickett complained directly to Lee. On July 9, Lee responded: "It was with reluctance that I imposed upon your gallant division the duty of conveying prisoners to Staunton." Although Lee professed regret "to assign them to such a service," he urged Pickett that he and his division concentrate their energies on the work before them. "No one grieves more than I do," Lee assured him, "at the loss suffered by your noble division in the recent conflict or honors it more for its bravery and gallantry." Lee needed stronger and larger units to lead the army should fighting resume.[75] Survivors of Pickett's division marched in the rear.

Pickett's formal report of the battle contained a tirade of complaints.

He criticized fellow officers and bemoaned the ill-fated circumstances that brought his division to its badly broken state.[76] Pickett's relationship with Lee had reached a boiling point, and Lee had little patience for the major general's complaints and lack of self-restraint. He could not tolerate the cantankerous tones inherent in Pickett's statements. Angry accusations would only pour salt on the wounds of a bloodied and exhausted army. Lee requested that Pickett destroy the report, "both copy and original, substituting one confined to casualties merely." Lee harshly rebuked: "We have the enemy to fight and must carefully at this critical moment, guard against dissensions which the reflections in your report would create."[77] Pickett refused to submit a new one.[78]

Waiting at home for word of the battle, LaSalle remembered that early rumors from the front pronounced a southern victory. She wrote, "I could hear nothing of the General except the vague rumor that he had been killed in the final charge."[79] Mail was slow, she claimed, but late in July a bundle of letters allegedly arrived, recounting the fate of Pickett's division. Again, the authenticity of these letters is difficult to establish, but there is one letter, perhaps the only one, where the handwriting and content appear entirely legitimate. In the letter dated July 23, 1863, George described the Gettysburg campaign as "short but terrible." He mused: "Would that we had never crossed the Potomac. . . . If the charge made by my gallant Virginians on the fatal third day of July had been supported, or even if my other two Brigades had been with me[,] we would have been in Washington and the war ended."[80]

George Pickett had little to do with the charge's planning or its failure, but he saw himself as criminally maligned. In his mind, he and his division suffered because of someone else's error. Pickett rarely proved an especially introspective or forgiving man. He arrived on the battlefield already paranoid, distracted, and overly anxious. His behavior just prior to the charge supported the contention that he was fully confident of a dramatic victory; instead, he witnessed a terrible disaster. The loss of his division only exacerbated old feelings of disillusionment and failure. Field officer T. G. Barham remarked of Pickett: "After the battle of Gettysburg where his division lost so many men he seemed to lose his snap."[81]

It did not take long for the charge to become part of Confederate and southern mythology. LaSalle Pickett later played a major role in creating the romanticized picture of Pickett's Charge. But there were others who played a part.[82] William Faulkner's *Intruder in the Dust* contains one of the best-known passages on Pickett's Charge at Gettysburg:

> For every Southern boy, fourteen years old, not once but whenever he wants it there is an instant when it's still not yet two o'clock on that July afternoon in 1863, the brigades are in position behind the rail fence, the guns are laid and ready in the woods and the furled flags are already loosened to break out and Pickett himself with his long oiled ringlets and his hat in one hand probably and his sword in the other looking up the hill waiting for Longstreet to give the word and it's all in the balance, it hasn't happened yet, it hasn't even begun yet, it not only hasn't begun yet but there is still time for it not to begin against that position and those circumstances, which made more men than Garnett and Kemper and Armistead and Wilcox look grave yet it's going to begin, we all know that, we have come too far with too much at stake and that moment doesn't need even a fourteen-year-old boy to think *This time, Maybe this time* with all this much to lose and all this much to gain.[83]

George Pickett had much to gain at Gettysburg, and he lost. The immortality he later attained proved more valuable to his widow than to himself.

CHAPTER 10

North Carolina, 1863–1864
You Will Hardly Ever Go Back There Again

After the disastrous battle of Gettysburg, LaSalle claimed, George was even more eager that they marry. "The future is uncertain," she recalled him saying, "and it is impossible for me to call a moment my own. Again, with all the graves I have left behind me, and with all the wretchedness and misery this fated campaign has made, we would not wish anything but a very silent, very quiet wedding, planning only the sacrament and blessing of the church, and after that, back to my division and to the blessing of those few of them, who by God's miracle, were left."[1] Though not quite the dutiful, humble soldier LaSalle idealized, George Pickett was a man increasingly sobered and sickened by war. Marriage to the vivacious, outgoing Sallie Corbell was perhaps his only salvation.

LaSalle's published accounts of their wedding stressed George's impatience, her youth, and the ceremony's hastiness. Her literary reconstruction of her and her husband's life repeatedly emphasized how they defied odds and acceptable behavior to be together. Still, she felt obliged to defend the absence of a proper courtship and a traditional ceremony. "Had we been living under the old regime," she explained to readers, "nothing would have been easier than to prepare for a grand wedding in the stately old Southern style." War dramatically changed the plans for many southern couples, and there probably was little time or resources for an ornate ceremony.

LaSalle's insistence on her young age is more difficult to explain. Calling herself the "child bride of the Confederacy," she claimed to be fifteen or sixteen on her wedding day, when she was, in fact, twenty or twenty-two in 1863.[2] LaSalle consistently portrayed herself in her autobiographical writings as a child prone to mindless prattle, naively

George and LaSalle Pickett, circa 1863
(The Museum of the Confederacy, Richmond, Va.)

gullible, and overly dramatic. Telling readers she was only six when she first met George, LaSalle maintained: "Almost from babyhood I knew him and loved him."[3] When they finally married, she remembered feeling like a child "who had been given a bunch of grapes, a stick of candy. Oh, I was happy."[4]

By falsely presenting herself as a little girl in her writings, LaSalle perhaps sought to hide the assertiveness and independence she later attained as a successful writer and single woman. By emphasizing her own delicacy and fragility, she could bolster, through contrast, her troubled husband's strength and thus defend repeated attacks on his manhood and courage.[5]

LaSalle further enhanced the picture of her wedding day by describing difficulties she and George allegedly faced as the ceremony drew near. According to LaSalle, George could not obtain a furlough but instead received permission for "special duty" to leave the front. Word leaked to Union troops that General Pickett might try to reach her family home near Federal-held Suffolk. So, instead, Sallie became a "smuggled bride," sneaking with family members across enemy lines, traveling by mule, ferry, and train to reach Petersburg from Chuckatuck. LaSalle's father, John, two uncles, and a female chaperone accompanied her; her mother, Elizabeth, had to stay behind to care for her baby brother. At St. Paul's Episcopal Church in Petersburg the wedding party assembled, including George's brother Charles, his uncle Andrew, and his aunt Olivia. Another delay almost derailed the entire event: since neither George nor LaSalle were Petersburg residents, they required a special court decree to obtain a license. A frayed and nervous Sallie wept inconsolably. Finally, LaSalle Corbell married her soldier on September 15, 1863. A crowd of "thousands" cheered the event. The newlyweds left Petersburg by train, hailed by "the salute of guns, hearty cheers, and chimes and bugles."[6]

More celebration followed in Richmond. A fine array of Confederate luminaries, including President and Mrs. Davis, congregated to toast the happy couple. Robert E. Lee's wife, Mary, gave the Picketts a fruitcake. Guests ate and danced, "dancing as only Richmond in the Confederacy could dance. With a step that never faltered she waltzed over the crater of a volcano." LaSalle observed, "If people could not dance in the crises of life, the tragedy of existence might be even darker than it is." The contrast was striking but not unusual; famed Civil War diarist Mary Chesnut also described Richmond's elite lavishly entertaining while war raged around them.[7]

Yet the only part of LaSalle's colorful account that can be corroborated is the occurrence and date of their marriage. On September 22, 1863, a Richmond newspaper listed the event under wedding announcements with little fanfare: "In Petersburg, at St. Paul's Church on Tuesday 15th inst. by the Rev. Mr. Platt, Maj. Gen. George E. Pickett to Miss Sallie Corbell, daughter of J. David Corbell, Esq. of Nansemond Co., VA."[8]

LaSalle's published recollections of those first months of marriage show a young wife trying to live, as much as the war would allow, a normal traditional married life. Soon after their wedding, George received a new assignment as head of the Department of North Carolina, headquartered in Petersburg.[9] LaSalle accompanied her husband to Petersburg, assuming the role, she assured readers, of moral superior. She worked to check her husband's bad habits and monitor his drinking and swearing. In her autobiography she recounted a member of George's staff remarking, "Before the General was married he would not allow any of us to swear at all. He said he would do the swearing for the whole division. Now that he is married we have not only to do our own swearing but his, too."[10]

Even though she was close to George's headquarters, LaSalle recalled long hours, sometimes days, spent apart from him. To fill her time, she befriended other officers' wives, read novels and newspapers, took long walks, rode horses, and even danced—anything to distract her from the war. The friendships forged during these dark days were special to LaSalle; she bonded with other women brought together through war. LaSalle recounted visiting hospitals and prisons, bringing buttermilk, soap, clean shirts, flowers, and any sort of small comfort to ragged and needy prisoners. These passages from LaSalle's wartime experiences ring true. Many other white southern women faced similar trials and sought ways to feel useful and stay busy as the war raged on.[11]

No doubt LaSalle also provided constant comfort and support to her troubled husband. George's new assignment brought new headaches. His department encompassed southeastern Virginia as well as eastern North Carolina. By late 1863, Unionists and Confederates had splintered the Tar Heel State into warring factions. Disaffection so plagued its troops that North Carolina earned the distinction of having the most desertions in the Confederacy. By the fall of 1863, President Davis's suspension of habeas corpus and freedom of speech, conscription, military defeats, and economic hardships took a heavy toll on North Carolina's poor whites. Bands of destitute deserters roamed communities, plundering homes and wreaking havoc, often upon their own neighbors. These were trying circumstances for anyone in command. For an embittered man like George Pickett, they were doubly straining.[12]

To make matters worse, Pickett's shattered division was at subpar strength; very few troops remained at his disposal. By the fall of 1863, the War Department struggled to meet enemy threats over vast areas of the Confederacy, and it became apparent that units in Pickett's command would be shifted out of his jurisdiction at any time to aid other departments and districts. Already he had lost Micah Jenkin's brigade to Longstreet in the west.[13] In September, Pickett received instructions to send troops to W. H. C. Whiting, who was nervously bracing for attack at Wilmington, North Carolina.[14] Finally, when the possibility arose that his entire division might go west to rejoin James Longstreet's corps, Pickett exploded.[15] He complained to Adjutant and Inspector General Samuel Cooper that plans to reorganize the division had just begun. Few recruits had appeared, and new officers had little time to learn their responsibilities. It would take more time and many more men to refill the ranks before it could again become "the crack division it was." He protested, "I decidedly would not like to go into action with it."[16] In mid-October Pickett lost another brigade to the Department of Southwestern Virginia.[17] Reports of an enemy offensive at key points within his department's jurisdiction increased his frustration.[18] On October 21, Pickett notified Cooper that, despite assurances to the contrary, "numbers of applications for the return of detailed men on work in the Navy Department, etc. have been sent back disapproved." Secretary of War Seddon could only respond by assuring the agitated general: "I am endeavoring to return detailed men as far as the interest of general service will possibly allow."[19]

By November 1863, Pickett had merely a single brigade under his command when he was notified of a large Federal advance above Richmond.[20] Secretary of War Seddon ordered Pickett to send troops north to Hanover Junction and keep another unit ready to protect Petersburg. Pickett, unaware of the reason for this latest request for troops, expressed his vexation in a telegram to Richmond. He implored Seddon: "If I am to take my division into the field, I wish to take the whole division, and not a portion of it, as I did at Gettysburg, and I beg of you not to split it up when going into action. If I am to keep command of this department, do not entirely denude it."[21] Pickett's reaction was not necessarily uncommon. Many departmental commanders felt undercut by the larger needs of the Confederate army and frequently interpreted these demands as personal threats to their authority.[22]

Pickett had good reason to be concerned about the strength of his command. Federal raids against the towns of Suffolk, Virginia, and Elizabeth City, North Carolina, commenced in October and continued through the winter.[23] Under the orders of Union major general Benjamin "Beast" Butler, Brig. Gen. Edward A. Wild visited plantations to offer freedom to all slaves and Union guns and uniforms to black men.[24] A white woman from Elizabeth City described Union soldiers who "looked and behaved more like deamons [sic] than any thing else" and threatened to burn and rob her home. She declared: "It would make your blood boil to see them rush on your premises throw out your pickets at any door and have your house completely surrounded by them white and black."[25]

The burning and pillaging of private homes continued into the winter. On December 15, 1863, a colonel of a Georgia cavalry unit sent disturbing news to Pickett. He described the presence of enemy forces south of Suffolk, in Gates County, North Carolina. Yankees were destroying property and "committing all kinds of excesses; insulting our ladies in the most tantalizing manner."[26] In addition, Wild's men took two white female hostages in retaliation for a black soldier held by Confederates. Wild ordered the women shackled with irons and confined "with negro men."[27]

These raids enraged George Pickett. Here again was the dishonorable enemy violating the "rules of war" and defying the slaveholding South's patriarchal and racist ideology. Just the thought of arming blacks and insulting ladies disgusted and frightened Pickett, and he requested permission from the War Department to clear slaves out of the northeast region of North Carolina. This plan sounded strikingly similar to his idea of banning northern Indians from Bellingham Bay; and his feelings of impatience and powerlessness also had a familiar ring. "Whatever is determined," he urged, "should be carried out at once, as everyday loses so much valuable property to the Confederacy." He deemed it an "emergency," with no time to waste. "Butler's Plan," Pickett warned, "is to let loose his swarms of blacks upon our ladies and defenseless families, plunder and devastate the country."[28] Butler already threatened his wife's family home in Suffolk. Pickett saw only one recourse to combat such "heathens": "to hang at once everyone captured belonging to such expeditions and afterwards anyone caught who belongs to Butler's department." He immediately issued orders to Colonel Griffin that "any one caught in the act (negroes or white men) of burning houses or maltreating women must be hung on the spot, by my order."[29]

But the "outrages" continued.[30] These Federal raids were meant to suppress supposed guerrilla activities in the eastern portions of Virginia and North Carolina. On December 18, General Wild captured a man described as "about thirty, a rough stout fellow, [who] was dressed in butternut homespun, and looked the very ideal of a guerrilla." Though this man was an enlisted member of the Georgia cavalry, Wild decided to make an example of Pvt. Daniel Bright. Union soldiers left Bright's body hanging from a post, a slip of paper pinned to his back: "This guerrilla hanged by order of Brigadier General Wild. Daniel Bright of Pasquotank County."[31]

On December 19, Pickett learned of Bright's death and shot off another angry dispatch to Richmond.[32] He bitterly described "the most brutal outrages" committed "upon our loyal citizens." He announced his intentions "to spare no one," but he feared the enemy "too wary" to stop. In a revealing reference to his days on the western frontier, Pickett added: "They, like the Indians, only war on the defenseless." The Union was no longer a respectable and worthy opponent: this civil war had spun out of control. "It makes my blood boil," he exclaimed, "to think of these enormities being practiced, and we have no way of arresting them."[33]

Colonel Griffin followed Pickett's instructions to hang anyone caught committing such outrages. Within a week after he had issued the order, a group of Unionist citizens from Pasquotank County, North Carolina, notified Federal officials that they had found the hanged body of a black Union soldier with a wooden placard around his neck. The placard read: "Here hangs Private Samuel Jones of Company B. Fifth Ohio Regiment, by order of Major General Pickett in retaliation of [Private Daniel Bright,] Company L, Sixty-Second Georgia Regiment, hung December 18, 1863, by order of Brigadier General Wild."[34]

In the midst of these strained circumstances, Lee ordered an attack on New Bern, North Carolina. New Bern had fallen into Union hands in February 1862 when Union general Ambrose Burnside led an amphibious assault on the coastal town. On January 20, 1864, Lee sent Pickett detailed instructions that explained his plan to capture the Federal garrison guarding the town. Lee essentially gave Pickett another chance to prove his ability as a commander. Yet, while Lee allowed Pickett to "mod-ify [the plan] according to circumstances developed by investigation, and your good judgment," he sent Brig. Gen. Robert Hoke with written orders to "explain" the movement to Pickett. Lee's plan called for infan-try, artillery, and naval units to converge on New Bern and its vicinity in careful coordination. Lee urged the utmost "secrecy, expedition and boldness" in preparation and execution.[35]

When it became clear to LaSalle that her husband had serious busi-ness in North Carolina, she insisted on accompanying him. "I would not be left behind," she recalled, "when the journey to the old North State was made." LaSalle traveled to the home of another Confederate general outside New Bern and waited with his wife. During her brief stay in North Carolina, she recounted withstanding hostility from Unionists who, she felt, greatly resented her and her husband's presence in the region.[36]

By January 30, Pickett had organized an attack force of 13,000 men and 14 cutter ships. Land troops were to assault enemy positions north-west, southwest, and northeast of the city, while navy vessels moved down the Neuse River to challenge enemy gunboats. If all went as planned, a surprised and surrounded enemy would quickly surrender New Bern to the victorious Confederates.

During the early morning hours of February 1, Pickett's offensive got under way. Fog and light rain obscured movement, but briefly it seemed the scheme might work. Northwest of town, Pickett accompanied Robert Hoke's successful crossing of Batchelder's Creek. Below New Bern, Seth Barton swept over enemy outposts, halting within view of the main defenses.

Soon there were signs of trouble. The four-pronged land and water attack failed to occur simultaneously, and any element of surprise disap-peared. Alarmed by the Confederate offensive, Union commanders rushed reinforcements by railroad to strengthen defensive positions. Naval commander J. Taylor Wood, initially finding the river free of gun-boats, waited until the next morning before capturing and destroying one enemy vessel. Maj. James Dearing, expecting to take Fort Anderson, northeast of town, discovered a stronger force than anticipated. Barton, positioned outside the city's main defenses, refused to attack as ordered. As LaSalle described, "Through a whole day of torture Pickett waited in deathlike suspense with the prize of Newbern almost within his grasp."[37]

On February 2, an exasperated George Pickett sent an aid to Barton to prod him into action. Barton stood his ground, claiming that preliminary reports of Federal strength were woefully inaccurate. Pickett then ordered Barton to join Hoke's forces across the Trent River to take New Bern from the northwest. Barton, nearly twenty-five miles from Hoke's position, moved only slowly. On February 3, when Pickett learned of Barton's seemingly snail-like pace, he canceled his plans and ordered a complete withdrawal. Pickett's expedition against New Bern was over.[38]

Pickett's initial report of the action around New Bern belied the attack's failure: "Met a reconnaissance within a mile and a half of New Berne. . . . Met the enemy in force at Batchelder's Creek; killed and wounded about 100 in all; captured 13 officers and 280 prisoners, 14 negroes, 2 rifled pieces and caissons, 300 stands of small arms, 4 ambulances, 3 wagons, 55 animals, a quantity of clothing, camp and garrison equipage and 2 flags. Commander Wood, C.S. Navy, captured and destroyed U.S. gun-boat Underwriter. Our loss, 35 killed and wounded."[39]

Pickett's superiors were not pleased when they realized what had happened. President Jefferson Davis expressed his disappointment to Lee: "General Pickett has returned from his expedition unsuccessful in the main object."[40] Lee was also unhappy with the results. He wrote Robert Hoke: "I regret very much that success did not attend the whole expedition." But he admitted, "It is difficult in a combined attack to regulate and harmonize on an extreme field all the operations."[41]

In retrospect, George Pickett seemed ill-suited for a task that required such careful boldness and expediency. Lee had repeatedly emphasized the need for swiftness and secrecy in detailing the original battle plan.[42] Yet Pickett's official report of the battle revealed that he had had reservations from the start. He complained that "there were too many contingencies," adding, "I should have wished more concentration, but still hope the effect produced by the expedition may prove beneficial."[43] Pickett also blamed Seth Barton, chiding him for this unwillingness to push forward and for his delay that prevented a final "coup de main on the enemy."[44] Pickett concluded: "Had I have had the whole force in hand I have but little doubt that we could have gone in easily, taking the place by surprise."[45] The truth beyond Pickett's rhetoric was all too clear, however. Entrusted with his first real offensive operation as department head, Pickett stumbled.

George Pickett's actions and words over the next several weeks seemed to show a man on the edge of despair. Little in this war had gone the way he planned. These battles were not the sort of honorable fighting he had envisioned as a young cadet at West Point, nor what he experienced as a hero in Mexico. Rather than offering affirmation, this war brought personal attacks on his manhood, strained relations with his superiors, and seemingly senseless death and destruction. Simple frontal assaults did not succeed, and the enemy ignored "rules of war." An outlet for his frustration came soon after his inglorious retreat from New Bern.

Not mentioned in either Pickett's cursory report to General Cooper on February 3 or his official report on the 15th was his capture of twenty-two North Carolina soldiers during the abortive expedition. These men had once donned the colors of the state's home guard but, when threatened with Confederate conscription, opted for Union blue. The U.S. government refused to view Confederate draft evaders who joined the Union army as deserters. Union officials insisted that Confederates treat these men as any other prisoners of war.[46] Subtle legalities meant little to Pickett. He had found a scapegoat for frustrations and failures that had been mounting for months. Two weeks after his failed expedition on New Bern, he court-martialed and hanged all twenty-two men for desertion.

Union major general John J. Peck first voiced his suspicion that something was seriously wrong when he wrote to Pickett on February 11 to inquire about a recent article he had seen in a Richmond paper. The newspaper had reported that during the action around New Bern, black troops shot and killed Confederate colonel H. M. Shaw.[47] The newspaper stated that incensed Confederates singled out the black soldier who fired the fatal shot and followed, captured, and subsequently hanged him. Peck included with his letter a copy of President Lincoln's warning to Confederates to make no distinction based on color in the treatment of war prisoners. Lincoln threatened "retaliation upon the enemy's prisoners" by executing rebel soldiers for every Union soldier killed "in violation of the laws of war." Peck closed, "Believing that this atrocity has been perpetrated without your knowledge, and that you will take prompt steps to disavow this violation of the usages of war and to bring the offenders to justice, I shall refrain from executing a rebel soldier until I learn your action in the premises."[48] Union officials already knew about the hanging of Private Jones.[49] Peck gave Pickett the benefit of the doubt

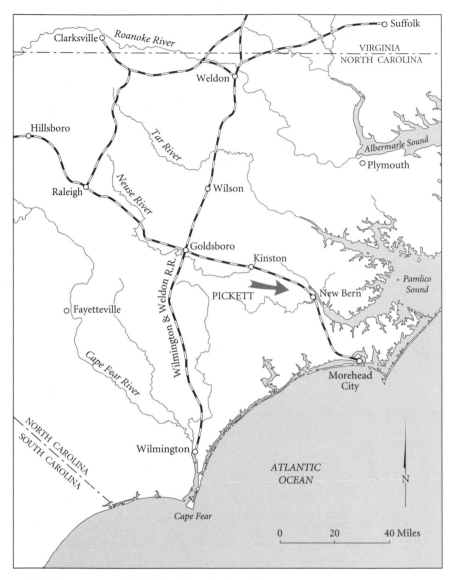

The Department of North Carolina, Spring 1864

about his participation in this new atrocity. Before Pickett could reply, Peck wrote him again about the captured North Carolinians. Peck reminded Pickett of Union policy toward such prisoners of war and asked for special consideration for this case.[50] He anxiously awaited a response.

Pickett must have had a chilling laugh. Here was the enemy, these "heathens," asking *him* to respect their rules of war! On February 16 he sharply denied that he had had any part in the hanging of Colonel Shaw's killer. He deemed the story "not only without foundation, but so ridiculous that I should scarcely have supposed it worthy of consideration." In the confusion of a battle how could anyone single out Shaw's killer, follow, and capture him? Nevertheless, Pickett coldly added that if he had caught any black soldier, "I should have caused him to be immediately executed." He indignantly answered Peck's threat of retaliation as expressed in Lincoln's proclamation: "I have in my hands and subject to my orders, captured in the recent operations in this department, some 450 officers and men of the United States Army, and for every man you hang, I will hang 10 of the United States Army."[51] These were serious threats, but as a member of Pickett's division remarked, "Pickett is not a man to back out from any step that he may take."[52]

On February 17, Pickett responded sarcastically to Peck's plea for special consideration for the North Carolina prisoners:

> General: Your Communication of the 13th instant is at hand. I have the honor to state in reply that you have made a slight mistake in regard to numbers, 325 having "fallen into your (our) hands in your (our) hasty retreat from before New Bern"; instead of the list of 53 with which you so kindly furnished me, and which will enable me to bring to justice many who have up to this time escaped their just deserts. I herewith return you the names of those who have been tried and convicted by court-martial for desertion from the Confederate service and taken with arms in hand, "duly enlisted in the Second North Carolina Infantry, United States Army." They have been duly executed according to law and the custom of war.

Pickett ended the communication: "Extending to you my thanks for your opportune list, I remain, very respectfully, your obedient servant."[53] He later told Peck that if Peck killed any southern prisoners in retaliation, he would make good his threat of ten Union dead for every one Confederate.[54]

Before Peck received Pickett's communications, the Union general heard disturbing news of the executions. A newspaper carried an account of the trial and hanging of two of the North Carolinians. Peck cautioned Pickett that if he failed to treat the men as prisoners of war, Confederate officers imprisoned at Fort Monroe would suffer the consequences.[55] Pickett ignored Peck's threats and diligently sent copies of all their correspondence to the War Department.[56] Only this time he wanted no intervention from Richmond: "The whole of the prisoners captured in this department will be held at my disposal."[57] He wanted complete control.

Details of the executions reveal just how much energy Pickett exerted to take full control of the prisoners' fate.[58] After his retreat from New Bern, Pickett marched the prisoners thirty miles west to Kinston, where he had them incarcerated in a local jail and then ordered court-martial proceedings to begin immediately. He allowed little food or coverings for the men and ignored the pleading of town officials, relatives, and subordinate army officers. Most of these men resided nearby, and wives came to visit them and provide what little comfort they could offer. Within two weeks of their capture, Pickett decreed three separate hangings of the prisoners in a public square, where they were surrounded by their wives, mothers, children, and townspeople. A Confederate army chaplain offered baptism to several of the condemned men and told them that "they had sinned against their country, and their country would not forgive them but they had also sinned against God, yet God would forgive them if they approached with penitent hearts."[59] After each execution, Pickett allowed his soldiers to strip corpses of all clothing and shoes. Confederates jeered and taunted widows who attempted to gather their husbands' bodies for proper burial.[60] Pickett's men hastily buried unclaimed bodies in a single grave beneath the gallows.[61]

In court months later, when the Federal government sought to indict Pickett for war crimes in 1865–66, widows of the condemned men recalled the horrific experience. Catherine Summerlin spent less than two hours with her husband, Jesse, before his death. The Confederacy, she testified, had already taken her property, conscripted her husband by force, and finally killed him. "My feelings," she remembered, "would not permit me to see them hanged."[62] Elizabeth Jones brought bedding to her husband, Stephen, so he would not have to sleep on the floor. She, too, could not bear to witness his hanging: "I did not see them hung, for I could not stand to see it. I carried my husband's body home with me that same day."[63] Nancy Jones recalled that when she retrieved her husband's body from the gallows, "he had nothing on but his socks."[64]

When Peck's superior, Gen. Benjamin Butler, learned of the executions, he wrote directly to the Confederate commander of prisoner exchange. He asked Col. Robert Ould whether the Confederacy was fully aware of Pickett's disturbing actions and threats toward Union prisoners. Butler began to sense the anger expressed in Pickett's acts and words, and he warned Ould of the larger implications of his behavior: "The question will be whether he [Pickett] shall be permitted to allow his personal feelings to prevail in a matter now in our hands."[65] A comparison of the records of Confederate court-martials kept at the National Archives appears to justify Butler's concern. The twenty-two men who died at Kinston were tragic exceptions to the rule that most soldiers sentenced to death were eventually spared. The haste in which Pickett ordered the executions and his denial of clemency made this case even more unusual. Desertion from state service was not even a crime in North Carolina.[66]

A Federal officer later accused George Pickett of belonging to a group of slaveholding aristocrats who used terror tactics to subdue poor whites sympathetic to the Union.[67] Certainly there was an element of class resentment in Pickett's earlier behavior and pronouncements against nonslaveholding whites in the Northern Neck. By February 1864, civil war had rocked the very foundation of his military judgment and personal restraint. Rage and frustration overshadowed any notions of discretion. "God damn you, I reckon you will hardly ever go back there again, you damned rascals; I'll have you shot, and all other damned rascals who desert," a Confederate soldier heard Pickett yell at two of the prisoners before court-martial proceedings started.[68]

LaSalle Pickett never mentioned publicly the hangings in Kinston. This was just another troubling detail from her husband's life she omitted in her writings. At sometime during their marriage or after his death she determined that she would be George Pickett's champion, through right or wrong. It is unclear how much she knew about the incident, yet during their intimate moments together she had to have seen her husband's bitterness, anger, and resentment.[69] She would make it right again, though, many years after his death, when she wrote her books and her short stories and lectured to masses of Americans. Then she would make him a better man than he ever could have been.

CHAPTER 11

Virginia, 1864–1865

Is That Man Still with This Army?

With the graves at Kinston still fresh, George Pickett's troubles were far from over. His failed attempt to wrest New Bern from Federal hold had serious military repercussions. When Braxton Bragg, newly appointed military adviser to President Davis, laid plans to attack Plymouth, North Carolina, he selected Brig. Gen. Robert Hoke to lead, instead of the department head. Bragg explained to Pickett that he chose the younger, less experienced officer for the mission merely "so as not to withdraw you from supervision from your whole department at this critical time."[1] Why Confederate high command did not dismiss Pickett entirely from active duty is unclear. Perhaps his twenty years of professional army experience and early war record convinced some that he would recover from his setbacks. His close friendship with James Longstreet may have been another factor. Still, there was enough doubt surrounding George Pickett to demote him to spectator as Hoke skillfully seized Plymouth on April 20, 1864.[2]

While Hoke's forces surrounded Plymouth, Federals began their own spring offensive. A massive deployment of troops on the south side of the James River was part of Gen. U. S. Grant's overall plan to coordinate Federal forces throughout the South. Ben Butler's 30,000-man Army of the James would steam up the James River, feinting an attack on Petersburg, while Meade's Army of the Potomac moved in from the north. The main Federal objective was to capture Richmond while Lee's army was bled into nonexistence.[3]

Since November 1863, Pickett had predicted an enemy assault up the York-James Peninsula toward Petersburg. Throughout the autumn and winter months of 1863, he tried to convince Richmond authorities of his fears. He visited the secretaries of war and navy personally, but all of his pleas fell on deaf ears.[4] Word must have gotten out that George Pickett was not a man to trust.

On April 13, 1864, Pickett received reports at his headquarters in Petersburg of renewed Federal activity in southeastern Virginia. Without a second thought, he passed the report on to Richmond. Most of Pickett's troops had gone with Hoke to Plymouth, leaving Petersburg largely unprotected. Pickett complained to General Bragg and begged that troops be rushed to Petersburg to aid in its defense. Initially, Bragg responded to Pickett's warnings favorably, instructing him: "Your scouts should be very active and vigilant to keep us advised of all movements about Suffolk and Portsmouth, especially during the absence of troops from their regular positions."[5] Bragg did not realize how literally Pickett would interpret this statement.

Pickett dutifully sent word of all reports from scouts and Union deserters. Over a twenty-four-hour period he forwarded eight separate telegrams. Much of the information was blatantly contradictory or ambiguous in its content. He thoughtlessly sent them anyway, without offering his own assessment of their reliability. After the last several months of stress, failure, and anger, he seemed capable only of instant reaction without careful reflection.[6]

Braxton Bragg was not a patient man. After a full day of Pickett's barrage of alarming telegrams, he had had enough. Bragg bluntly advised, "You should keep the enemy closely watched and report his movements frequently, but I must warn you of the evil resulting from exaggerated and unreliable reports."[7] Chastened by Bragg's harsh tone, Pickett explained that he had only followed orders. He hoped that keeping Bragg fully informed, "would enable you to form your own conclusions."[8] Pickett appeared incapable of forming any lucid conclusions for himself —except that the Federals were dangerously close and he had no protection. He must have hoped that someone else might take the situation in hand and tell him what to do.

A few days later, the secretary of war deemed it time to make a change. On April 23, 1864, Gen. P. G. T. Beauregard officially took charge of the Departments of North Carolina and Cape Fear and renamed them the Department of North Carolina and Southern Virginia. Beauregard relieved Pickett of departmental command, leaving him with district command of Petersburg. George Pickett's plight had gone from bad to worse.

Once the proud leader of a full division of battle-hardened veterans, he now led a ragtag force of regular soldiers, local militia, and civilian volunteers. As district commander he had only 2,000 men under his authority to fight the 30,000 well-equipped and confident Yankees headed directly for Petersburg.[9]

Pickett frantically sought a way out. He filed a request to be transferred back to Longstreet's corps with the Army of Northern Virginia and resume command of his old division. Perhaps he hoped to erase the terrible memories of the last twelve months. Longstreet and Pickett had been friends for many years, and "Old Pete" would not scold him or reprimand him for following orders. Why could he not simply return to that secure place he held only a year earlier? Pickett must have voiced his feelings candidly to his friend. On May 1, Longstreet wrote directly to Lee and asked that he restore Pickett to field command. Three days later, Pickett received orders to resume command of his division in the Army of Northern Virginia.[10]

Relief would not come so easily. General Beauregard, en route for Petersburg, stopped at Weldon, North Carolina, and notified Pickett that he was ill. Feeling helpless, Pickett knew it "would have been impossible" to leave Petersburg without a commanding officer. He stayed. It was the very day the Federals launched their offensive on the James.[11]

Pickett had excitedly acknowledged his orders to rejoin his division at Hanover Junction, stating, "Shall lose no time."[12] Neither would the Federals. Pickett dispatched eight telegrams to Richmond describing Union boats steaming up the James. The War Department sent no response. This time, perhaps more than any other, his concerns were well-founded: a powerful enemy offensive was under way. But like the boy who cried wolf too often, Pickett found his ardent pleas for help ignored, perhaps even derided, by Richmond. During the early afternoon on May 5, he wrote despairingly, "I have telegraphed you four times this morning and received no answer. Please answer this."[13]

By 3:00 P.M., Pickett's nerves were near shattering. No doubt he wanted to escape this crisis, but there was no way out. He had been in these situations too many times before—at San Juan, the Northern Neck, and North Carolina—where he had pleaded for help but few seemed to care. At Gettysburg he stood by helplessly with no support as the hated foe reaped bloody victory. He dispatched another message: "I have sent you numerous telegrams this morning and fail to obtain an answer. The emergency is so great that I sent a courier by train to say that the enemy in force are coming up the river. You had better send troops." Bragg scribbled the word "seen" across Pickett's telegram and filed it.[14] Before the day ended, Pickett hurried another appeal for help to the War Department. Again, there was silence and no signs of reinforcements.[15]

On May 6, relief finally came to George Pickett in the form of Maj. Gen. D. H. Hill, who had recently volunteered to serve on Beauregard's staff. Special Order No. 3 stated: "Gen'l Hill is specially charged with communicating to Maj-Gen'l Pickett the views of the commanding General."[16] Beauregard tried to ease Pickett's anxiety by expressing his full confidence in Hill to "aid you in the discharge of your onerous duties in the present emergency."[17] On May 7, Secretary of War Seddon confessed to General Bragg that he felt "some distrust of Pickett's adequacy to the load upon him." Seddon hoped Beauregard might soon relieve Pickett and take control of the situation at Petersburg.[18]

The next several days passed in a blur. Pickett rushed his few troops to the crucial railroad junction near Petersburg. He scraped together a group of mounted and armed civilians for a makeshift cavalry screen, and ran locomotive cars in and out of town to give the semblance of arriving reinforcements. Reportedly, Pickett personally rode along the lines, perhaps hoping that by rallying the men's spirit his anxieties might lessen. With a total of 1,400 men, Pickett braced for the arrival of Butler's army. He continued to bombard Richmond with frenzied descriptions of the enemy's imminent approach.[19]

LaSalle Pickett later recounted these tension-filled days in her published books and articles. She celebrated her heroic husband as risking all to save Petersburg. According to LaSalle, her soldier was constantly cool and courageous, even prophetic.[20] She wrote with conviction, "Though my Soldier had been ordered a few days before to report to the Army of Northern Virginia, he could not leave Petersburg to destruction. In defiance of orders he remained in the beleaguered city."[21] He refused sleep, she maintained, so concerned was he with protecting "a whole city full of helpless, defenseless women and children at the mercy of an oncoming army."[22] LaSalle wrote dramatically of joining other "heroic, unselfish wives and daughters of the Confederacy" who carried dispatches, conveyed food to hungry soldiers, and cheered on imaginary troops at the railroad station.[23] She barely saw her husband at all, except "when I carried to him on the lines a dispatch or his bread and soup and coffee."[24]

Yet, as she had in recounting other crises, LaSalle maintained that George's thoughts remained solely on her. In the published Pickett letters, he allegedly beseeched her, in the middle of the enemy attack, to explain why she had quipped "Never mind" to him at their last meeting. "It troubled me all night," he claimed. "I wanted to follow after you and ask you what you meant, but couldn't. I would have jumped on Lucy [his horse] and ridden in to Petersburg and found out if it had been *possible* for me to leave. I was so troubled about it that I was almost tempted to come in anyhow." He asked, "Were you aggrieved because your blundering old Soldier told you there was no necessity for your coming out to bring dispatches, any longer, that, thank heaven, the recruits and reinforcements were coming in now and that we could manage all right?"[25]

In reality, George Pickett was not managing well at all. His fears were not entirely unfounded, his actions not entirely unwarranted. But after months of tension and stress, the bitterness of Gettysburg, the disappointment of New Bern, and anger of Kinston, his system could take no more. As LaSalle later ascertained, he had had little sleep and probably little food. On May 9, he sent orders to attack and then mindlessly canceled them. On May 10, Pickett collapsed, mentally and physically exhausted. He crawled into bed and blotted out the turmoil surrounding him. Seven days later, he described himself as being "far from well" and "confined to my bed."[26] Word of Pickett's illness spread quickly. Confederate chief of ordnance Josiah Gorgas recorded in his diary, "Pickett is very dissipated, it is asserted."[27] Beauregard, who had finally arrived at Petersburg on the 11th, wrote Bragg: "He [Pickett] has been confined to his room since."[28]

LaSalle Pickett was partly right: George's meager forces did manage to protect Petersburg from a superior enemy offensive until reinforcements arrived. Out of sheer desperation, George took control and succeeded in his task. Two recent studies of the campaign applaud Pickett for his "heroic exertions" as "the man who . . . saved Petersburg for the Confederacy."[29] Clifford Dowdey credits Pickett for his "key part in saving Richmond by unheroic actions performed in bureaucratic chaos."[30] A member of Pickett's command told his wife, "General Pickett deserves much credit for having successfully defended with a very small force the

George Pickett, circa 1864
(The Museum of the Confederacy, Richmond, Va.)

town till the arrival of reinforcements."[31] LaSalle Pickett described townspeople passing an official resolution of thanks and presenting gifts of silver to her and her soldier "for his brave defense of the city."[32] But what use would George Pickett have had for silver mugs or city resolutions? These probably would seem empty gestures for all he had suffered. As soon as he was able, he left for Hanover Junction. By May 19, George Pickett had his division back with the Army of Northern Virginia.[33]

Pickett's division was markedly smaller than the one he had commanded at Gettysburg. After the disaster in Pennsylvania, his brigades spent the winter rebuilding their broken ranks. By mid-May 1864 the division totaled about 5,000 men, including returned wounded, returned prisoners, and a few conscripts.[34] The First Corps had changed too. James Longstreet was absent from command due to a serious wounding on May 6 in the battle of the Wilderness. South Carolinian Richard H. Anderson temporarily assumed command of the corps until Longstreet's return.

This was not the same enemy Pickett had led his division against in 1862–63. Ulysses S. Grant, general-in-chief of the armies of the United States, now accompanied George Meade's Army of the Potomac. In the past, Union commanders had retreated to Washington to lick their wounds as soon as they engaged the Confederates. Thus, no decisive victories had been won by the Federal troops. Unlike his predecessors, however, the aggressive Grant viewed the war as a single battlefield and no longer based Union strategy solely on the capture of Richmond. Instead, he sought to destroy the Confederate armies piece by piece. This strategy dictated that Meade's Army of the Potomac lock itself into almost daily combat with Lee's forces in order to weaken and eventually break Lee's ability to wage successful battle.[35] As Pickett traveled north from Petersburg to resume field command, Grant prepared to destroy Lee's army swiftly and decisively.

Soon after Pickett rejoined Lee's army, he resumed his complaining. Pointing to contradictory orders, Pickett bemoaned instructions that "had to be corrected." Perhaps Lee had questioned Pickett's whereabouts and health, for Pickett added: "I considered myself as much with my division as to have gone as contemplated, as to have been anywhere on the road, the division going as it is in detachments." He closed with a testy assurance: "Had it been intended for me to stop at Hanover Junction, or any other point with the Division and such instructions, given me, I would have carried them out."[36] On May 28, he dispatched three couriers and two staff officers to the First Corps headquarters, demanding rations for his brigades. He claimed that "the men are calling loudly for bread." "We must get something," he declared, "or the division will be worse than useless."[37]

Prior to Pickett's return to his division, Grant had initiated a series of flanking movements on Lee's Army of Northern Virginia. Lee responded with his own counteroffenses. From early May to mid-June 1864, Lee and Grant clashed, and clashed again, at the battles of the Wilderness, Spotsylvania Courthouse, and Cold Harbor.[38] As the spring turned to summer and casualties began to mount, Pickett's men essentially served as a "mobile reserve" under the direct command of Lee, missing the most intensive combat. Portions of the division shifted frequently to lend support north of Richmond and outside Petersburg.[39] Morale was initially high despite the soldiers' lack of battle action. Blair Burwell, Pickett's brother-in-law and division surgeon, wrote his wife on May 26, 1864, that the entire army remained confident: "Genl Lee's army is in fine condition & full of enthusiasm & only awaits the opportunity to crush Grant when they get a fair chance at him."[40]

One of the division's few opportunities to prove its renewed fighting capacity came on June 17, 1864, when it was ordered to retake Confederate lines at the Bermuda Hundred. The division's success came after Lee canceled the order for their attack. Confederate engineers realized at the last minute that they could build lines around the targeted enemy battery. The cancellation came too late for Pickett's men, and they rushed forward to recapture the lines easily with little blood loss.[41] Lee congratulated the unit by writing corps commander Anderson: "General I take great pleasure in presenting you my congratulations upon the conduct of the men in your corps. I believe they will carry anything they are put against." Lee added, "We tried very hard to stop Pickett's men from capturing the breastworks of the Enemy but could not do it."[42] Charles Pickett proudly remembered this dispatch as "one of the highest complements Genl Lee ever paid to a command."[43] In August, a portion of Pickett's division, while occupying trenches near Fussell's Mill, again had the chance to pursue the enemy. "Don't fire," several soldiers reportedly shouted across the battlefield, "we're Pickett's Division," hoping to instill fear in their foe.[44] His men were full of vigor and fight despite the many months that had passed since that fateful day at Gettysburg.

By mid-June, Pickett's division settled into its place on the Howlett Line northeast of Petersburg.[45] LaSalle remembered how she and George occupied first a tent, then a log cabin near the front lines. She claimed that she had the company of several other officers' wives who also joined their husbands at the front. Although in close proximity to the sieges, LaSalle recalled that "there was no lack of social diversions. In a small way we had our dances, our conversaziones and musicales, quite like the gay world that had never known anything about war except from the pages of books and the columns of newspapers. True we did not feast."[46] She emphasized yet again how she looked for the "rifts of sunshine to break the gloom."[47]

Pickett's soldiers made the most of the monotony, too, although they lacked ample provisions. A private in the 18th Virginia described "the dull monotony of camp life." "We have nothing around us to engage our attention," he wrote, "other than the discharge of the regular routine of military duty."[48] Pickett's division was stretched out over three miles, and occasionally Pickett ordered attacks on the enemy line to straighten his own line or feel for weakness. Daily existence became a test in patience and durability. There was constant shelling by artillery and gunfire from enemy sharpshooters. Pickett and his men remained on the Bermuda Hundred lines until March 1865. Despite his earlier protest against splitting his division, Pickett's brigades were occasionally shifted during the winter and early spring.[49]

There is little in the available public and private record to lend insight into the Picketts' daily life during these long months of siege warfare. Still, it is apparent that a cloud of uncertainty lingered over George Pickett as a reliable field commander. Even though he was the army's most senior major general, Lee did not entrust Pickett with any sort of independent command following his shaky performance at Bermuda Hundred in May 1864. In June, Lee moved his headquarters to Drewry's Bluff to supervise the occupation of the Bermuda Hundred line and, it would seem, to supervise the division's actions. For a little while at least, Pickett would be under the watchful eye of General Lee.[50]

LaSalle's record of these long months reinforced her celebratory images of the dutiful soldier-husband, loyal wife, and with the birth of her son, good mother. During the summer of 1864, her "new little soldier," George Jr., was born, and she alleged that "cheer after cheer went up for the 'General's baby.'" According to LaSalle, her son, dubbed the "little general" by Pickett's men, was a favorite among the troops. During a visit to camp she claimed that several soldiers clamored for the chance to hold the baby. "I am ashamed to confess it," she wrote, "but, notwithstanding the gentleness of the soldiers, baby's quiet, peaceful mien, and the General's continued assurance that he was all right, I, his very new and solicitous mother, suffered agonies of torture and anxiety until he was back again in my arms; and oh, dear, what a greasy, dirty, grimy little bundle it was when I did get it back."[51] Here again were the striking contradictory images found through much of her writings of female nurturing and male war making.

Marriage and motherhood had not lessened LaSalle's stubborn rebelliousness. She alleged that she came frequently to the front, alone or with her baby. She later described accompanying George once as he inspected the lines. Shells began to explode dangerously close, and he pleaded with her to leave. "No indeed," Sallie said. "I'm not a bit afraid, and if I were do you think I would let Pickett's men see me run?" To which George replied: "Come, dear, please! You are in danger, useless danger, and that is not bravery."

She told readers that she stayed at the front, snatching a pair of field glasses to gaze across the lines, allegedly catching a glimpse of General Grant and his wife.[52]

Notwithstanding her efforts to stress only positive aspects of her husband, her marriage, and her wartime experience, traces of terror and pain lingered in her writings. In one of her most macabre stories, LaSalle recounted witnessing the decapitation of a young officer, just after he, too, had warned her of the danger of her visiting the front. She watched him "riding in that graceful way which the Southerner has by inheritance from a long line of ancestors who have been accustomed to ride over wide reaches of land."[53] Regretting her "obstinate resistance to his appeal" that she take shelter, she was mortified to see his death. "Impulsively I sprang from my horse," she wrote, "and ran and picked up the poor head, and I solemnly believe that the dying eyes looked their thanks as the last glimmering of life flickered out." This gruesome memory, she wrote, haunted her the rest of her life.[54]

This is indeed a strange and disturbing story for LaSalle to have included in her autobiography, but perhaps it underscores the vast destruction, death, and personal suffering she experienced firsthand. In many ways, this war truncated her dreams and hopes as a white southern lady. Her husband was a failed, short-tempered, and complaining general. His health was poor, and he probably continued to drink. LaSalle was utterly devoted to her soldier, or at least the ideal of him, but she knew there was no turning back to those seemingly carefree years of her youth. She, and other white southerners, would do their best to celebrate their idealized, racist past in the myth of the Lost Cause. Occasionally, the raw pain of civil war came back in full force, and no amount of romanticizing could excise the ghosts.[55] "Years away from that time of anguish and terror," she wrote, "I awaken suddenly with the crash of those guns still in my ears, their fearful sounds yet echoing in my heart, only to find myself safe in my soft, warm bed."[56]

LaSalle Pickett's postwar writings omitted any mention of the large number of men deserting her husband's division during the fall and winter of 1864–65. Desertion in general was a disturbing problem for the Confederate army during that final winter of war, but the number of men defecting Pickett's division was staggering. Many of these soldiers were conscripts and looked for any opportunity to leave. Others answered desperate pleas from loved ones by returning home. Still others had simply grown tired of the stagnancy of siege warfare. In November 1864, Assistant Adjutant and Inspector General Walter Harrison informed Pickett of men "straggling to the rear of the line for several miles and committing depredations." The problem was so serious that Harrison sent out patrols, using up a "number of the more active and efficient men" in the process. From March 9 to 18, 1865, over 500 men, nearly 10 percent of Pickett's total strength, deserted his division.[57]

There were few bright spots. In November 1864 Harrison reported that James Kemper's brigade, under the command of Col. William R. Terry, was "in the best condition I have ever seen it," with clean camps and sufficient food, clothing, weapons, and horses.[58] Unfortunately, this single favorable report did not speak for the division as a whole nor did it address the predicament of its leader.

On January 19, 1865, Lee wrote to Longstreet of his deep dissatisfaction with the conditions in Pickett's division. In one brigade, Lee chided, "the articles of war were seldom read, accommodations for the sick bad, and religious exercises neglected." He labeled another "unsoldierly & unmilitary, lax in discipline & loose in military instruction." Lee suggested that Pickett and his officers were not "sufficiently attentive to the men" and "not informed as to their condition." Lee warned Longstreet that "unless the division and brigade commanders are careful and energetic, nothing can be accomplished." Pickett was Longstreet's responsibility as a subordinate and as a friend. Lee directed Longstreet to do all in his power to "correct the evils in Pickett's division."[59]

By late March 1865, Grant was determined to drive Lee from his entrenchments at Petersburg. The Union commander sent Philip Sheridan's cavalry around the Confederate right to tear up railway and turn Lee's flank. On March 30, Sheridan had his cavalry at Dinwiddie Courthouse with infantry from the II and V Corps nearby. To meet the renewed Federal threat, Lee ordered three of Pickett's four brigades to the extreme right of the Confederate line. By daybreak, March 30, Pickett's men arrived from a tiresome march through mud and pouring rain. Pickett then joined with his cousin Harry Heth and Dick Anderson to discuss with Lee their next move.[60]

Lee promptly unveiled his plan to his subordinates to send a combined force of cavalry, artillery, and infantry, some 19,000 men, to oppose the enemy's movement. Longstreet predicted: "I believe that such a force, in proper hands, will be able to frustrate [the] object of [the] enemy, as nearly all of his horses must be somewhat exhausted."[61] Surprisingly, Lee selected George Pickett to lead the mission. Existing records reveal some disagreement between Longstreet and Lee as to whether Pickett's division could be spared for the offensive, but at least formally, Longstreet did not give any preference as to who should command the special task force. Perhaps Longstreet suggested his old friend casually to Lee, and against his better judgment, Lee agreed. Lee's reasons for choosing Pickett as the leader are unclear.[62]

Pickett was to take three of his brigades, plus two from Bushrod Johnson's division, and six guns from Col. William J. Pegram's artillery to Five Forks. Cavalry from Thomas Rosser, W. H. F. "Rooney" Lee, and Fitz Lee would join Pickett there. Together, with Pickett as overall commander, the combined force would advance toward Dinwiddie Courthouse and assail the Federals. "It was," historian Douglas Freeman writes, "an order in the old spirit of the Army—to disdain odds and attack."[63]

A few years before, Pickett would have eagerly welcomed such an assignment. As a brigadier general he had proven aggressive and zealous, even while rumors swirled around him of his cowardice and incompetence. Battle was a chance to silence both his critics and his insecurities. At Gettysburg his shaky confidence was at its height, despite the apparent risk his men faced in charging across an open field. Only when he perceived himself unsupported and alone on the killing field did his certainty shatter, and then anxiety took over, it would seem, permanently. New Bern was a fiasco, and his desperate actions at Bermuda Hundred were successful almost by accident. Continual desertion plaguing his division and spotty inspection reports further weakened his record. His physical health was not good either. He continued to suffer after his collapse in May 1864. As late as March 20, 1865, his brother Charles reported: "Genl Pickett is in Richmond sick."[64] His chief surgeon, M. M. Lewis, notified corps headquarters the next day that Pickett had been "quite sick for several days with disease of the bowels and is still too unwell for duty."[65] Five Forks was the final opportunity for George Pickett to prove his worth and competence as a general, and as a man. In the past he had faced deep personal grief and loneliness, but he repeatedly sought direction, purpose, and identity on the battlefield. Now more than ever he needed a military victory.

Around noon on March 30, Pickett set out with his five brigades of infantry and a single artillery battery toward Five Forks. "The march," Pickett explained later, "was necessarily slow, on account of the continual skirmishing with the enemy's cavalry, both in front and flank."[66] Capt. W. Gordon McCabe, Pegram's adjutant, disagreed. Frustrated at the delay, McCabe confided to his diary, "General Pickett, instead of pushing on, stopped, formed a regiment in line of battle, and awaited some attack." Rather than post skirmishers on his flanks, Pickett wasted "much valuable time."[67] Already Pickett's judgment was in question.

A cold rain continued to fall as the Confederates marched westward along the White Oak Road. By 4:30 P.M., Pickett arrived at Five Forks. Only Fitz Lee's cavalry had reached him, and Pickett deemed his men "in much need of rest, having been marching nearly continuously for eighteen hours." He decided to wait until morning before attacking enemy cavalry concentrated around Dinwiddie Courthouse, five miles south of Five Forks. By driving the enemy from the courthouse, Pickett hoped to protect the Southside Railroad and halt Grant's offense on Lee's lines.[68]

At daylight, Pickett determined that Federal cavalry, reinforced by infantry, held a strong position on the Dinwiddie Courthouse Road, just outside town. Pickett advanced southward from Five Forks along the Scott Road, turning southeast at Ford Station Road toward the courthouse. Around 2:00 P.M., he readied his troops to cross Chamberlain's Bed in a two-pronged attack on Sheridan's west flank. Coordination failed, and Fitz Lee's cavalry moved toward Fitzgerald's Ford before the infantry was ready. Mounted and dismounted troopers fought stubbornly on opposite sides of the riverbank. Federals initially yielded to the weight of the Confederate assault, but a Union counterattack pushed the southerners back over the ford. Meanwhile, Confederate infantry waded across Danse's Ford farther north on Chamberlain's Bed. Montgomery Corse's brigade stormed enemy outposts, soon followed by Pickett's remaining troops. Federals hurriedly prepared a battle line to meet the Confederate flank attack. Hot fighting raged through the afternoon, with Federals giving up ground only grudgingly. By sunset on March 31, Pickett had successfully wrestled the initiative and driven the enemy back to Dinwiddie Courthouse. "This engagement," Pickett wrote in his report, "was quite a spirited one, the men and officers behaving most admirably."[69]

Pickett halted the advance with the onset of darkness. Veterans were surprised at the order; many could still see the Federals in retreat. Pickett later admitted, "Half an hour more of daylight and we would have gotten to the Court-House." He argued in his report that once he realized infantry was rapidly reinforcing enemy cavalry, he pulled back to Five Forks, where he believed he could better protect the Confederate right flank and the vital Southside Railroad. "The enemy," Pickett reported, "was . . . pressing upon our rear in force."[70]

Lee could not have been pleased with Pickett's decision. A telegram from Lee, which appears only in LaSalle Pickett's *Pickett and His Men*, urged: "*Hold Five Forks at all Hazards*. Protect the road to Ford's Depot and prevent Union forces from striking the South-side Railroad. Regret exceedingly your forced withdrawal, and your inability to hold the advantage you had gained."[71] Pickett later claimed that he assumed Lee would rush reinforcements to aid him in this task. He alleged that he informed "the general commanding of the state of affairs, that the enemy was trying to get in between the main army and my command, and asking that a diversion be made or I would be isolated."[72]

No acknowledgment from Lee exists to support Pickett's assumption that reinforcements were en route. Lee notified Secretary of War John C. Breckenridge on April 1 of Pickett's situation at Five Forks without mention of sending support, nor that Pickett had even asked for it.[73] After the fiasco that subsequently occurred at Five Forks, Pickett looked for others to blame, unwilling to admit any mistakes on his own part. Just as he had after Gettysburg, he convinced himself that he and his men had been left alone for the slaughter.

Pickett's carelessness can be seen in his hasty arrangement of troops for the day. To cover a gap of some three miles between himself and the main Confederate line, Pickett posted a small cavalry force. The division of W. H. F. Lee's cavalry covered his other flank, and in between he entrenched the infantry along the White Oak Road. Harrison described men "throwing up a temporary breastwork. Pine trees were felled, a ditch dug, and the earth thrown up behind the logs."[74] Then, completely losing all sense of the importance of his responsibilities, Pickett left the field. Sometime between noon and 1:00 P.M., he and Fitz Lee went to a shad bake hosted by cavalry commander Tom Rosser. Rosser's location was north of Hatcher's Run, at least one mile to Pickett's rear. While he ate fish and perhaps drank whiskey, Pickett ignored repeated reports of the enemy advance. Several officers did not even know that Pickett had left the front, nor his location.[75]

Pickett's official report of Five Forks made no mention of the shad bake or his whereabouts on the afternoon of April 1. He acknowledged receiving word that the enemy had "pushed steadily from the Court-House and commenced extending to our left." After several couriers visited the party, Fitz Lee finally left to assess the position of his cavalry, and if necessary, "cover the ground at once." Pickett recalled: "I supposed it had been done, when, suddenly the enemy in heavy infantry column appeared on our left front, and the attack which had, up to that time been confined principally to our front towards the Court-House now became general."[76] Fitz Lee later explained: "When we moved towards Five Forks, hearing nothing more of the infantry's move which we heard of the night before, I thought that the movements just there, for the time

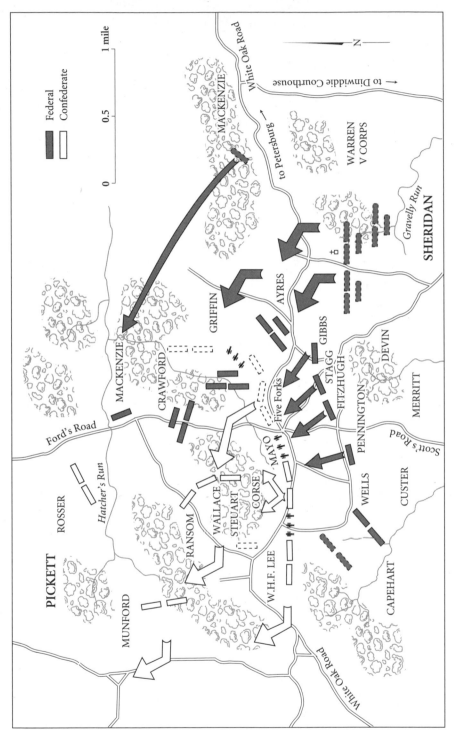

The Battle of Five Forks, Virginia, April 1, 1865

being, were suspended, and we were not expecting any attack that after-noon, so far as I know." He maintained: "Our throwing up works and taking position were simply general matters of military precaution."[77]

Fitz Lee's words and Pickett's actions show that neither anticipated any serious enemy attack despite Pickett's insistence that he demanded reinforcements and diversions. Even when he received word that an enemy attack was in progress, Pickett refused to believe its seriousness. Rosser admitted: "One would have thought that he [Pickett] would have been on the alert in the presence of the enemy he had so recently [been] fighting."[78] Pickett's later claim that he assumed reinforcements were on their way was a shoddy attempt to cover his own misjudgment

Federals were amassing a large offensive upon the Confederate lines at Five Forks. After some intermittent skirmishing, Sheridan sent an entire corps of infantry to storm Pickett's vulnerable left flank. Simultaneously, cavalry feinted toward the right, followed by a frontal assault by another division of Federals. Sheridan hoped that by hurling his entire command upon Pickett's lines he would drive the Confederates westward and iso-late them from the rest of Lee's Army of Northern Virginia. It was about 4:00 P.M. when Sheridan's offensive got under way.[79]

Picket finally realized the seriousness of the situation when he watched two couriers he had just dispatched to the front captured before his eyes. A line of Federals came swarming through the woods. Pickett bolted for his horse and raced across the stream toward Five Forks. Hunched for-ward on his saddle, he ran a gauntlet of enemy infantry fire to reach his own lines. One of Rooney Lee's staff officers tried to stop the harried general to deliver a message. Pickett barked at the young officer "not to talk to him," and rapidly rode on.[80]

By the time Pickett arrived on the scene, the enemy had broken his left line and began rolling up his flank. He desperately tried to form a new battle line, but the Federal strength was overwhelming. Union cavalry blocked Ford's Road, Pickett's retreat route north toward Hatcher's Run.[81] "Charge after charge of the enemy was repulsed," Pickett re-ported, "but they still kept pouring up division after division, and press-ing around our left."[82] He attempted, as he had at Bermuda Hundred, to rally the men on his own accord. He exhorted Col. C. C. Floweree of the 7th Virginia: "I depend upon your regiment to save the day."[83] It was far too late for anyone to play savior. Pickett's soldiers panicked and ran; others merely surrendered in helplessness. A colonel recalled that "each private could see for himself the odds against him."[84] By nightfall, Sheridan's victory was complete. He captured 4 cannon, 11 flags, and over 5,000 Confederates, and successfully cut Pickett off from the rest of Lee's army. The Southside Railroad was lost, and Grant could quickly move on Lee's right flank.[85]

Could Pickett have prevented this fiasco had he been at the front when the Federal attack began? It is doubtful given the size of the force his men faced. Certainly as the general in command of the Confederate forces at Five Forks, entrusted by Lee to hold the position at all costs, he should have been accessible and on the field at all times.[86]

Historian Douglas Freeman, who offers the most insightful discussion of Five Forks to date, concluded that Fitz Lee and Pickett "cherished the general belief of the Army—a belief which had helped to create high morale—that . . . [Robert E. Lee] would continue to achieve the 'impossible' even though in this case, the line was stretched to the breaking point." Freeman defends their decision to attend the shad bake because of their "overconfidence," "lack of understanding" of the military situation, and downright hunger.[87]

This explanation of Pickett's behavior at Five Forks is far too charitable. Even if the odds were against him, he acted irresponsibly as the senior ranking major general. Of course this was not inconsistent with his past performances. This was a man who two years earlier habitually left his division command to visit his lover. This was someone who repeatedly held a distorted view of his responsibilities and the threats he faced. In the immediate aftermath at Gettysburg, Pickett was so consumed with his own grief that he wandered about the field aimlessly, sobbing openly. Throughout the Civil War, and his entire military career, he proved to be an officer unwilling to admit error or take responsibility for his actions. At New Bern and Gettysburg, Pickett lashed out at others for his own mistakes, and Five Forks was no different. In his report he reproached Lee for failing to send reinforcements and criticized him for choosing Five Forks rather than a position behind Hatcher's Run. Pickett even blamed his lunch partner, Fitz Lee, for failing to protect the left flank.[88] This was probably the same sort of unproductive and unprofessional complaining with which Pickett filled his infamous "lost" report from Gettysburg.

While her husband faltered and failed at Five Forks, LaSalle recalled waiting anxiously in Richmond for news. On April 2, 1865, the Confederate government abandoned their capital, and the next day, Union troops entered the city. LaSalle described being alone with her baby; her slaves had long gone, and rumors circulated that her soldier was dead. Fires set by Confederates spread, and frenzied crowds looted stores and warehouses. Broken furniture, shattered glass, and other wreckage filled the muddy streets. LaSalle likened the experience to a "reign of terror": "The yelling and howling and swearing and weeping and wailing beggar description. Families houseless and homeless under the open sky!"[89] The surreal, hellish picture was made complete by the presence of black Union soldiers. LaSalle remembered, "They were the first colored troops I had ever seen, and the weird effect produced by their black faces in that infernal environment was indelibly impressed upon my mind."[90]

LaSalle's description of the Confederacy's last days includes one of her most blatant and oft-repeated fabrications. The day after the city fell, she maintained, she had an unexpected visitor. "With my baby on my arm," she wrote, "I opened the door and looked up at a tall, gaunt sad-faced man in ill-fitting clothes." It was President Abraham Lincoln, who, LaSalle repeatedly told her readers, was an old friend of her husband's and had taken time to check on Pickett's young family. Kissing George Jr., Lincoln declared, "Tell your father, the rascal, that I forgive him for the sake of your bright eyes." She asserted that Lincoln was instrumental in obtaining George his appointment to West Point and that George would never allow anyone to speak badly of the Yankee president.

LaSalle's Lincoln-Pickett stories have no factual basis. George's uncle Andrew Johnston did apparently know Lincoln, and George may have met the Illinois lawyer during his brief stay in Quincy. Most of LaSalle's postwar writings date from the turn of the century, when national feelings of reconciliation were at their peak. Making the martyred president her husband's close friend was probably her deliberate attempt to reflect renewed nationalism and to attract northern audiences. It was yet another way for her to lessen publicly the magnitude of George's failings.[91]

After Five Forks, Lee made his last desperate move westward. He evacuated his lines at Petersburg and Richmond and marched toward Amelia Courthouse, where, supposedly, badly needed supplies waited. On April 4, tired and hungry Confederates arrived to find no supply trains. Lee then determined to move southwest to Rice Station, obtain supplies via the railroad from Lynchburg, and continue south to unite with Joseph E. Johnston's Army of Tennessee. Grant, in close pursuit, hurried to block Lee's retreat. On April 6, Sheridan's cavalry interrupted the Confederate's escape route, forcing a confrontation at Sayler's Creek.[92]

George Pickett and his men stumbled through these final days of war. A fellow officer spotted Pickett after Five Forks and described him as "hopeless, demoralized and prostrated. He did not look like Pickett, but like an old and broken man."[93] After Five Forks, Pickett was to join Lt. Gen. Richard H. Anderson en route to the Amelia Courthouse. Survivors of the once proud division did fight at the battle of Sayler's Creek, but weak with hunger and lack of sleep, these remaining tattered veterans were hardly in their best condition.[94] Brig. Gen. Henry Wise attested that at Sayler's Creek "we had hardly formed and begun to move in his rear before Pickett's whole command stampeded."[95]

Just before the Confederate surrender at Appomattox, Lee relieved Pickett of command. A staff officer who drafted the order later recalled Lee's strong dissatisfaction with Pickett not only for Five Forks but also for failing to measure "up to the occasion requiring supreme devotion," and instead proving "a source of weakness and demoralization."[96] Pickett refused to leave. One historian wonders whether Pickett ever received the order. In light of his mental and emotional state, it would be safe to assume that he indeed received it but refused to obey. He would stay with the pathetic remnants of his division until the end. Pickett's division numbered approximately 1,031 officers and men on April 9, 1865, with 60 men actually surrendering weapons. At Appomattox, Pickett signed his soldiers' paroles with the words "Maj. Genl. Comdg.," even though it was a lie.[97] Lee reportedly spotted Pickett at the surrender and asked bitterly, "Is that man still with this army?"[98]

James Longstreet would later argue that Five Forks was George Pickett's "greatest battle." He described his friend's dubious performance as "masterful and skillful," adding that if Pickett had been allowed to exercise his own plans and operations, "there might have been no Appomattox." Sounding like Pickett himself, Longstreet reasoned that "despite the disparity of overwhelming numbers a brilliant victory would have been his, if reinforcements which he had every reason to expect had opportunely reached him." He concluded: "It was cruel to leave that brilliant and heroic leader and his Spartan band to the same hard straits they so nobly met at Gettysburg."[99] George and LaSalle Pickett could not have agreed more.

CHAPTER 12

Canada, Virginia, and Washington, D.C., 1865–1889

We Have Suffered Enough

After Lee's surrender at Appomattox, George Pickett made his way back to Richmond. LaSalle joyfully remembered their reunion and her relief that her husband had returned to her safely. Just hearing his voice, she wrote, swept away "all the privation and starvation and bloodstains of the past four years, all the woes and trials, griefs and fears, of the last dreadful days." In true tomboy fashion, LaSalle excitedly slid down the banister to greet her soldier with open arms. She wrote: "I do not know how to describe the peace, the bliss of that moment—it is too deep and too sacred to translate into words."[1]

Again, LaSalle was trying to hide painful reality; any happiness they shared at George's homecoming must have been short-lived. George's childhood home at Turkey Island was in ashes, and after nearly twenty-five years in uniform, he had no occupation. He had lost the one thing that had repeatedly given him direction and purpose throughout his life: the army. LaSalle confessed: "We had no plans for the future."[2] Without home or income, the couple sought temporary shelter with LaSalle's parents in Nansemond County, Virginia.

In late May 1865, the U.S. government issued an amnesty proclamation to Confederate soldiers under the rank of colonel and individuals with taxable property valued under $20,000. George Pickett found himself, by rank and by class, exempted. On June 1, he made a special application to President Andrew Johnson for an individual pardon. In a long, rambling letter, he recounted his days as a regular army officer in the Pacific Northwest. He stated that if his native state had never seceded, he never would have left his beloved U.S. Army. "No one," Pickett professed, "was more attached to the old service, nor ever stood by and fought for it with more fidelity, nor could any one have been sadder and more loath to leave it than I, who, from my youth, had been devoted to it."[3]

These words contain a great deal of truth. From the age of seventeen, George Pickett had known no other life except that of a soldier. The military brought structure to his life during his careless youth, it brought excitement and direction to his early adulthood, and it affirmed his manhood. When death claimed two wives and a child, he had the army to ease his pain and loneliness and give him purpose. The army allowed him to cross cultural and societal boundaries while simultaneously providing rigid rules and codes of conduct. Through it all, he had attempted to maintain a balance between civilization and frontier, rebellion and conformity. Civil War destroyed this balance and rewrote the rules. With his prewar life in ruins, Pickett wanted to "renew my allegiance as a loyal citizen, to the United States Government, . . . to take the oath of allegiance—and observe with scrupulous truth its stipulations, and to faithfully obey the laws of their country." He wanted a second chance.[4]

The Picketts were soon horrified to learn that the federal government was investigating George for war crimes. Fearing indictment for his actions at Kinston, George and LaSalle fled to Canada. LaSalle could not bear to admit publicly the real reason for their self-imposed exile; instead she alleged that Ben Butler wanted her husband "indicted for treason" because George joined the Confederacy before the Federal government accepted his resignation from the U.S. Army.[5]

Details of their escape to Canada are sparse and difficult to document. LaSalle's published writings offer the only complete account of this experience, but her descriptions, as always, must be used with great caution. She wrote that George went alone, asking her to remain behind with relatives in Baltimore until he sent word that he had secured them a safe place in Canada.

The tale of her trip northward was one of her favorites to recount, full of familiar themes of unquestioning loyalty and determined faith. An unchaperoned white southern woman journeying with her baby, she experienced a palpable sense of fear: "Perhaps no timid little waif thrown out upon the deep sea of life ever felt more utterly desolate."[6] She recalled the noise of the train keeping her up much of the night, reminding her "of the sound of the executioner's axe. All night long it rose and fell through seas of blood—the heart's blood of valiant men, of devoted women, of innocent little children." When LaSalle finally drifted off to sleep near morning, she dreamed that "it was I who had destroyed the world of people whose life blood surged around me with a maddening roar, and that I was destined to an eternity of remorse."[7]

In another incident on the train to Montreal, LaSalle alleged that passengers glared at her suspiciously, seeming to question whether little George was her son. She explained to her readers that she had trouble calming him because he was teething, suffering a cold, and missing his black mammy. The more he fussed, the more unwanted attention she drew. In a surprising and controversial passage, LaSalle recounted how she breast-fed her baby to prove to her fellow passengers, her readers, and perhaps herself that she was indeed his mother and not an impostor. She wrote: "I, who had never nursed my baby in the presence of even my most intimate friends, bared my bosom before all those strange men and women and nursed him as proof that I was his mother."[8]

These strange and disturbing stories show LaSalle again striving to conform her literary self-portraits to traditional southern ideals of female passivity, innocence, and domesticity. Yet that decidedly powerful and active voice resonates throughout her works. In the dream excerpt, she blamed herself for the suffering and death that America, not just her native South, had endured in its bloody civil war. In the train story, she revealed a certain ambivalence toward motherhood, apparently more comfortable playing that role to her husband, George, than to her two sons. LaSalle sought ardently to celebrate her husband, their marriage, and the Confederacy, but the personal pain and humiliation seeped through the lines.

LaSalle made no mention of the War Department's court of inquiry and its investigation of the "murder" of Union soldiers at Kinston. By March 1866, Federal investigators had questioned widows, townspeople, soldiers, and government officials from both North and South. The court went to great pains to determine whether the Confederate army denied the dead men rights guaranteed by military law to prisoners of war, and if so, who was to blame. Evidence revealed that these twenty-two men had been members of a partisan ranger unit organized early in the war as a state home guard. Initially, the Confederate government could not remove such units from their home vicinity. When Richmond ordered their disbandment, members could either enlist voluntarily in a regular army unit or suffer conscription. Those who refused to enlist were taken from their homes at gunpoint and sent to conscription camp. The North Carolinians George Pickett captured had felt so betrayed and disgruntled that they deserted to Union lines soon after their forced conscription. Judge Advocate Joseph Holt maintained that the Confederate military court-martial had no jurisdiction over men who, he believed, had never been Confederate soldiers.[9]

The court also paid special attention to correspondence between Peck and Pickett. Judge Holt ruled that Pickett's letters revealed an "imperious and vaunting temper" and indicated "his readiness to commit this or any kindred atrocity." They also revealed "his boastful admissions" that he would kill ten Union prisoners for every one Confederate executed by the Federals in retaliation. Witnesses accused Pickett of being solely responsible for the hangings.[10] "All tend to show," Holt concluded, "that he was in responsible command, and furnishes evidence upon which it is believed charges can be sustained against him." On December 30, 1865, Holt recommended Pickett's immediate arrest.[11] A second court of inquiry continued proceedings for three more months to gather additional evidence against Pickett.

While these investigations progressed, the Picketts remained in Montreal. LaSalle's published writings and other sources recount how they rented a modest room in a boardinghouse, ate cold leftovers, and borrowed money from family and other exiled Confederates. George was too ill to work, LaSalle wrote, and he stayed in bed, weak and depressed. She told her readers that she secretly sold her jewelry and took a job teaching Latin to support her family. Whether or not LaSalle actually provided financial support, she must have at least bolstered her husband emotionally. The experience no doubt was humiliating for the forty-year-old man, dependent on others and reduced to an ostensibly purposeless existence. LaSalle admitted: "I could not help thinking of the time when my Soldier had been served by butlers and waiters, each anxious to anticipate his wishes, and all feeling amply rewarded for every effort by a pleasant word or an appreciative smile. I wondered how any one of those obsequious attendants would feel to see us now."[12] LaSalle described her husband cheering briefly one day when he overheard martial music outside his window and watched a military dress parade. She observed him as he lost himself to the cadence of drums and marching men.[13] Although those months in Canada had to have been extremely difficult, LaSalle declared publicly and privately that they were the happiest times of her life. She had her soldier to herself, and she could freely nurture and support him, and perhaps quiet his demons.[14]

As George and LaSalle endured exile, family and friends visited Washington and tried to intervene on the general's behalf. In the past, these connections had been immensely valuable to George, aiding him with his appointment to the academy and several promotions. This time his political affiliations were not strong enough to sway Johnson to intercede. The president had thus far ignored George's initial request for a pardon because of the pending investigation. In November 1865, a family friend, former senator Orville Browning, tried again to exert some influence on the president. Browning spoke to both Johnson and Grant, but neither felt tempers had cooled sufficiently to warrant a special pardon.[15]

Sometime in December 1865, George and LaSalle came back to Virginia. Perhaps they felt too far from family and friends, or perhaps their money had run out and they hoped tempers had cooled enough for them to return. Perhaps it was the prospect of facing a cold winter in a strange and foreign place. It may not only have been George's poor health, but LaSalle's, too, that prompted their return to Virginia.[16]

How could the Picketts begin their life again with Judge Holt demanding George's arrest for war crimes? In desperation, George turned for help from his West Point classmate and Mexican War comrade Ulysses S. Grant. On March 12, 1866, Pickett pleaded with Grant to intercede and procure a "guarantee that I may be permitted to live unmolested in my native State, where I am now trying to make a subsistence for my family, (much impoverished by the War), by tilling the land." Pickett described "certain evil disposed persons [who] are attempting to reopen the troubles of the past, and embroil me for the actions taken whilst the Commanding Officer of the Confederate Forces in N.C." He insisted that he had merely followed the rules of war by executing the deserters. Pickett pledged his honor "as an officer and a gentleman" and asked for "some assurance, that I will not be disturbed in my endeavor to keep my family from Starvation, and that my parole, which was given in good faith, may protect me from the assaults of those persons desirous of still keeping the War which has ended in my humble opinion *forever*." Grant sent an endorsement to President Johnson on the day he received Pickett's letter. Admitting that Pickett had used poor judgment in ordering the hangings, Grant asked the president, as a personal favor, to overlook the incident. He immediately issued Pickett a parole exempting him from arrest unless ordered by the president or secretary of war. Johnson received the request and let the matter stew for several more months.[17]

George also visited Washington personally to make his case. He took a great risk coming to the capital, but he was apparently eager to meet with his supporters. He received assurances from several congressmen and former army comrades that "all may be right again" and that they would do what they could to "keep the wolf from the door."[18] LaSalle resentfully blamed northerners, who seemed "mad with grief and rage," for seeking to punish the weak and defenseless in their wrath.[19]

Through the summer of 1866, the "madness" continued. The House of Representatives passed a resolution requesting President Johnson to report on the status of Pickett's pardon.[20] William Doherty, a Unionist from North Carolina, wrote Judge Holt and demanded to know why "this bad and cruel man" had not been arrested and brought to trial. Doherty declared: "The poor whites of the south will lose confidence in the federal power if they are thus forsaken and their murdered friends unavenged."[21] By December 1866, Attorney General Henry Stanberry notified the president that no action had been taken against Pickett.[22] Secretary of War Stanton explained that he was hesitant to arrest Pickett until he was sure the Supreme Court would back the findings of the military commission that had conducted the investigations. "The magnitude of the offense alleged against Pickett," Stanton wrote, "is such that there should be no reason to contest the jurisdiction of the tribunal to whom their trial may be committed."[23]

In the end, the U.S. government never did press formal charges against George Pickett; nor did he ever succeed in obtaining a personal pardon. It appears that Grant's endorsement saved him. Pickett eventually obtained a full pardon under Johnson's general amnesty in December of 1868.[24]

George and LaSalle came back to Turkey Island and built a small cottage near the ruins of the plantation house. George and his brother Charles initially tried to farm their father's land, but as LaSalle conceded, George was no "expert with plowshares."[25] He had no money to pay laborers, black or white, nor did he have funds to buy equipment or seedlings. He sold some family property in the city but lamented the loss of the plantation. George wrote to friend Benjamin Starke: "Everything has been swept clean by the ruthless war, houses, dwellings, barns, stables, ice house and negro quarters; fences of course, and every fruit or ornamental tree, vineyard and shrubs and flowers." He hoped that with God's help, and "the clemency of the President," they could have a roof over their heads and begin life again.[26]

Besides farming, George tried a variety of occupations and business ventures to support his family, but he failed at each one. He turned down state and federal government positions, including, according to LaSalle, the governorship of Virginia. He finally settled on selling insurance and became an agent for a New York–based firm with an office in Norfolk.[27]

As the weeks turned to months, and to years, George seldom spoke publicly about the war, although he was active in organizing the Association of the Army of Northern Virginia and served as president of the Southern Historical Society. While other Confederates made speeches, wrote memoirs, and increasingly grew sentimental about the Lost Cause, George Pickett remained largely silent. LaSalle alleged that her husband "did not like to fight his battles over." She claimed that he wanted to rest and recover from the war, and perhaps years later they might "take up the pen again and write down our memories for our children and perhaps for the children of the old division."[28] His silence may have been out of gratitude toward his northern friends who saved him from indictment. It may have been because of his financial problems, or perhaps it was his continued bewilderment and resentment that such a senseless war had ever occurred. In private correspondence to friends he spoke fondly and proudly of his "noble" division, yet the bitterness never completely disappeared.[29]

In one of his rare public appearances, George presented a banner from the "fair daughters of our City of Richmond" to former members of his division. He told a crowd of onlookers that he was "proud beyond measure that it fell to my lot to command such men as yourselves and your brother Virginians." His speech dwelled on the war's loss and suffering. He described Gettysburg as "the awful conflict" where his men "marched in line of battle as on dress parade down that slope and across the stone wall one mile into the jaws of death, under fire from two hundred pieces of ordinance, and upon the centre of the foe (who had been 3 days preparing) without support and *without faltering*[,] oh grand but fatal day." In his speech, Pickett alleged that when Lee proclaimed, "You have covered yourself with glory," he could only say, "Alas, what will ever repay Virginia for her best & noblest blood poured out for naught[?]" He praised his former soldiers for not dwelling on the past: "You have kept silent on wrongs either real or imaginary, and have still maintained your dignity." This was behavior he himself probably tried to emulate, not always successfully.[30]

George Pickett still brooded about his failed charge at Gettysburg. As Robert E. Lee became the patron saint of the fallen Confederacy, Pickett continued to nurse his resentment toward his former commander. One March day in 1870, Pickett saw Lee again, briefly and accidentally, in a Richmond hotel. John Mosby, who witnessed the strained exchange between the two officers, recalled that Lee was capable of "freezing out a man he did not like." As Pickett left, he allegedly remarked to Mosby, "He had my division massacred at Gettysburg." Mosby sharply replied, "Well, it made you immortal."[31]

Such immortality was a cold comfort to the Picketts. They had little money, their health was poor, and they had another mouth to feed with the birth of their second son, Corbell.[32] George wrote a friend that he and LaSalle tried to resign themselves to God: "It is not in our power to control the wills of man any more than that of the almighty." He only hoped that God would "shortly think we have suffered enough."[33]

Private correspondence shows that stress and hard work were taking their toll on LaSalle's health, too. She worked daily, probably for the first time in her life, perhaps helping George with the farming, doing household chores, and caring for the two boys. Unaccustomed to manual labor, LaSalle could at one point "scarcely hold a pen, her fingers being very sore from hard work." Her concerned husband confided to his brother-in-law that he felt "miserable" for not providing her with "the comforts which I expected for my darling wife when I married." He had failed as a southern husband and chief provider. He admitted: "I must say that she bore up bravely under her trials."[34]

At times George seemed overwhelmed. He faced an uncertain future with his helpmate and lover weak and sick and his own health precarious. He confessed to a former comrade that he dreaded the future "a

George Jr. and Corbell Pickett
(The Museum of the Confederacy, Richmond, Va.)

thousand times more than I did any battle I have ever been in." The
"physical discomforts" and "personal dangers" of war paled "when a
women is in danger and duress," particularly "one [who] is so dear." It
made George feel helpless to the point that he declared, "I *am* a child."[35]
A sympathetic family member expressed his concern over the Picketts'
"domestic troubles," maintaining that these were particularly difficult for
the man of the family to bear. "The[se] infernal hard time[s] are bad
enough to make a man mad," the cousin stated, "without having family
afflictions to to[r]ment his feelings."[36]

As he had his entire adult life, George looked to the battlefield to ease those feelings of pain and despair. He hoped that the United States would engage in a foreign war so that he could resume soldiering. He rather simplistically felt that this would solve not only his personal plight but all the nation's problems as well, and reunite the country. "If Grant should inaugurate a new foreign policy and get the general attention diverted from the wooly head, by a skirmish with something outside. Why then we may hope for 'peace' at home and some of us . . . may get occupation abroad."[37] Even after the destruction and death he had witnessed in the Civil War, George clung to the old, familiar longing for a foreign war with an honorable but easily vanquished foe.

In 1874, James Tilton, George's old friend from the Pacific Northwest and the namesake of his eldest son, suggested that the Picketts leave the country permanently and that George take a position in the Egyptian army. Tilton maintained that George could begin as a colonel and quickly move up. "I feel sure that you can take a fresh start," Tilton wrote. "You're one of the best infantry officers of our time." Tilton assured him that Alexandria and Cairo were fine cities in which to raise a family and that the Egyptian prince "appreciates Americans."[38]

It is unknown how seriously George and LaSalle considered going to Egypt. In the published Pickett letters, George quoted LaSalle as declaring, "We have had glory enough, and war enough, with its hardships and separations and dangers, and now we just want each other forever and forevermore."[39] LaSalle said this or wished she had said this; either way, George did not pursue the offer.

Their hardships, however, had not ceased. In the spring of 1874, Corbell became severely ill with measles and died. LaSalle's version of her son's death is again less important for its verity than for the meaning it conveys. Corbell was only eight years old, but according to LaSalle, he had a Christlike quality, withstanding his suffering without complaint. While Corbell lay dying on Good Friday, he supposedly asked his parents to help a stranger whom he had heard scuffling with police outside his window. He also picked out his pallbearers and cheerfully asked that they wear white and bring flowers to cast on his grave. LaSalle dramatically described her son's final moments as Easter Sunday dawned: "Through the open window the voices were sounding 'Christ is risen' as he turned his head and laid his face against mine and reached out his little hand to

George E. Pickett, sometime during the postwar period
(Virginia Historical Society, Richmond, Va.)

my Soldier and [his nurse] Mary. I felt his spirit flutter and go." Her
perfect marriage could only produce perfect, angelic children.[40]

In July 1875, George was in Norfolk on business when he, too, fell
seriously ill, with "gastric fever." The Picketts had planned to vacation at
White Sulphur Springs, but unexpectedly, George had to go to Norfolk.

LaSalle recalled: "Very much against his advice, I insisted on accompanying him." George died two days later. LaSalle claimed that his last request was to be alone with her: "I do not want anybody but my wife." He was fifty years old.[41]

George Pickett's death brought an outpouring of public grief. In Virginia and other parts of the South he was eulogized as a Confederate hero alongside the likes of Robert E. Lee and Stonewall Jackson. At his interment, the Episcopal priest declared that Pickett's heroism, sense of duty, determination, and brilliance made him immortal. Capt. George D. Wise remarked, perhaps with unintended irony: "General Pickett was one who moved so noiselessly along that some of us had forgotten that we had a hero among us."[42] Despite his uneven military record, questionable battlefield behavior, and personal troubles, Pickett, the man, was being transformed into Pickett, the myth. The *Atlanta Daily Constitution* announced: "He is dead, but his deeds will live forever."[43] Later, LaSalle would build and expand on these same sentimental memories to spread her own idealized image of her husband. For now she perhaps could take some comfort in the kind words and acclamation expressed toward George, even if they were part of something larger and more symbolic.[44]

A few months after Pickett's death, his remains were moved from Norfolk to Richmond's Hollywood Cemetery to lie alongside other Confederate dead. The procession and interment service on October 24, 1875, attracted thousands: Approximately 1,500 "official" mourners attended, with over 40,000 spectators. Stretching over a mile, the procession included members of black militia units, the Virginia Military Institute corps of cadets, Knights Templar, and survivors from the Army of Northern Virginia. Later, a group of veterans erected a six-sided granite stone over his grave, memorializing Pickett's Charge and his Virginia division.[45]

Despite the pomp and circumstance surrounding her husband's funeral and burial, LaSalle felt desperately alone. When George died, she and their eleven-year-old son had little financial support. "The future is a dark one to me," she confessed privately. "I dare not look into it, for I see only loneliness and desolation if I do." LaSalle lamented, "The light of my life is gone out."[46] When she later published her autobiography in 1917, she ended her life story with George's death. As he sighed his last breath, LaSalle recalled: "Darkness came."[47]

LaSalle Corbell Pickett, sometime during the postwar period
(Virginia Historical Society, Va.)

In reality, LaSalle Pickett's life did not end in 1875. She lived for five more decades, facing her uncertain future with her stubborn determination. She broke a time-honored southern taboo by setting out to support herself and her son without a man. LaSalle left her native Virginia, traveled to Washington, D.C., and found a job as a government clerk in the Federal Pensions Office.[48]

Historians continue to debate whether the American Civil War opened new opportunities for women; most agree that it did not provide lasting ones for white southern women. However, whether through choice or not, LaSalle Pickett gained autonomy in the postwar period and enjoyed the self-determination she celebrated in her published writings. She was the main actor in her life story.[49]

LaSalle left little public or private record of her first twenty years of widowhood. Her primary responsibility after George's death was raising their son. She apparently taught George Jr. at home for a time, and when he reached college age she enrolled him in the Virginia Military Institute. Following his father's example, George became a professional army officer.[50]

LaSalle also maintained contact with her husband's first son, who had remained in the Pacific Northwest. James, or "Jimmie" as some friends called him, had grown to manhood without seeing his father again after 1861. James Tilton assured his godson and namesake that George wanted to bring him to Virginia, but poverty prevented him from ever doing so. "Your father loved you and told your mother, that is his widow who writes to you, all about you."[51] Sadly, it seems, George had little contact with James after he left the Pacific Northwest. A white foster family raised James from the time he was about eighteen months old. It is unlikely he had any lasting memory of his father.[52]

Friends and his adopted mother remembered James as a sensitive, quiet, and uniquely talented young man. He attended Union Academy in Olympia as a teenager and excelled in his studies. Excerpts from his diary reveal a young man striving for perfection and bitterly disappointed that he fell short. "No one knows how I suffer these defeats," he wrote.[53] His biographer, Thomas Bibb, noted his "serious disposition" and frustration with boys his own age. Unlike his gregarious father, Jimmie preferred study over play. Bibb attests that young James had "more in common with the girls."[54]

After graduating from the academy, James lived in boardinghouses and took odd jobs up and down the Pacific Northwest coastline. He worked on farms and labored in lumber yards. He tried to put his natural talents to work painting glass and houses and illustrating books, but steady employment was difficult to find. James studied photography but yearned to paint and sketch. A childhood friend recalled that young James's passion for art was so great that, lacking paper or canvas, he would draw on walls of the house and barn. He attended the San Francisco School of Design, hoping that he could attain skills necessary to become a professional lithographer. He was so devoted to excelling that he vowed to cut the normal time of schooling in half. James eventually secured a position with the *Seattle Post Intelligencer* and the *Portland Oregonian*, but he continued painting. His passion was landscapes, and several of his works are now in the possession of the Washington State Capital Museum in Olympia, Washington.[55]

A half-Indian living in the white world, James never quite found his place. Ironically, if his father had ever tried to have a relationship with his son, he would have found perhaps some similarities between them.

LaSalle Pickett did not publicly acknowledge James, nor did she include any stories about him or his mother in her publications. But existing private correspondence shows that LaSalle attempted to maintain a long-distance relationship with George's son over a span of nearly fifteen years. Illness prevented her from ever visiting her stepson, but George Jr. allegedly did travel to see James some time in the 1880s. Local historian Lelah Edson writes, "Young George E. apparently had a southerner's contempt for a mixed race, and to Jimmie's notion, it seemed, treated the latter accordingly. At least he never recovered from the fancied slight."[56] Nonetheless, privately, LaSalle wrote James, addressing him as son and signing her letters "your loving" and "your devoted mother."[57] She assured James that she would do what she could to support his attending art school, and despite George's snub of his half brother, she warmly promised to tell her son "all about the young artist whom I loved and whom he was to [love too]."[58] W. D. Campbell, who knew James when he was a teenager, recalled "the fine letters Jimmie received from his step-mother in the East, who seemed very fond of him, and they corresponded regularly."[59] In 1888, LaSalle and George Jr. quit-claimed one of George's Whatcom County lots to James.

In the summer of 1889, tuberculosis struck the young artist. As James lay sick and dying in a Portland boardinghouse, fellow boarders took turns sitting up with him, trying to comfort him. H. C. McReavy recalled, "During one night he asked me to read him a couple of letters from his father, General Pickett, and some others from his stepmother, describing the General and announcing that he was to have his father's saber, worn in the battle of Gettysburg."[60] On August 28, 1889, just four months short of his thirty-second birthday, James Tilton Pickett died. He was buried near one of his favorite spots in view of Mount St. Helens.[61] Novelist Archie Binns referred to George Pickett's abandoned son as someone "who has been lost out of history all these years. And lost out of life."[62]

LaSalle Pickett lived on, not yet intent on a writing career. Poor health and financial concerns plagued her, but she continued working in Washington and never remarried. Limited personal correspondence before 1890 shows her mildly depressed and haunted by the loss of her husband. Confederate defeat and emancipation had destroyed her and her husband's childhood world of planters and slaves; their families' wealth was long gone. Still, it was the loneliness that seemed most difficult to face. She once confided to James that although she had "lost a portion of the little left to me," the financial strain was "nothing in the balance where a heart is so bowed down with sorrow as mine is—such things do not alter to the smallest fraction the point of the scale."[63]

The war experience and loss of her husband scarred LaSalle, but at some point during her widowhood she decided to turn the trials and sufferings she endured into something positive. It is not known if her reasons were purely financial; it seems that there were other factors at work. Just as the nation was entering a new period of reconciliation and nationalism, LaSalle Pickett decided to bring her revised and reconstructed story of love and war to the public stage. Her timing was perfect.

CHAPTER 13

Washington, D.C., 1887–1931
I Have Had All and Lost All

In the summer of 1899, LaSalle Pickett published *Pickett and His Men*. She plagiarized large passages of Walter Harrison's *Pickett's Men* to describe military movements and introduced readers to her mythical heroic husband. Her soldier was affectionate and amiable, a man of "classic taste and perfect harmony and simple, pure heart" who loved nature, singing, and most of all, his wife, Sallie.[1] He fought because duty bade him to but preferred peace over war making and never felt anger or bitterness toward his enemy, only love and respect. LaSalle dedicated the book to her husband and his men but confessed: "I would gladly inscribe this book—to him alone, to whom my life has been dedicated."[2]

Reviews were mostly favorable; the 1890s American reading public generally extended Civil War generals' widows deferential respect. James Longstreet's introduction praised Mrs. Pickett and other ex-Confederate widows who had "fought as fierce a battle as ever their warrior husbands waged, for in the silent passages of the heart many severer battles war waged than were ever fought at Gettysburg."[3] Pickett seemed both pleased and a little surprised by the warm reception her book received: "All parties say kind things etc., etc., and such beautiful tributes have been paid me that I can hardly realize that I am myself."[4]

In many ways LaSalle Pickett was no longer herself. With the successful publication of *Pickett and His Men*, she constructed a new public identity for herself as much as for her husband. Sallie Pickett became the charming and charismatic Mrs. General George E. Pickett, "child bride of the Confederacy," professional widow, and author. In her writings, she idealized herself as the loyal and dependent white southern daughter, wife, and devoted mother. To her readers she fondly recounted growing up on a large Virginia tidewater plantation surrounded by faithful slaves and affectionate relatives. Her father, John Corbell, was "always my ideal" southern patriarch: handsome, stately, and refined.[5] Her father was "always courteous and gallant, always solicitous of and interested in his people, and always thoughtful and considerate of everyone."[6] Her mother, Elizabeth, was pale, beautiful, well-bred, and a bit aloof. Before her marriage to George, LaSalle was the educated and gay southern belle. Once married, she fit the prototype of the elite white southern lady who was delicate, deferential, and wholly dependent on men.[7]

From 1899 to 1931, Pickett brought her mythologized past to a national audience. She toured the Chautauqua lecture circuit and published articles in *Cosmopolitan*, *McClure's*, and other popular magazines. Pickett remained in Washington, D.C., and took up residence in the "Ontario" hotel. Her travels brought her to Washington State, Gettysburg, and other important places in her late husband's life. By 1926, she had written over a half dozen books, including her own autobiography, entitled *What Happened to Me*. She made enough money to live independently, support herself and her son, and never remarry.[8] There were rumors of her venturing onto the vaudeville stage, but there is only evidence of her association with the vaudeville education circuit, although LaSalle probably would have proven a fine actress.[9]

LaSalle Pickett's public career paralleled a time of renewed nationalism and sentimentalism. White Americans were redefining the Civil War as a heroic struggle, empty of troubling racial or political questions. Memorialization of the war included statue building and reunions and an outpouring of books by survivors. Virginians successfully transformed Pickett's Charge from a failed infantry attack into *the* dramatic turning point of the war and an affirmation of southern sacrifice and manhood. George's death in 1875 had brought an outpouring of praise, and fifteen years later the adulation had not stopped. In death, George Pickett was more popular than he had ever been during his own lifetime.[10]

LaSalle Pickett both benefited from and actively contributed to this romanticization of the Confederacy and her husband. In 1887, she and her son George Jr. attended a veterans' reunion at Gettysburg, and as the *New York Times* reported, "Mrs. Pickett was the centre of attraction on the field."[11] Pickett basked in the attention from both northerners and southerners who clamored for a glimpse of the widow. She happily gave autographs as her son displayed a gold watch allegedly worn by George

Sr. during the charge. Survivors of Pickett's division readily responded to an appeal for donations to pay the Picketts' expenses.[12]

LaSalle had constant requests for George's photographs and signature, and it seems, complied as much as possible. In 1889 she explained to Lida Perry: "I will try and send you both a picture and an autograph of my noble husband. I have tried to grant so many like favors to those who loved his memory and honored his name that I have no letters I could spare and but few names left."[13] Six years later, she again wrote Perry of her inability to meet the demand for autographs. She wrote that the "only way I have been able to send autographs of the General to anyone is to cut the addresses from the envelope of an old letter written to me." Perry must have suggested that LaSalle simply forge George's signature, for LaSalle wrote: "I wish that I could do the forgery act as you suggest, but fear that I have not the sufficient skill."[14]

In fact Pickett's writings and lectures showed great skill and deliberation. The images and words she selected were never carelessly presented. Pickett knew her Gilded Age audiences' penchant for sentimental nostalgia and yearning for national reconciliation, and she went to any length to entertain them. To relay romantic and intimate stories of her husband, their courtship and marriage, she altered and/or entirely created wartime correspondence from George. To reveal "the heart of a Soldier" to the public she carefully reconstructed personal details of her courtship and marriage and may have even forged her husband's handwriting to promote the letters' authenticity. Her plagiarizing of other military histories was probably no accident either; a woman writing with any authority about war was highly unusual, and using veterans' language bolstered her books' legitimacy.[15]

Her heroic husband made appearances in all of her works, but she also mimicked the "plantation tradition" of Joel Chandler Harris and Thomas Nelson Page. Celebrating "de good ole times 'fo' de wah," LaSalle Pickett put herself and her husband in a setting of paternalistic slaveowners and loyal, passive slaves. These were racist images eagerly bought up by the white reading American public, North and South, at the turn of the twentieth century. She sprinkled her books and short stories with black dialect, claiming a special understanding of southern blacks' "pathetically musical speech." In her four-part series, "In De Miz," she informed readers: "I have tried to portray the quaint and homely humor, their strange exaltation of mind and temperament, their pathetic and sympathetic natures, their superstitions and sentiment, their strange characteristics."[16] Harris, author of "Uncle Remus," commended her: "In dialect work she is at her best."[17]

Thousands attended Pickett's lectures. Brochures produced by her sponsors included commendations from prominent northerners and southerners. "Having heard the most distinguished dialect readers of our country," Mississippian and former congressman Charles E. Hooker stated, "I feel capable of saying that Mrs. Pickett's work is nearer to the real life of the ante-bellum Southern darkey than any other that has been produced." Oliver O. Howard, former Union general and head of the Freeman's Bureau, also endorsed her: "I not only commend your marvelous compilation of truth, your exactness and justice, but the subtle charity with which you cover and silence any mistakes which may have been made by others."[18] Newspapers applauded her magnetic presence and vivid descriptive abilities. The Xenia, Ohio, *Daily Gazette* reported of one of her speaking engagements: "The address was marvelous in diction and delivered with force and eloquence."[19]

Her gender and marriage to a well-known albeit controversial Civil War general silenced most critics. She outlived many of the Civil War generation and could speak with special insight and personal connection. Occasionally, some people publicly challenged her accuracy. A North Carolina journalist questioned her description of Gettysburg, adding, "She doubtless records what she believes to be true."[20] Mainly she gained acclamation and approval for her efforts. A 1903 poem in the *Confederate Veteran* heralded her and other soldiers' wives and mothers as more heroic and self-sacrificing than their dead husbands.[21] Another writer called her "the last link connected with the tragedy at Gettysburg —the charge of Pickett's Brigades."[22]

She used her identity as Pickett's widow and newfound celebrity status to meet and claim acquaintance with other famous people. Her books *Literary Hearthstones of Dixie* (1912) and *Across My Path: Memories of People I Have Known* (1916) told of her personally visiting a wide range of well-known authors and actors, no doubt individuals who influenced her own writing. *Literary Hearthstones* included at-home interviews with William Gilmore Simms, Joel Chandler Harris, Sara Evans Wilson, and Margaret Junkin Preston. *Across My Path* focused on twenty-five women actors, writers, and other prominent females whom she alleged to have met. She applauded Julia Ward Howe's capacity to learn from the past but not live in it, and Fannie Kemble's freedom to meet so many "charming people" and have so many "beautiful experiences." She admired Varina Davis's pride and Mary Lee's patience and calm sincerity.[23]

As Pickett aged and her books gained prominence, the tension between the world she created and the actual life she lived grew more apparent. Her writings blurred lines between fact and fiction, myth and reality. Even her personal correspondence mirrored her published works. Passages appear in her private letters that echo the same stylized language and imagery found in her books. In 1911, she responded to an inquiry about her husband's physical appearance. She described George's hair as "fine and waving and curly, with a glimmering of gold when the sun shone on it," and his eyes as "dark gray, sometimes blue and sometimes hazel; like a tiger's eyes, but gentle and loving; piercing and with a twinkle in them." He had a "beautiful" neck, throat, and ears, and "the most wonderful figure and hands and feet that I ever saw." Pickett added that her husband "sang and whistled and played almost every musical instrument," and spoke "three languages beautifully and translated Mother Goose into Spanish and made a translation of the Lord's Prayer into Chinook."[24]

She may have become unable to distinguish fact from fiction. While her husband lived, Pickett no doubt repeatedly assured him of his worth and innocence in the face of frightening accusations and disappointments. The private pain and humiliation she suffered had to have affected her. As the years progressed, LaSalle Pickett may have found, as Shirley Leckie has written of another famous widow, Libbie Custer, that "after decades of revising her husband on paper and in her speeches (and herself in the process), she lost much of her ability to separate fact from myth in the popular sense."[25]

While Pickett kept a hectic schedule of writing, lecturing, and promoting her books, poor health and money problems continued to plague her. Private correspondence alludes to frequent sickness and ailments. In 1904, she suffered an accident that put her on crutches for several months; in 1907, illness prevented her from answering her mail. In 1912, she battled pneumonia for weeks, "so near death that the physicians regard my recovery as miraculous."[26]

Her stubborn determination to live was only matched by her efforts to persist writing. She did not seem as desolate and alone as those first two decades of widowhood, but the years took their toll. In the spring of 1911, yellow fever struck LaSalle's only surviving son, Maj. George E. Pickett Jr., while he was stationed in Manila. LaSalle found herself helpless and far from her ailing son: "I am praying and trusting that this sorrow may pass from me."[27] It did not. LaSalle buried forty-seven-year-old George in Arlington National Cemetery, "where the peace of God falls gentle upon him and his comrades."[28] In 1925, she confessed to a close friend: "I have prayed and hoped our Heavenly Father might feel it was time to take me, but, alas, I seem destined to remain longer yet."[29]

Although Pickett must have earned considerable money from her writings, she apparently did not manage it very well. She complained repeatedly about her poor financial situation. She once confided to a close friend that her main income came from her modest government pension, forcing her to sell everything but her engagement ring, and to consider moving into a smaller apartment.[30]

In 1926, poet Arthur Crew Inman sought to edit a revised version of the George Pickett letters. His wife, Evelyn, journeyed to Washington to visit the aging widow and speak to her about the project. Inman met Pickett in her bedroom amidst a disorderly array of boxes and drawers. The frail, white-haired Pickett was alone, almost lost in the large arm-chair in which she sat. Faded photographs and framed documents covered the walls. Inman noted velvet and silk clothing draped carelessly over the bed and chairs. "Hello Darlin'," Pickett greeted Inman, her dark eyes sparkling, her voice soft yet animated. "Where did you come from? Come in here with all this mess if you love me enough to."

"What am I doin'?" the old woman demanded, and then promptly answered her own question. "Sewing, child. Look! This is the lace mantilla that Mrs. Jefferson Davis gave me on my wedding day!" Pickett confessed that the young bride to whom she was going to give it may not appreciate its value: "But I don't know whether she'll like this or not, she's so stylish and so prosperous, she may not care for old things like I do!" Inman spent several hours with Pickett, who chattered aimlessly of the past, repeating familiar stories from her books. She described the two happiest times in her long life: her wedding day and her months in Canada.[31]

Surviving into the modernizing twentieth century, Sallie Pickett refashioned herself yet once again. No longer the "child bride of the Confederacy," she became "Mother Pickett," protector of her husband's memory and nurturer of the antebellum South. Her closest friend, Selma Lewisohn, described Pickett during her final years: "She lives in the past. Her courage is that of youth, and her 'Soldier' her one inspiration."[32]

Although she wrote of "what happened to her," most of Pickett's writings centered on what she actively did and sought to accomplish as a white southern woman in a man's world and war. Her published memoirs were more subjectively "true" than objectively so, accurately conveying her private hopes, desires, and fears. In her 1916 book *Across My Path*, Pickett claims to quote author Margaret Sangster summing up Pickett's actual and fictitious existence:

> You have had a wonderfully rich life and you are yet a child. You have had the black mammy, and the little colored playmates, the old atmosphere of the romantic South and the plantation life that is all over now. You have had the romance of war, the excitement of the battlefield, the love of the soldiers, the nursing of the wounded in the hospital. You have known a new country, a new president and cabinet and all the great changes of South and North alike. You have been the wife of a hero, the mother of children, the mother of an angel and now the greatest of all sorrows has come to chasten you, widowhood, and last, the highest boon that could come with all these things, the necessity for work. It is only through pain and loss that we gain the joy of effort and the triumph of winning.

Pickett responded by saying, "I have had all and lost all." Sangster insisted, "You cannot lose what you have had," and urged her to "pass it on to the world before you forget and let the people see the old life as it was."[33] Sangster's words expressed Pickett's sentiments. Pain and loss were indeed her lot, but she turned them around to recreate the life and marriage she wanted instead of the one she endured.

LaSalle Corbell Pickett's life was far from ideal. As the educated daughter of a Virginia planter she no doubt looked forward to assuming the role of the elite white southern lady. Instead, she endured war, exile, poverty, and early widowhood. The pain at times was hard to hide. She once admitted, "It is our helplessness in the storms of life that breaks our hearts."[34] Pickett refused to be helpless. Sometime in her life she devel-

LaSalle Corbell Pickett, circa 1917
(portrait from her autobiography, What Happened to Me*)*

oped a fierce determination to set things right again and make order out of life's chaos, disillusionments, and disappointments. She demonstrated an amazing resiliency, and only late in life did poor health and dwindling finances make her dependent on friends and family. Profit was obviously one of the main reasons she published and toured; but other, more personal factors, seemed to drive her. An intelligent and ambitious woman, her writing career gave her social acceptance and purpose outside traditional gender roles. Her career justified her life and her troubled marriage. And it gave her an opportunity to repay her husband's undeniable loyalty and devotion to her; she publicly made him the Confederate hero he never was. She deliberately molded the way subsequent generations would view her husband, herself, and her marriage. LaSalle Pickett used racism and celebration of the Lost Cause to fabricate and lie about her and her husband's past. A measure of success came through these literary reconstructions of a man and a marriage. In the process, she reconstructed herself and gained, at least briefly, economic and social autonomy.

LaSalle Corbell Pickett died in 1931, and it seemed only natural that she be laid to rest beside the man she spent decades memorializing. In her 1917 autobiography she had told readers that she looked forward to the afterlife when she would reunite with her beloved soldier. "When I have gone through all these dark days of privation and of starvation of heart and soul here, victorious," she wrote, "and at last am safe within the golden gates and waiting and listening shall hear again the voice that said, 'Whoa Lucy!' here, bidding me welcome there as I welcomed him after the perilous waiting."[35] In the afterlife they may indeed be together, but they were not initially buried together. The Ladies Hollywood Memorial Association, fearing that they would set a precedent for other soldiers' wives, refused to allow LaSalle's remains to be placed alongside George in the venerated soldiers' section of the cemetery. Relatives raised a ruckus and tried to dig up George and re-bury the two together in Arlington National Cemetery in Washington, D.C. George E. Pickett III and Longstreet's son, Robert Lee Longstreet, proposed building a monument to Lee in Arlington, flanked by graves of Longstreet and Pickett. In the end, George's grave was not disturbed and LaSalle's ashes were placed in the Abby Mausoleum near Arlington Cemetery. Over the years the mausoleum became dilapidated, and plans were made for its permanent closure. In 1998, the Virginia Division of the United Daughters of the Confederacy removed LaSalle's cremated remains from the neglected vault and had them re-interred next to George's grave in Hollywood. The UDC division president stated: "The motto of the Virginia Division is 'Love Makes Memory Eternal.' For us to bring Mrs. Pickett back is a very inspiring thing."[36]

Upon her death LaSalle left behind her "most colorful work" yet: an unfinished manuscript entitled "My Memory Chain."[37] To date, her final effort at rewriting the past is lost to the historical record.

NOTES

LIST OF ABBREVIATIONS

AL   Alderman Library, University of Virginia, Charlottesville, Va.

BC   Buswell Collection, Center for Pacific Northwest Studies, Western
           Washington University, Bellingham, Wash.

BL   Brenner Library, Quincy University, Quincy, Ill.

BPL   Bellingham Public Library, Bellingham, Wash.

EGSL   Earl Gregg Swem Library, College of William and Mary, Williamsburg,
           Va.

EU   Emory University, Atlanta, Ga.

F&S   Fredericksburg and Spotsylvania National Military Park, Va.

HHL   Henry H. Huntington Library, San Marino, Calif.

HQAC   Historical Society of Quincy and Adams County, Quincy, Ill.

JHL   John Hay Library, Brown University, Providence, R.I.

LOC   Library of Congress, Washington, D.C.

MC   Museum of the Confederacy, Richmond, Va.

ML   Morris Library, Southern Illinois University, Carbondale, Ill.

MVC   Michael Vouri Private Collection, San Juan Island, Wash.

NA   National Archives, Washington, D.C.

NHHS   New Hampshire Historical Society, Concord, N.H.

OHS   Oregon Historical Society, Portland, Oreg.

OR   *War of the Rebellion: A Compilation of the Official Records of the Union
           and Confederate Armies.* 128 vols. Washington, D.C.: Government
           Printing Office, 1880–1901. (All citations to *OR* are to series 1, unless
           otherwise noted.)

PL   Perkins Library, Duke University, Durham, N.C.

SHC   Southern Historical Collection, Wilson Library, University of North
           Carolina, Chapel Hill, N.C.

USMAA   United States Military Academy Archives, West Point, N.Y.

UWL   Manuscripts and University Archives Division, University of
           Washington Libraries, Seattle, Wash.

VHS   Virginia Historical Society, Richmond, Va.

VSL   Virginia State Library, Richmond, Va.

WSCM   Washington State Capital Museum, Olympia, Wash.

INTRODUCTION

1. Pickett, *Ebil Eye*, 24.

2. The Slayton Lyceum Bureau, "Announcement," Meany Papers, UWL.

3. Pickett, *Pickett and His Men*, 7.

4. Faulkner, *Intruder in the Dust*, 194–95; Shaara, *Killer Angels*, 56; McPherson, *Battle Cry of Freedom*, 662.

5. Gramm, *Gettysburg*, 199; Reardon, "Image of 'Pickett's Charge,' " 74.

6. Gallagher, "Widow and Her Soldier," 334, 344. Eleven letters in the Arthur Crew Inman Papers at Brown University, which Gallagher accepted as legitimate, are also suspect. Their style and handwriting match a collection recently rejected by archivists at the Virginia Historical Society as fraudulent. Richard Selcer and Glenn Tucker have accepted the letters as bona fide, with varying degrees of LaSalle's "editing." George Stewart, R. E. Stivers, and Douglas Southall Freeman rejected them and opted not to use them in their books. See Tucker, *Lee and Longstreet at Gettysburg*, 44–45; Stewart, *Pickett's Charge*, 297–98; Freeman, *R. E. Lee*, 4:563; and George R. Stewart to Glenn Tucker, November 22, 1958, Tucker Papers, SHC.

7. Selcer, "George Pickett," 73.

8. Longacre, *Pickett*, xi.

9. Longacre justifies his use of the published Pickett letters by stating: "Because portions of the published letters appear to contain authentic material, selected passages have been incorporated into the present work when they tally with known facts, when they present a reasonably accurate account of events, and when they offer a plausible interpretation of Pickett's frame of mind." How he decided what was "reasonably accurate" and a "plausible interpretation of Pickett's frame of mind" is unclear, although this author has tried at times to do the same. Longacre also cites LaSalle's autobiography without any qualifications. See Longacre, *Pickett*, 182, 5 n. John C. Waugh, in his recent book, *Class of 1846*, notes that "it is not considered safe to believe Pickett's wife." He then retells several stories concocted by LaSalle in his chapter on George, including one linking him to Lincoln. Waugh complains, "If he [Pickett] didn't write such eloquent letters, he should have" (*Class of 1846*, 459, 577, 14 n).

10. Bertram Wyatt-Brown observes: "Influenced by the self-questioning taking place in English, historians recognize the problematic nature of their enterprise and yet are free from the old constraints, so that almost anything can be called a fact if it sheds light on the new kinds of problems we ask about the past" (*Literary Percys*, 37).

11. Lowenthal, *Past Is a Foreign Country*, 200, 206, 210.

12. Kammen, *Mystic Chords of Memory*, 132, 162, 224; Leckie, *Elizabeth Bacon Custer*, xxii.

13. "Confederate Military History," 459.

14. The city of Harrisburg, Pennsylvania, recently purchased a considerable number of Pickett family papers, but at the time this book went to press, the mayor had banned scholarly access to them. In 1957, George and LaSalle's grandson, George III, wrote that R. E. Stivers had seen this private collection and was allowed to transcribe them. R. E. Stivers donated copies of over 100 transcribed letters to the Virginia Historical Society in 1991, although archivists there questioned their legitimacy. This author has accepted those transcriptions as authentic. See George E. Pickett III to H. E. Buswell, May 25, 1957, BC.

CHAPTER ONE

1. Andrew Johnston to Mary Pickett, August 31, 1837, Pickett Family Typescript Notebook, VHS.

2. Turkey Island originally belonged to Col. William Randolph, the great grandfather of John Randolph of Roanoke. See Stivers, "Turkey Island Plantation," 46; Armistead C. Gordon, *Memories and Memorials*, 52–53; *Inventory of Early Archi-*

Alexander, *Exploring Washington's Past*, 246–47; Murray, *Pig War*, 7, 53, 56; Elliot, *Winfield Scott*, 665–66.

25. Lorenzo Thomas to Samuel Cooper, October 22, 1859, *Executive Document No. 10*, 56; Murray, *Pig War*, 58–60; Special Orders, November 5, 1859, *Executive Document No. 10*, 67; Kirk and Alexander, *Exploring Washington's Past*, 246–47; Murray, *Pig War*, 58–60; Edson, *Fourth Corner*, 104–5. Post returns and newspaper reports show that Pickett was on detached duty at Fort Vancouver from August 10 to December 5, 1859, leaving command of his company to Lieutenant Forsythe. See Fort Bellingham Post Returns, typescript copies of originals, BC, and *Daily Alta Californian*, November 23, 1859.

26. Alfred Pleasonton to George E. Pickett, April 10, 1860, *Executive Document No. 98*, 36th Congress; Murray, *Pig War*, 63; McCabe, *San Juan Water*, 56–57. Harney also capitalized on some inhabitants' dislike of Pickett's replacement, Capt. L. C. Hunt. When Hunt tried to crack down on drunkenness, illegal trading, robberies, and general disorder on the island, a handful of disgruntled Americans signed a petition demanding Hunt's removal on March 7. Scott dismissed the attacks on Hunt, deeming him a man "remarkable for firmness, discretion and courtesy." See "Petition," March 7, 1860, *Executive Document No. 98*, 36th Congress, 18; Alfred Pleasonton to L. C. Hunt, March 21, 1860, ibid., 23; L. C. Hunt to Alfred Pleasonton, March 30, 1860, ibid., 24–26; L. C. Hunt to E. D. Keyes, April 24, 1860, ibid., 22; and Winfield Scott, "Remarks," May 14, 1860, ibid., 21.

27. Adams, "General William Selby Harney," 290, 304. George's cousin Henry Heth referred to Harney as a "singular man; if he liked you, all that you did pleased him; if not[,] the reverse" (Morrison, ed., *Memoirs of Henry Heth*, 127). For more on Harney and San Juan, see Warner, *Generals in Blue*, 208–9; Murray, *Pig War*, 15–16, 21; and Skelton, *American Profession of Arms*, 335. Other historians who have studied the "Pig War," or the "War That Was Never Fought," agree that it was Harney who pushed both sides to the brink of war. See Murray, *Pig War*, 21, 32–36; Dawson, *War That Was Never Fought*, 107; Edson, *Fourth Corner*, 99; and McCabe, *San Juan Water*, 56–58.

28. Murray, *Pig War*, 42; Withers, *Autobiography of an Octogenarian*, 164–65. Edson cites historian Fred John Splitstone, who argues that the combination of the "belligerent Pickett" and the "practical" and "calm" British admiral Baynes prevented catastrophe (*Fourth Corner*, 105). On the other hand, James McCabe implies that Pickett did allow for some leeway when he arrived on the island the second time. If he had followed Harney's orders literally, demanding the British to acknowledge the island as part of Whatcom County, McCabe predicts, "All the pacific work of Scott and Baynes would be nullified, for Scott had advised Hunt that he was to remember that no officials of Washington Territory were to interfere in any way with British subjects on San Juan so long as the title remained unsettled" (*San Juan Water*, 56). In this case, it seems that, thanks to the British hesitation and some hasty diplomatic work behind the scenes, open conflict was again avoided. It is unclear what Pickett thought of the situation, as no correspondence exists from the time of his arrival in April to Harney's removal from command in June. Given his earlier concerns, he may have been hesitant to take the first move, despite Harney's orders.

Later in his military career, this stubbornness, insistence on following "the rules of war," and strict interpretation of orders would backfire.

29. George E. Pickett to Alfred Pleasonton, July 27, 1859, Letters Received, Adjutant General's Office, RG 94, NA.

30. Skelton, *American Profession of Arms*, 330, 338–39.

31. Scott added that if an armed confrontation did not occur on the island, it would only be "due to the forbearance of the British authorities." He offered no praise for Pickett's ability or leadership during the crisis. See Winfield Scott, "Remarks," May 14, 1860, *Executive Document No. 98*, 36th Congress, 21; Special Orders, November 5, 1859, *Executive Document No. 10*, 67; and George E. Pickett to George W. Cullum, February 19, 1860, Cullum Papers, USMAA.

32. George E. Pickett to George W. Cullum, February 19, 1860, Cullum Papers, USMAA.

33. William S. Harney to Winfield Scott, August 18, 1859, *Executive Document No. 10*, 24; Evans, ed., *Confederate Military History*, 3:651.

34. Silas Casey to Alfred Pleasonton, August 22, 1859, *Executive Document No. 10*, 46.

35. House Joint Resolution of the Washington Territorial Legislature, No. 15, undated, in Cullum Papers, USMAA; George E. Pickett to Henry M. McGill, January 25, 1860, *Washington Historical Quarterly* 1 (October 1906): 74.

36. Special Orders No. 115, June 8, 1860, *Executive Document No. 98*, 36th Congress, 22; Murray, *Pig War*, 64–65. In October 1860, Secretary of War Floyd formally censured Harney's actions at San Juan and denied Harney's claim that Scott had left no instructions when he left the island in September. Harney's reassignment placed him in command of the Department of the West, but he did not serve actively during the Civil War (see John B. Floyd to William S. Harney, October 27, 1860, Letters Sent, Adjutant General's Office, RG 94, NA, and Warner, *Generals in Blue*, 209).

37. George E. Pickett letter, April 21, 1860, typescript copy of original, Pickett Papers, MVC.

38. George E. Pickett letters, June 1 and 19, 1860, typescript copies of originals, ibid. Pickett banned Northern Indian women with the intention of cutting down on Indian prostitution. See Murray, *Pig War*, 68; Blackman, *During My Time*, 43–44; and George E. Pickett letter, July 18, 1860, typescript copy of original, Pickett Papers, MVC.

39. Pickett complained incessantly of "unfit" horses, inadequate men, and inaccurate maps. See George E. Pickett letters, July 18, August 28, September 26, 1860, typescript copies of originals, Pickett Papers, MVC; Vouri, "Raiders from the North," 36; Peck, *Pig War*, 105; and Edward D. Warbass to Benjamin Alvord, April 14, 1863, *OR* 50 (2):427. On November 23, 1859, the *Daily Alta Californian* described the town of San Juan as having "20 odd buildings and huts," a bakery, a grocery, a theater, "fruitery," "one aristocratic two-bit house," and four saloons.

40. Pickett, *Pickett and His Men*, 123–24; Edson, *Fourth Corner*, 105.

41. For example, George E. Pickett to Benjamin Starke, March 16, 1866, Pickett-Starke Letters, OHS, and George E. Pickett to Henry Coalter Cabell, March 4, 1869, Cabell Family Papers, VHS.

42. Alexander, *Military Memoirs*, 4.

43. George E. Pickett to Benjamin Alvord, February 13, 1861, Pickett Family Type-script, VHS. Vermont native Alvord was an 1833 graduate of the USMA and served in the Mexican War in the 4th Infantry. In 1861, Major Alvord was paymaster in the Department of Oregon. See Warner, *Generals in Blue*, 4–5.

44. John D. S. Spencer to George Wright Jr., January 24, 1861, *OR* 50 (1):435.

45. Albert Sidney Johnston to John D. S. Spencer, February 18, 1861, ibid., 445.

46. W. W. Mackall to George E. Pickett, February 22, 1861, ibid., 449.

47. Maury, *Recollections*, 128.

48. Andrew Johnston to Mary S. Boggs, April 26, 1861, Pickett Family Typescript Notebook, VHS; emphasis in original.

49. Special Orders No. 9, June 11, 1861, *OR* 50 (1):512; E. V. Sumner to Lorenzo Thomas, June 10, 1861, ibid., 506–7; Murray, *Pig War*, 69.

50. Cullum, *Biographical Register*, 2:305. It is unclear if the slowness of communication prevented Pickett from learning of Virginia's secession until late June.

51. Don Carlos Buell to George Wright, June 21, 1861, *OR* 50 (1):519; Special Orders No. 13, June 21, 1861, ibid.; George Wright to Don Carlos Buell, June 22, 1861, ibid., 519–20; Don Carlos Buell to George Wright, June 22, 1861, ibid., 521; Henry M. McGill to Edward V. Sumner, June 24, 1861, ibid., 522; Special Orders No. 18, July 11, 1861, ibid., 533; George E. Pickett to J. S. Mason, July 26, 1861, ibid., 544–45.

52. George E. Pickett to Goldsborough, July 2, 1861, letter reproduced in Edson, *Fourth Corner*, 117.

53. Murray, *Pig War*, 69. Edson, *Fourth Corner*, 116–25; James Tilton to Mrs. Collins, August 8, 1861, quoted in Edson, *Fourth Corner*, 117. Novelist Archie Binns recounts a group of Haida women, including Morning Mist's mother, bringing James to the Collinses' home on Pickett's request. Binns's story implies that, at least temporarily, the boy lived with his mother's tribe, although there is no other source to confirm this. See Binns, *Laurels Are Cut Down*, 4–9.

54. James Tilton to Mrs. Collins, August 8, 1861, and James Tilton to Mrs. Collins, September 23, 1861, both quoted in Edson, *Fourth Corner*, 117–18. Pickett, *Bugles of Gettysburg*, 30–49. E. P. Alexander and Private Peck followed a similar eastward route from Fort Steilacoom, minus the side trip to Canada (see Alexander, *Military Memoirs*, 7–8, and Peck, *Pig War*, 208–9).

CHAPTER SIX

1. Freeman, *Lee's Lieutenants*, 1:158; George E. Pickett to Samuel Cooper, September 20, 1861, Letters Received, Adjutant and Inspector General's Office, and Compiled Service Record of George E. Pickett, RG 109, NA; Special Orders No. 160, September 23, 1861, *OR* 5:877. Pickett's compiled service record also contains evidence that he almost went to Pensacola, Florida, to serve under Braxton Bragg. It is unclear why his rank and assignment altered, but the uncertainty probably resulted from the Confederate War Department's inexperience and early disorganization. LaSalle alleged that George enlisted as a private, immediately received commission to captain, and then received commission to colonel. See Pickett, *What Happened to Me*, 90.

2. Archer, "Letters," 88.

3. Freeman, *Lee's Lieutenants*, 1:158–59, 718. Examples of his concern for his men include George E. Pickett to Benjamin Alvord, February 13, 1861, and George E.

Pickett to Benjamin L. Larned, May 20, 1861, Pickett Family Typescript Notebook, VHS.

4. Pickett commanded the District of the Lower Rappahannock, a subdivision of the Department of Aquia. See O'Sullivan, *55th Virginia Infantry*, 10–11.

5. Ibid., 12; Judah P. Benjamin to Theophilus H. Holmes, October 27, 1861, *OR* 5:923; Samuel Cooper to George E. Pickett, October 27, 1861, *OR* 51 (2):359; Judah P. Benjamin to Joseph E. Johnston, October 28, 1861, *OR* 5:923–24.

6. False alarms were common during that first winter of war, and government officials in Richmond often overestimated the enemy's strength. Judah P. Benjamin, October 28, 1861, *OR* 5:925; Samuel Cooper to George E. Pickett, October 29, 1861, ibid., 927. Pickett's original telegram requesting help has not been found.

7. Theophilus H. Holmes to Samuel Cooper, December 12, 1861, ibid., 993.

8. "Proceedings of Meeting of the Citizens of Lancaster and Northumberland Counties, Virginia," October 21, 1861, ibid., 910–11.

9. R. L. T. Beale to [D. H. Maury], November 30, 1861, ibid., 972.

10. Theophilus H. Holmes to Samuel Cooper, December 12, 1861, ibid., 993.

11. George E. Pickett to D. H. Maury, December 10, 1861, ibid., 991; see also D. H. Maury to George E. Pickett, December 3, 1861, in Compiled Service Record of George E. Pickett, RG 109, NA.

12. In his Indorsement to Samuel Cooper, December 13, 1861, *OR* 5:992, Holmes explained that this "certain class" were the "poor and nonslaveholders."

13. George E. Pickett to D. H. Maury, December 10, 1861, ibid., 991–92.

14. George E. Pickett to Samuel Cooper, December 13, 1861, ibid., 994.

15. George E. Pickett to [W. W. Mackall], May 21, 1857, BC.

16. George E. Pickett to Samuel Cooper, December 13, 1861, *OR* 5:994; see also Indorsement of Theophilus H. Holmes to Samuel Cooper, December 13, 1861, ibid., 992.

17. Judah P. Benjamin to Theophilus H. Holmes, December 16, 1861, ibid., 997. Secretary Benjamin referred to Holmes's proposal to send a regiment to the Northern Neck, but Pickett had first suggested this plan in George E. Pickett to D. H. Maury, December 10, 1861, ibid., 991.

18. Special Orders No. 203, December 24, 1861, ibid., 1006.

19. Indorsements of Theophilus H. Holmes to [Samuel Cooper], December 31, 1861, and January 4, 1862, *OR* 51 (2):428.

20. George E. Pickett to Samuel Cooper, December 28, 1861, ibid., 427.

21. Receipt for W. N. Ward to Samuel Cooper, January 6, 1862, Letters Received, and Samuel Cooper to Joseph E. Johnston, January 10, 1862, Letters Sent, Adjutant and Inspector General's Office, RG 109, NA.

22. Robert K. Krick writes in *Lee's Colonels*, 360–61: "Ward's wife and 12 children were stranded behind enemy lines on the Northern Neck while he stayed in Richmond seeking a position, with glowing referrals from several generals and from Rev. Charles Minnigerode." Ironically, 15 percent of Ward's 55th Virginia Infantry, Pickett's principle regiment in the region, were illiterate, nonslaveholding yeomen farmers from Essex and Middlesex Counties. See O'Sullivan, *55th Virginia Infantry*, 3, 5, 10, 157.

23. Freeman, *Lee's Lieutenants*, 1:158; Indorsement by Theophilus H. Holmes on George E. Pickett to Samuel Cooper, December 28, 1861, *OR* 51 (2):428.

24. Joseph E. Johnston, *Narrative*, 78–79, 483; Freeman, *Lee's Lieutenants*, 1:137.

25. George E. Pickett to Samuel B. French, February 12, 1862, *OR* 51 (2):467.

26. His appointment was to rank from January 14, 1862. See Warner, *Generals in Gray*, 239; Wright, *General Officers*, 69; and George E. Pickett to R. M. T. Hunter, February 12, 1862, *OR* 51 (2):466.

27. Samuel Cooper to Joseph E. Johnston, February 10, 1862, Letters Sent, Adjutant and Inspector General's Office, RG 109, NA.

28. Joseph E. Johnston to Samuel Cooper, February 15, 1862, Johnston Papers, EGSL.

29. Joseph E. Johnston to Samuel Cooper, February 25, 1862, *OR* 5:1081.

30. Special Orders No. 63, February 28, 1862, ibid., 1085–86.

31. Longstreet biographers Piston and Wert recount this story, but LaSalle's postwar letter to Helen Longstreet is the only source that they both uncritically cite. See LaSalle Corbell Pickett to Helen Longstreet, January 3, 1903, in Helen D. Longstreet, *Lee and Longstreet*, 337; Wert, *General James Longstreet*, 97; and Piston, "Lee's Tarnished General," 1:148.

32. Pickett, ed., *Heart of a Soldier*, 32.

33. Besides her own books and her obituaries, there is no corroborating evidence that LaSalle actually attended the academy. There does not seem to be any reason to question this, nor any reason for her to lie. Her writings show that she had some formal education. Established in 1837, Lynchburg Female Academy became the Lynchburg Female Seminary in 1847. See Potter and Potter, *Lynchburg*, 1, and Pickett, *What Happened to Me*, 83. For more on elite white women's education in the South, see Farnham, *Education of the Southern Belle*, 72–73, 174, and Scott, *Southern Lady*, 71.

34. Pickett, *What Happened to Me*, 89–92; Morris and Foutz, *Lynchburg in the Civil War*, 10. Drew Faust states that many ladies' seminaries thrived during the war, offering a refuge for southern white girls away from the battlefront and enemy invasion. LaSalle's family home in Chuckatuck did fall under enemy hands by 1862, and that may explain why she continued to attend the school until, she alleged, the spring of 1863. See *Mothers of Invention*, 39.

35. Elshtain, *Women and War*, 10. Elshtain's book lends fascinating insight into American cultural symbols of the "male fighter" and "female noncombatant," and males as life takers and females as life givers, from the Civil War to the 1980s. Mary Elizabeth Massey was one of the first scholars to discuss the changes and challenges women faced during the Civil War, and recent scholars have expanded the discussion. See Massey, *Bonnet Brigades*; Faust, *Mothers of Invention*; Whites, *Civil War as a Crisis in Gender*; and Rable, *Civil Wars*. Another pioneering book on women and war in American history is Norton, *Liberty's Daughters*.

36. Pickett, *What Happened to Me*, 92. Mary Ryan maintains that for white women, North and South, the war provided greater opportunity to enter the public arena, even if that meant merely assuming traditional female tasks like rolling bandages or sewing uniforms. The point was that women did these things publicly, with clear political implications (*Women in Public*, 142).

37. Clinton and Silber, eds., *Divided Houses*, 136; Faust, *Mothers of Invention*, 231–32.

38. Pickett, *What Happened to Me*, 99–100.

39. "Organization of the Army of Northern Virginia, commanded by General Joseph E. Johnston, near Richmond, Va., May 21, 1862," *OR* 11 (3):531.

40. James Conner to his mother, March 4, 1862, in Conner, *Letters*, 82.

41. Robert K. Krick, *Lee's Colonels*, 28, 73, 336; Warner, *Generals in Gray*, 69–70, 146–47.

42. Joseph E. Johnston, *Narrative*, 101–4.

43. Joseph E. Johnston to Jefferson Davis, February 23, 1862, *OR* 5:1079.

44. James Longstreet, *From Manassas to Appomattox*, 63.

45. Alexander, *Military Memoirs*, 66.

46. G. W. Smith to D. H. Hill, March 10, 1862, *OR* 5:1096.

47. Howard, *Recollections*, 68.

48. Joseph E. Johnston, *Narrative*, 103–4; James Longstreet, *Manassas to Appomattox*, 65; Freeman, *Lee's Lieutenants*, 1:146; Sears, *George B. McClellan*, 167.

49. Shotwell, *Papers*, 1:170–71.

50. Joseph E. Johnston, *Narrative*, 111–16; Freeman, *Lee's Lieutenants*, 1:149–51.

51. David Johnston, *Four Years a Soldier*, 117; General Orders No. 1, April 18, 1862, *OR* 11 (3):448.

52. Alexander, *Military Memoirs*, 64.

53. Robert A. Toombs to Alexander Stephens, May 17, 1862, in Phillips, ed., *Correspondence*, 594–95.

54. James Dearing to "Uncle," April 28, 1862, Dearing Family Papers, VHS.

55. Freeman, *Lee's Lieutenants*, 1:155.

56. Ibid., 155, 174–76; Current, ed., *Encyclopedia of the Confederacy*, 4:1724–25.

57. James Longstreet, *Manassas to Appomattox*, 72–74; Report of the Battle of Williamsburg, George E. Pickett to Moxley Sorrel, May 1862, *OR* 11 (1):584.

58. Report of the Battle of Williamsburg, George E. Pickett to Moxley Sorrel, May 1862, *OR* 11 (1):584, 587; "Organization of Army of Northern Virginia Commanded by General Joseph E. Johnston, on the Peninsula, about April 30, 1862," *OR* 11 (3):481, lists 2,460 men under Pickett's command.

59. Report of the Battle of Williamsburg, George E. Pickett to Moxley Sorrel, May 1862, *OR* 11 (1):585.

60. Ibid., 586.

61. Ibid.; Current, ed., *Encyclopedia of the Confederacy*, 4:1725.

62. Report of the Battle of Williamsburg, George E. Pickett to Moxley Sorrel, May 1862, *OR* 11 (1):586–87.

63. Report of the Battle of Williamsburg, James Longstreet to Thomas G. Rhett, May 16, 1862, ibid., 567.

64. Report of the Battle of Williamsburg, George E. Pickett to Moxley Sorrel, May 1862, ibid., 587.

CHAPTER SEVEN

1. Johnston's army numbered about 60,000. See Freeman, *Lee's Lieutenants*, 1:214, and Current, ed., *Encyclopedia of the Confederacy*, 3:1402.

2. Freeman, *Lee's Lieutenants*, 1:225–43; Faust, ed., *Historical Times Illustrated Encyclopedia*, 668, 1402.

3. Report of the Battle of Seven Pines, George E. Pickett to Joseph E. Johnston, 1862, *OR* 11 (1):982.

4. Ibid.; Newton, *Battle of Seven Pines*, 86–88.

5. Report of the Battle of Seven Pines, George E. Pickett to Joseph E. Johnston, 1862, *OR* 11 (1):982.

6. Ibid.; Organization of the Army of the Potomac, July 21, 1861, *OR* 2:469.

7. Withers, *Autobiography of an Octogenarian*, 177.

8. In his report, Pickett further censored their behavior by claiming that they had "evidently been on a plundering expedition" and thus not legitimately part of the fight (Report of the Battle of Seven Pines, George E. Pickett to Joseph E. Johnston, 1862, *OR* 11 [1]:982).

9. Ibid.

10. Newton, *Battle of Seven Pines*, 92.

11. Ibid., 88–89; Report of the Battle of Seven Pines, George E. Pickett to Joseph E. Johnston, 1862, *OR* 11 (1):983; Withers, *Autobiography of an Octogenarian*, 177–78; Fields, *28th Virginia Infantry*, 14–15.

12. Pickett reported that D. H. Hill "asked me if I could not withdraw my brigade," and he protested that he would lose many more men in the process. See George E. Pickett to Joseph E. Johnston, 1862, *OR* 11 (1):983. Colonel Withers of the 18th Virginia later denied ever seeing Pickett on the field of battle at Seven Pines, claiming that the brigade waited for two long, deadly hours before receiving any word from Pickett to charge or retreat. See Withers, *Autobiography of an Octogenarian*, 178.

13. Report of the Battle of Seven Pines, George E. Pickett to Joseph E. Johnston, 1862, *OR* 11 (1):983.

14. Newton, *Battle of Seven Pines*, 93.

15. Report of the Battle of Seven Pines, George E. Pickett to Joseph E. Johnston, 1862, *OR* 11 (1):984. His casualties for Seven Pines were nearly 20 percent of his aggregate strength of 1,700 men. The Federals lost 286 killed and wounded from their 2,200 men, apparently suffering most of these after Pickett had fallen back, not before, as Pickett's report implied. See Newton, *Battle of Seven Pines*, 93.

16. Withers, *Autobiography of an Octogenarian*, 178.

17. Freeman, *Lee's Lieutenants*, 1:243.

18. Report of the Battle of Seven Pines, Joseph E. Johnston to Samuel Cooper, June 24, 1862, *OR* 11 (1):935.

19. Report of the Battle of Seven Pines, James Longstreet to Thomas G. Rhett, June 10, 1862, ibid., 940–41; James Longstreet, *Manassas to Appomattox*, 108.

20. James Longstreet to Samuel Cooper, June 15, 1862, Compiled Service Record of Richard H. Anderson, RG 109, NA.

21. Report of the Battle of Seven Pines, D. H. Hill to James Longstreet, 1862, *OR* 11 (1):945. In a public address to veterans, Hill repeated his account of Pickett at Seven Pines, stating: "There was no fighting on the second day to speak of except by Pickett who started on his own accord and stopped when he pleased or after he had driven the enemy to the brush, as he expressed it" (D. H. Hill, address at "Reunion of the Virginia Division of the Army of Northern Virginia Association," October 22, 1885, *Southern Historical Society Papers* 13 [1885]: 265).

22. Boatner, *Civil War Dictionary*, 651.

23. Pickett, *Pickett and His Men*, 170.

24. Pickett, "Wartime Story of General Pickett," *Cosmopolitan* 56 (January 1914): 178.

25. Ibid., 179.

26. Ibid., 180. LaSalle repeated this same passage in her 1917 autobiography, *What Happened to Me*, 104–8; see also Pickett, *Pickett and His Men*, 170–74.

27. Current, ed., *Encyclopedia of the Confederacy*, 1:76. For more on the resulting Seven Days battles and the Peninsula campaign, see Sears, *To the Gates of Richmond*.

28. Buel and Johnson, eds., *Battles and Leaders*, 2:352.

29. Ibid., 347–52; see also Freeman, *Lee's Lieutenants*, 2:503–16, and Current, ed., *Encyclopedia of the Confederacy*, 3:1020–21.

30. Freeman, *Lee's Lieutenants*, 1:517–37; Current, ed., *Encyclopedia of the Confederacy*, 2: 653.

31. Quote from Report of the Battle of Gaines's Mill, John B. Strange to G. Moxley Sorrel, July 15, 1862, *OR* 11 (2):767; see also Current, ed., *Encyclopedia of the Confederacy*, 653, and Dowdey, *Seven Days*, 228, 231.

32. Harrison, *Pickett's Men*, 29. See also Report of the Battle of Gaines's Mill, John B. Strange to G. Moxley Sorrel, July 15, 1862, *OR* 11 (2):767.

33. Harrison, *Pickett's Men*, 29.

34. Withers, *Autobiography of an Octogenarian*, 187–88.

35. Quoted in Wert, *General James Longstreet*, 138.

36. Harrison, *Pickett's Men*, 29.

37. Report of the Battle of Gaines's Mill, John B. Strange to G. Moxley Sorrel, July 15, 1862, *OR* 11 (2):767–68.

38. Harrison, *Pickett's Men*, 29–30; emphasis in original.

39. Pickett, *Pickett and His Men*, 182.

40. Ibid., 181–82; Pickett, *What Happened to Me*, 110.

41. Haskell, *Memoirs*, 32.

42. The editors of Haskell's diary praise him for his frank and unapologetic honesty. Haskell also censured Pickett's behavior at Gettysburg, implying that the general skulked in a barn during the infamous charge. See ibid., viii–ix, xi–xiii, 51–52. Haskell composed his memoirs forty years after the war ended; LaSalle's *Pickett and His Men* appeared at about the same time, in 1899.

43. Pickett, *What Happened to Me*, 110–11.

44. LaSalle's constant postwar affirmation of her late husband's bravery coupled with outside attacks on his manhood seem to indicate something was awry, although I do not agree with Richard Selcer's notion that Pickett suffered from a sort of nineteenth-century posttraumatic stress disorder. See Selcer, "George Pickett," 61. Several excellent studies explore the way the war experience (and southern defeat) tried, tested, and redefined traditional concepts of masculinity. See Linderman, *Embattled Courage*; Foster, *Ghosts of the Confederacy*; Clinton and Silber, eds., *Divided Houses*; Reid Mitchell, *Vacant Chair*; and Silber, *Romance of Reunion*. The author also thanks Michael Vouri for his insight into this issue.

45. Quote from W. H. Cocke to [parents and sisters], October 7, 1862, Cocke Family Papers, VHS. See also Harrison, *Pickett's Men*, 65, 69, and Pickett, *What Happened to Me*, 115.

46. Freeman, *Lee's Lieutenants*, 2:284–86; Faust, ed., *Historical Times Illustrated Encyclopedia*, 167.

47. Freeman, *Lee's Lieutenants*, 2:257, 264, 269. The author thanks Carol Reardon for her view that Lee had no reason *not* to trust Pickett in this early part of the war.

48. Edward Baird to "My Dear Aunt," November 11, 1862, Baird Family Papers, EGSL.

49. Inman, ed., *Soldier of the South*, 25.

50. Abstract from Monthly Return of the Department of Northern Virginia, December 31, 1862, *OR* 21:1082; Compiled Service Record of George E. Pickett, RG 109, NA. Division staff officers included his brother Charles and cousins W. Stuart and Thomas Symington. His brother-in-law, Dr. Blair Burwell, was also nearby as surgeon for the 8th Virginia Infantry. See George E. Pickett to Samuel Cooper, February 21, 1862, Adjutant and Inspector General's Office, RG 109, NA; Edward Baird to "My Dear Aunt," November 11, 1862, Baird Family Papers, EGSL; Pickett, *Pickett and His Men*, 206; Crute, *Confederate Staff Officers*, 151–52; "Staff Officers," *Southern Historical Society Papers* 38 (1910): 176; and "Paroles of the Army of Northern Virginia," *Southern Historical Society Papers* 15 (1887): 70–71.

51. Edward Baird to "Father," November 25, 1862, and Edward Baird to "Willie," December 4, 1862, Baird Family Papers, EGSL.

52. Cooke, *Life of Gen. Robert E. Lee*, 184.

53. Osmun Latrobe Diary, entry for December 13, 1862, VHS; capitalization in original. For more on the battle see, Current, ed., *Encyclopedia of the Confederacy*, 2:637–40, and Gallagher, ed., *Fredericksburg Campaign*.

54. Longstreet did detach two of Pickett's brigades to reinforce other divisions, but their casualties were relatively light: fifty-four killed, wounded, or missing. See Report of the Battle of Fredericksburg, James Longstreet to R. H. Chilton, December 20, 1862, *OR* 21:570–71, and "Return of Casualties in Pickett's Division at Battle of Fredericksburg," December 18, 1862, ibid., 573.

55. Morgan, *Personal Reminiscences*, 148–49.

56. H. T. Owen to Harriet Owen, December 15, 1862, Owen Papers, VHS.

57. Harrison, *Pickett's Men*, 71.

58. Hunton, *Autobiography*, 83.

59. Harrison, *Pickett's Men*, 71.

60. Ibid., 71–72; LaSalle repeated this account, almost verbatim, in *Pickett and His Men*, 233–34.

61. Report of the Battle of Fredericksburg, James Longstreet to R. H. Chilton, December 20, 1862, *OR* 21:571.

62. Pickett, "Wartime Story of General Pickett," *Cosmopolitan* 56 (February 1914): 336–37.

CHAPTER EIGHT

1. Harrison, *Pickett's Men*, 72; James Longstreet, *Manassas to Appomattox*, 323–24; Bell, *11th Virginia Infantry*, 36; Hunter, *Johnny Reb and Billy Yank*, 326, 329–30; Wallace, *17th Virginia Infantry*, 43.

2. Samuel Cooper to George E. Pickett, February 18, 1863, Compiled Service

Record of George E. Pickett, RG 109, NA; see also Robert E. Lee to James Seddon, February 14, 1863, *OR* 18:876–77, and Freeman, *Lee's Lieutenants*, 2:468.

3. Orders given to Hill and Smith required them to be vigilant and respond to situations as they saw fit. Compare correspondence in Compiled Service Records of D. H. Hill, G. W. Smith, and George E. Pickett, RG 109, NA.

4. Lee wrote Secretary Seddon, "I must request you to give him [Pickett] orders" (Robert E. Lee to James A. Seddon, February 16, 1863, *OR* 18:880).

5. R. E. Lee to James Longstreet, February 18, 1863, ibid., 883.

6. Special Orders No. 44, February 21, 1863, ibid., 889.

7. Sorrel, *Recollections*, 58.

8. Ibid.

9. Quoted in Cormier, *Siege of Suffolk*, 9.

10. James A. Seddon to Robert E. Lee, February 22, 1863, *OR* 18:890.

11. Harrison, *Pickett's Men*, 72–73. John Cocke wrote his family, "We deserve a long rest for we had an awful time getting here, marching for one week over the worst roads I've ever seen" (John Cocke to [parents and sisters], March 19, 1863, Cocke Family Papers, VHS). Jedediah Hotchkiss recorded in his diary on February 28, 1863: "It is said that Hood's and Pickett's Division suffered much in their late march to Richmond" (*Make Me a Map*, 117).

12. Pickett, *Pickett and His Men*, 235.

13. Mary Elizabeth Massey, Gerald Linderman, Reid Mitchell, Drew Faust, and Elizabeth Leonard are just a few scholars who have explored the connections between civilians and soldiers, battlefront and home front, men and women. See Massey, *Ersatz in the Confederacy*; Massey, *Refugee Life*, vii–viii, 282; Linderman, *Embattled Courage*, 1–3; Reid Mitchell, *Vacant Chair*, 4, 71–87, 158–66; Clinton and Silber, eds., *Divided Houses*, 171–99; Faust, *Mothers of Invention*; and Leonard, *Yankee Women*, xix–xxi.

14. Longstreet essentially had an independent command, though he was still under Lee's supervision. See Cormier, *Siege of Suffolk*, 4, 12–16; Wallace, *17th Virginia Infantry*, 45; and Freeman, *Lee's Lieutenants*, 2:483.

15. Pickett, *What Happened to Me*, 121.

16. Quoted in Young and Young, *56th Virginia Infantry*, 74.

17. Sorrel, *Recollections*, 153.

18. Pickett, *Bugles of Gettysburg*, 66.

19. Pickett, *What Happened to Me*, 121.

20. John H. Lewis, *Recollections*, 60–61.

21. T. G. Barham Typescript, F&S.

22. James Thomas Petty Diary, entry for March 29, 1863, MC; see also Wallace, *17th Virginia Infantry*, 45.

23. At the age of eighty-two Eppa Hunton recited the story of his life to his son in 1904, so postwar bitterness may have colored his view of Pickett. Hunton was no fan of his division commander after failing to gain promotion to brigadier general in the fall of 1863. See Hunton, *Autobiography*, 85, 81; see also Tucker, *Lee and Longstreet at Gettysburg*, 336.

24. Hunton, *Autobiography*, 127. As Gerald Linderman notes, "A failure in courage in war was a failure in manhood" (*Embattled Courage*, 8).

25. Pickett, ed., *Heart of a Soldier*, 66.

26. Gary Gallagher recognizes Pickett's romantic side but dismisses letters he believes were written by LaSalle, partly because of their "overpowering sentimentality and gushy prose" (see Gallagher, "Widow and Her Soldier," 340–41). An archivist at the VHS assured this author that "no man" would write in such a sentimental manner. In 1925, an editor at Houghton Mifflin remarked to Arthur Crew Inman that *Heart of a Soldier* "as it stood had a woman's title and a man's content." He suggested cutting LaSalle's introduction in the new edition because "it detracted from the masculine spirit of the letters." See Inman, *Diary*, 1:261.

27. Lystra, *Searching the Heart*, 4–5, 7–9, 26–27, 35; quote from 20. Lystra discusses the "romantic self" in relation to the shift toward individualism and companionate marriage in the nineteenth century. She recognizes that her study perhaps best represents western, midwestern, and New England couples (5).

28. This is not to say that other soldiers and officers did not face these same struggles. But Pickett, as a major general and namesake of the most famous charge of the war, openly defied accepted behavior. His reputation suffered for it, and thanks only to the postwar writings of LaSalle Pickett, James Longstreet, promoters of the romanticized Pickett's Charge, and a few other determined admirers do some present writers refer to him as the "epitome of the mythic Southern soldier." See Gramm, *Gettysburg*, 199. See also Rotundo, *American Manhood*, 274; Reid Mitchell, *Vacant Chair*, 7, 12; and Reardon, *Pickett's Charge*, 79–83.

29. Robert E. Lee to Samuel Cooper, April 16, 1863, *OR* 25 (2):726. See also James A. Seddon to Robert E. Lee, April 6, 1863, ibid., 709; Robert E. Lee to James A. Seddon, April 9, 1863, ibid., 713–14; Samuel Cooper to Robert E. Lee, April 14, 1863, ibid., 720; and Cormier, *Siege of Suffolk*, 64.

30. Robert E. Lee to James A. Seddon, May 10, 1863, *OR* 25 (2):790. In March, Longstreet also briefly considered sending Pickett to command the siege of Washington, North Carolina, but instead kept him under his watchful eye in Suffolk. See James Longstreet to D. H. Hill, March 20 and 21, 1863, *OR* 18:931 and 932, and Freeman, *Lee's Lieutenants*, 2:479.

31. Richard Garnett's and James Kemper's brigades were detached from Pickett's during the spring. See James Longstreet to Robert E. Lee, March 21 and 22, 1863, *OR* 18:933 and 937, and Cormier, *Siege of Suffolk*, 61.

32. Henry T. Owen to Harriet Owen, March 14, 1863, Owen Papers, VHS. Owen, a member of the 18th Virginia Infantry, Garnett's brigade, also stated that the men in his brigade "prefer Pickett and ere hope the transfer is not permanent but will only last a few weeks and that we may return to Virginia and to Pickett."

33. Lee instructions included in Samuel Cooper to James Longstreet, April 29, 1863, *OR* 18:1029.

34. Cormier, *Siege of Suffolk*, 249–52; Freeman, *Lee's Lieutenants*, 2:494.

35. Special Orders, May 4, 1863, *OR* 18:1045.

36. Jones, *Rebel War Clerk's Diary*, 1:325–26. Pickett's exact hair color is difficult to document. Some referred to it as black, others auburn or red. Contemporary John S. Wise claimed it to be blond. Photographs seem to indicate it was dark. For references to Pickett's hair, see Wise, *End of an Era*, 338; Young, *Battle of Gettysburg*, 315; James Longstreet, "Introduction," in Pickett, *Pickett and His Men*, xi; James Longstreet,

From Manassas to Appomattox, 392–93; Withers, *Autobiography of an Octogenarian*, 165; and T. G. Barham Typescript, F&S.

37. Edgar Ashton to "Sister," May 11, 1863, Cocke Family Papers, VHS.

38. George E. Pickett to Arnold Elzey, June 2, 1863, *OR* 18:1091; Robert E. Lee to Jefferson Davis, June 2, 1863, *OR* 25 (2):848; see also McMurry, *John Bell Hood*, 71.

39. George E. Pickett to Arnold Elzey, June 2, 1863, *OR* 18:1090–91.

40. Ibid.

41. Robert E. Lee to George E. Pickett, June 3, 1863, *OR* 25 (2):852–53.

42. Robert E. Lee to A. P. Hill, June 5, 1863, *OR* 27 (3):859.

43. For discussion of the Confederate military situation in Virginia just prior to the Pennsylvania campaign, see Freeman, *R. E. Lee*, 3:18–27.

44. Arnold Elzey to James Johnston Pettigrew, June 5, 1863, *OR* 27 (3):861.

45. James Johnston Pettigrew commanded Hanover Junction. See J. J. Pettigrew to Arnold Elzey, June 6, 1863, ibid., 862. Pettigrew followed up with a second telegram saying, "General Pickett is still here" (J. J. Pettigrew to Arnold Elzey, June 6, 1863, ibid.).

46. Robert E. Lee to A. P. Hill, June 8, 1863, ibid., 869.

47. One of his brigades remained on the Blackwater near Suffolk, the other at Hanover Junction to protect Lee's crucial communication lines. See G. Moxley Sorrel to George E. Pickett, June 14, 1863, ibid., 888, and Robert E. Lee to James Longstreet, June 15, 1863, ibid., 890.

48. George E. Pickett to R. H. Chilton, June 21, 1863, ibid., 910.

49. There is evidence that both Lee and Davis tried to return Montgomery Corse's brigade to Pickett as late as June 23, 1863. See Jefferson Davis to Robert E. Lee, June 19, 1863, ibid., 904, and Robert E. Lee to Samuel Cooper, June 23, 1863, ibid., 925–26. Six days later, on June 29, Pickett received word that, "though Corse's may not be expected immediately, he [Lee] hopes that ere long it will be enabled to rejoin its division" (Walter H. Taylor to George E. Pickett, June 29, 1863, ibid., 944–45).

50. Pickett, *What Happened to Me*, 124.

51. Inman, ed., *Soldier of the South*, 51.

CHAPTER NINE

1. Pickett, "Wartime Story of General Pickett," *Cosmopolitan* 56 (May 1914): 762; see also Pickett, *Pickett and His Men*, 315.

2. Sorrel, *Recollections*, 57–58.

3. Raphael J. Moses, "Autobiography," 78, Moses Papers, SHC.

4. Fremantle, *Three Months in the Southern States*, 253.

5. Lois Banner discusses the tie between male hairstyles and beards and large-scale violence during the mid-nineteenth century. She argues that ostentatious hairstyles and beards stressed male virility, power, and maturity (*American Beauty*, 234–37).

6. Dawson added that the women had no interest in Pickett's hair anyway (*Reminiscences*, 90–91).

7. Domschcke, *Twenty Months in Captivity*, 29–30.

8. Ed Baird, "Gettysburg," speech to the Essex Chapter of the United Daughters of the Confederacy, n.d., Baird Papers, MC.

9. Charles Pickett to Editor, Richmond *Times*, November 11, 1894.

10. Pickett, *Bugles of Gettysburg*, 112. Lois Banner, in *American Beauty*, 227–28, notes a Byronic ideal of masculinity that became popular among white women in antebellum America.

11. Banner, *American Beauty*, 237–38; see also Moers, *Dandy*.

12. E. Anthony Rotundo refers to these "manly passions" and states, "Being a man, then, meant more than suppressing 'female' qualities and encouraging 'male' ones. It also meant strict control of some 'male impulses' and encouragement of others" (*American Manhood*, 180). David Pugh writes with significant insight that men would "displace their fear of being womanized or symbolically emasculated not by direct attacks against women but by describing male opponents in female terms. This projection mechanism not only demeaned its male victims in the eyes of other men, but also vented a largely unconscious male distrust of women" (*Sons of Liberty*, 103). This idea may also explain attacks on Pickett's masculinity, since the Civil War threatened white male gender roles and allowed women to take on traditionally "masculine" responsibilities and occupations, even if only temporarily.

13. Harrison, *Pickett's Men*, 87. Lee's order to respect civilian property is from General Orders No. 72, June 21, 1863, *OR* 27 (3):912–13; Dooley, *War Journal*, 97; and John H. Lewis, *Reminiscences*, 76–77. Reference to religious revivalism is from Irby, *Historical Sketch*, 26–27,

14. Boatner, *Civil War Dictionary*, 334; Faust, ed., *Historical Times Illustrated Encyclopedia*, 306.

15. Youngblood, "Unwritten History," 314; William Henry Cocke to John Cocke, July 11, 1863, Cocke Family Papers, VHS; Charles Pickett to Henry T. Owen, March 30, 1878, Owen Papers, ibid.; Irby, *Historical Sketch*, 27; quote from David Johnston, *Four Years a Soldier*, 240. Staff officer Walter Harrison estimated twenty-three miles; aide Robert A. Bright thought it to be twenty-eight (see Harrison, *Pickett's Men*, 87, and Robert A. Bright to Henry T. Owen, July 20, 1887, Owen Papers, VHS).

16. Harrison, *Pickett's Men*, 88; Robert A. Bright to Henry T. Owen, July 20, 1887, Owen Papers, VHS; Dooley, *War Journal*, 101; Charles Pickett to Henry T. Owen, March 30, 1878, Owen Papers, VHS. William Garrett Piston has suggested that Longstreet erred in failing to call Pickett to the front, so that by dawn on July 3 the division would be ready for action. See William Garrett Piston, "Cross Purposes: Longstreet, Lee and Confederate Attack Plans for July 3 at Gettysburg," in Gallagher, ed., *Third Day at Gettysburg*, 45.

17. Boatner, *Civil War Dictionary*, 335–37; Faust, ed., *Historical Times Illustrated Encyclopedia*, 306.

18. Coddington, *Gettysburg Campaign*, 462; Freeman, *Lee's Lieutenants*, 3:144–45. Boatner, in *Civil War Dictionary*, 338, estimates that 15,000 troops made the charge. Pickett's division numbered 5,800, according to Georg and Busey, *Nothing but Glory*, 8–9, and Dooley, *War Journal*, 102.

19. Diary entry for July 3, 1863, in Dooley, *War Journal*, 101.

20. James Longstreet to Henry T. Owen, April 21, 1878, Owen Papers, VHS.

21. Pickett, *Bugles of Gettysburg*, 64.

22. Pickett, *Pickett and His Men*, 298.

23. According to Bright, the officer warned Pickett, "My men have until lately been down on the seashore, only under the fire of heavy gun ships, but for the last

day or two they have lost heavily under infantry fire and are very sore and they will not go up to-day." This officer was George T. Gordon, of Scales's brigade, Pender's division. However, there is some question over which regiment Gordon spoke of. As George Stewart asserts, however, "There is no reason to suppose that Bright invented the story." See Bright, "Pickett's Charge," 229; Robert K. Krick, *Lee's Colonels*, 146; and Stewart, *Pickett's Charge*, 144–45.

24. B. D. Fry, "Pettigrew's Charge at Gettysburg," *Southern Historical Society Papers* 7 (February 1879): 92; B. D. Fry to John B. Bachelder, December 27, 1877, Bachelder Papers, NHHS. Fry had flunked out of Pickett's West Point class, but, as a member of the regular army, he joined his former classmates in the Mexican War. See Boatner, *Civil War Dictionary*, 318.

25. Quoted in Wise, *End of an Era*, 338–39.

26. Domschcke, *Twenty Months in Captivity*, 29–30.

27. Buel and Johnson, eds., *Battles and Leaders*, 3:343.

28. James Longstreet to E. P. Alexander, "about 12," July 3, 1863, copy from original, Alexander Papers, SHC.

29. E. P. Alexander to James Longstreet, July 3, 1863, ibid.

30. James Longstreet to E. P. Alexander, "about 12:30," July 3, 1863, ibid.

31. Alexander, *Fighting for the Confederacy*, 255.

32. Ibid., 258.

33. E. P. Alexander to George E. Pickett, 1:25 P.M., July 3, 1863, copy from original, Alexander Papers, SHC.

34. James Longstreet, *From Manasass to Appomattox*, 392; Alexander, *Fighting for the Confederacy*, 260. Longstreet explained, "I would not speak for fear of betraying my want of confidence to him" (*Annals of War*, 429–30).

35. E. P. Alexander to George Pickett, July 3, 1863, 1:40 P.M., copy from original, Alexander Papers, SHC.

36. Jean Bethke Elshtain discusses traditional roles of women in war as noncombatants but notes ways in which women took more active parts as nurses, wartime correspondents, and, occasionally, as soldiers themselves. Still, in American society, the military and war making remains "man-made." Drew Faust's recent book explores these roles for Confederate women. See Elshtain, *Women and War*, 180–93, and Faust, *Mothers of Invention*.

37. Inman, ed., *Soldier of the South*, 44.

38. According to LaSalle, he wrote: "If Old Peter's nod means death, good-by, and God bless you, little one." She maintained that this letter did reach her and remained "one of my most treasured possessions" ("Wartime Story of General Pickett," *Cosmopolitan* 56 [April 1914]: 619). But in the published Pickett letters, the letter dated July 3, 1863, is several pages long and does not include this phrase at all. See Pickett, ed., *Heart of a Soldier*, 91–96.

39. Pickett, *Pickett and His Men*, 302. A member of the 11th Virginia publicly inferred that Pickett and his staff members were loitering near the "whiskey wagon" while the battle raged. See Carol Reardon, "Pickett's Charge: The Convergence of History and Myth in the Southern Past," in Gallagher, ed., *Third Day at Gettysburg*, 73–75. Reardon observes that Otey nursed a grudge against Pickett for bringing court-martial charges against him for drunkenness. See below for the response of

Pickett defenders to these and other equally negative attacks about Pickett's actions at Gettysburg.

40. Although Carol Reardon rightfully notes the difficulty of piecing together accurate accounts of the charge because of "literary wars" between participants, I have based my description of the battle, and more specifically the details of the charge itself, on a variety of sources, both secondary and primary, hoping to find some middle ground. The reader should refer to Reardon's essay, "Pickett's Charge," in Gallagher, ed., *Third Day at Gettysburg*, 56–92, and her more complete study, *Pickett's Charge*, for excellent and thorough overviews of the biases inherent in much of the literature of the charge. The description of Pickett's words and actions just before the charge comes from David Johnston, *Four Years a Soldier*, 255; Easley, "Saw Pickett 'Riding Grandly Down,'" 133; McCulloch, "High Tide at Gettysburg," 474; Mayo, "Pickett's Charge at Gettysburg," 331; McPherson, "Private's Account of Gettysburg," 149; and Charles S. Peyton, Report of the Battle of Gettysburg, July 9, 1863, *OR* 28 (2):385–86.

41. Coddington, *Gettysburg Campaign*, 490, 503–4, maps 10 and 11; Tucker, *High Tide at Gettysburg*, 344; Boatner, *Civil War Dictionary*, 338.

42. Several Union soldiers recalled the charge with admiration and awe. For example, see Report of the Battle of Gettysburg, Theodore B. Gates, July 4, 1863, *OR* 27 (1):319, and Edmund Rice and Norman J. Hall, "Repelling Lee's Last Blow at Gettysburg," in Buel and Johnson, eds., *Battles and Leaders* 3:387–91.

43. Cowan, "Repulsing Pickett's Charge," 28.

44. Georg and Busey, *Nothing but Glory*, 97.

45. Coddington, *Gettysburg Campaign*, map 11.

46. In 1894, responding to public criticism of Pickett's behavior at Gettysburg, seven members of his staff published an editorial in the Richmond *Times*, hoping forever to "end all controversy about what sensible men could never have had any doubt about from the beginning." Ten years later, nine veterans from Pickett's division met in Richmond to lay to rest lingering questions surrounding Pickett's actions and location during the charge. One committee member stated, "I think it is absurd for anyone to deny the fact that General Pickett was in command." See Richmond *Times*, December 19, 1894, and "Committees Report on General Pickett and His Command and Participation in the Battle of Gettysburg, July 3, 1863," November 14, 1913, in Gregory Family Papers, VHS. Kathy Georg and John Busey devote an entire appendix to the subject in their book *Nothing but Glory*.

47. For example, see Haskell, *Memoirs*, 51–52.

48. Clayton Coleman to John W. Daniel, July 1, 1904, Daniel Papers, AL.

49. Coddington writes, "Many participants who studied the battle after the war worried over the question of Pickett's whereabouts, although none seemed to show the same concern for Pettigrew." Yet it is significant that attacks on Pickett's courage in battle predated Gettysburg and continued until Lee finally removed him from command in April 1865. Even if Pickett did not shirk his duty at Gettysburg, many believed him guilty of cowardice. LaSalle's dramatic defensiveness of her husband's heroism is also significant. See Sorrel, *Recollections*, 173; Coddington, *Gettysburg Campaign*, 504; and Stewart, *Pickett's Charge*, 286.

50. Thomas R. Friend to Charles Pickett, December 10, 1896, Pickett Papers, VHS;

F. M. Bailey to John W. Daniel, December 22, 1904, and W. P. Jesse to John W. Daniel, n.d., Daniel Papers, AL.

51. Stewart, *Pickett's Charge*, 199; Freeman agrees in *R. E. Lee*, 3:129, 122 n.

52. Coddington, *Gettysburg Campaign*, 505; Bright "Pickett's Charge," 233; W. Stuart Symington to Charles Pickett, October 17, 1892, Pickett Papers, VHS. Joseph Mayo, in "Pickett's Charge at Gettysburg," 332, recalled, "I saw a disorderly crowd of men breaking for the rear, and Pickett with Stuart Symington, Ned Baird, and others vainly trying to stop the rout."

53. Martin, "Colonel Rawley Martin's Account," 187–88; Rawley Martin to Sylvester Chamberlain, August 11, 1897, Daniel Papers, AL.

54. Bright, "Pickett's Charge," 231–32; Robert A. Bright to Charles Pickett, October 15, 1892, Pickett Papers, VHS.

55. Charles Pickett, "Letter to the Editor," Richmond *Times*, November 11, 1894.

56. One soldier later harshly criticized Pickett for allowing this time to pass without calling a retreat. H. C. Michie, who suffered capture and imprisonment at the hands of the Yankees at Gettysburg, wrote, "I have always blamed General Pickett for not giving the order to 'fall back' " (see H. C. Michie to John W. Daniel, February 21, 1904, Daniel Papers, AL).

57. Robert A. Bright to Charles Pickett, October 15, 1892, Pickett Papers, VHS. In Dearing's official report he claimed that he used his last rounds of ammunition "upon a column of infantry which had advanced on General Pickett's right flank." From all other accounts, it seems that he meant the left flank. See James Dearing, Report of the Battle of Gettysburg, August 16, 1863, *OR* 27 (2):389.

58. E. P. Alexander had readied several howitzers, complete with full chests of ammunition, to lend some strong support to the charge "when both the moral + physical effect of a prompt + close art[iller]y support are very powerful and decide an action." At some point during the day, William Pendleton, the chief of artillery, moved the guns and ammunition without notifying Alexander. Longstreet was horrified to learn of the weakened condition of the artillery just as the charge commenced, and stated that he would have "revoked [the order to charge] had I felt that I had that privilege." Lee professed that the ineffective state of the artillery "was unknown to me when the assault took place." See E. P. Alexander to John B. Bachelder, May 3, 1876, Bachelder Papers, NHHS; James Longstreet, Report of the Battle of Gettysburg, July 27, 1863, *OR* 27 (2):360; and Robert E. Lee to Samuel Cooper, January 1864, ibid., 321.

59. Coddington, *Gettysburg Campaign*, 519; Georg and Busey, *Nothing but Glory*, 104; Cadmus M. Wilcox, Report of the Battle of Gettysburg, July 17, 1863, *OR* 27 (2):620.

60. Clyde N. Wilson, *Carolina Cavalier*, 195; Freeman, *Lee's Lieutenants*, 3:149–51; Tucker, *High Tide at Gettysburg*, 375.

61. Tucker, *High Tide at Gettysburg*, 366, 393–94; Stewart, *Pickett's Charge*, 211, 213. Coddington, *Gettysburg Campaign*, 529–31. This was the common view among Confederate participants. For example, James Dearing wrote his mother three weeks after the fight, "If we could have held those heights, if Pickett had been supported . . . we would have destroyed their army" (see James Dearing to "Mother," July 26, 1863, Dearing Family Papers, AL). See also W. H. Cocke to [parents and sisters], July 11,

1863, Cocke Family Papers, VHS, and Hotchkiss, *Make Me a Map*, 157, for similar sentiments.

62. Dawson, *Reminiscences*, 97.

63. Poague, *Gunner with Stonewall*, 75.

64. Stewart, *Pickett's Charge*, 230.

65. Stewart goes on to state that Pickett "suffered some failure of stamina, though probably nothing that should be called cowardice; . . . not being a quick-thinking man, he merely became confused, and ended by doing what was not heroic" (ibid., 286). Accounts that attest to Pickett's crying include Wood, *Reminiscences of Big I*, 124; Henry T. Owen to Charles S. Marshall, January 27, 1878, Owen Papers, VHS; and Henry T. Owen, "Pickett's Charge," Philadelphia *Weekly Times*, March 26, 1881. Bernhard Domschcke wrote, "When I saw him [Pickett] a few days later on the Potomac, a pall seemed to cloak the ruddy features" (*Twenty Months in Captivity*, 30).

66. Historians have echoed the thoughts of Pickett's male contemporaries. George Stewart refers to Pickett's behavior as "almost a crack-up after the repulse" (*Pickett's Charge*, 274), and Clifford Dowdey describes Pickett as "almost out of self-control when he rode back among the shattered men" (*Lee's Last Campaign*, 234).

67. Youngblood, "Unwritten History," 317.

68. This account of the exchange comes from Bright, "Pickett's Charge," 234.

69. Pickett, *Bugles of Gettysburg*, 139.

70. Ibid., 126.

71. Coddington, *Gettysburg Campaign*, 535–39; Boatner, *Civil War Dictionary*, 339.

72. John W. Daniel, "Gettysburg," November 20, 1863, Daniel Papers, VHS.

73. Stewart, *Pickett's Charge*, 266–68; Georg and Busey, *Nothing but Glory*, 190.

74. Robert E. Lee to George E. Pickett, July 8, 1863, *OR* 27 (3):983; Stewart, *Pickett's Charge*, 274; Harrison, *Pickett's Men*, 105.

75. Robert E. Lee to George E. Pickett, July 9, 1863, *OR* 27 (3):986–87.

76. Although this report has never surfaced, Longstreet apparently read it. He recalled Pickett's "criticism of the lot assigned him." Longstreet admitted that, while Pickett's "report was not so strong against the attack as mine before the attack was made," Pickett made the mistake of putting his objections into writing; Longstreet expressed his orally to Lee. James Longstreet to Nash, September 3, 1892, Pickett Papers, VHS.

77. Robert E. Lee to George E. Pickett, n.d., *OR* 27 (3):1075. Coddington, in *Gettysburg Campaign*, 525–26, argues that Lee took complete blame for Gettysburg just to avoid such dissension and finger-pointing.

78. James Longstreet to Charles Pickett, October 15, 1892, Pickett Papers, VHS. W. Stuart Symington, Pickett's cousin and staff officer, remembered Pickett as "furious" that Lee returned his report (W. Stuart Symington to [?], December 21, 1903, Alexander Papers, SHC). LaSalle insisted that she had the original report, but it has never surfaced. James Longstreet wrote to George's brother, "His widow has told me that she had his report that General Lee returned to him, and would send it to me whenever she could get back to her old papers at home. But I fear that she was mistaken and that the General did not keep the original report" (James Longstreet to Charles Pickett, October 5, 1892, Pickett Papers, VHS).

79. Pickett, *Pickett and His Men*, 315. Gary Gallagher, in *Third Day at Gettysburg*, 1,

argues that most southerners did not see Gettysburg as a "catastrophic defeat" during the summer of 1863.

80. I accept this as the only fully authentic letter, based on correspondence with Gary Gallagher and my own comparison of handwriting. This "original" is George E. Pickett to LaSalle Corbell, July 23, 1863, located in Inman Papers, JHL; it is also reprinted in Inman, ed., *Soldier of the South*, 78.

81. T. G. Barham Typescript, F&S.

82. Reardon offers the best discussion of this phenomenon in "Pickett's Charge," in Gallagher, ed., *Third Day at Gettysburg*, 56–92, and *Pickett's Charge*, 3–4, 199–213.

83. Faulkner, *Intruder in the Dust*, 194–95; emphasis in original.

CHAPTER TEN

1. Pickett, *Pickett and His Men*, 318.

2. Her obituary also called her the "child bride" of the Confederacy. See "Obituary," *Confederate Veteran* 39 (April 1931): 151, and *Washington Post*, March 23, 1931; see also Pickett, *Pickett and His Men*, 318, and Rable, *Civil Wars*, 51.

3. Pickett, "My Soldier," 568. Her "childish" traits especially come through in her autobiography, *What Happened to Me*, 143–45, 191–99, 207–16.

4. Inman, *Diary*, 1:328.

5. David Pugh and Caroll Smith-Rosenberg have also discussed the "child-woman" (Smith-Rosenberg's term) image imposed on women during the nineteenth century in order to keep them submissive and dependent on men. Pugh argues that after the Civil War this notion gained even wider acceptance with the rise of social Darwinism. See Pugh, *Sons of Liberty*, 65–68, and Smith-Rosenberg, "Hysterical Woman," 655–56. See also Fox-Genovese, *Within the Plantation Household*, 109, and Wyatt-Brown, *Southern Honor*, 201–2.

6. Wedding details are gathered from Pickett, "Wartime Story of General Pickett," *Cosmopolitan* 56 (May 1914): 764, and *Pickett and His Men*, 320–21; Palmer, "Civil War Wedding of LaSalle Corbell," 53–54, and Massey, *Refugee Life*, 196.

7. Pickett, *Pickett's Men*, 320–21; see also Pickett, *What Happened to Me*, 126–29. Mary Chesnut includes several instances of Confederate elite entertaining despite war deprivations. For a few examples from the fall of 1863, see Woodward, ed., *Mary Chesnut's Civil War*, 486–87. See also Faust, *Mothers of Invention*, 244–45. Five weeks after the Picketts' alleged bountiful banquet, Pickett issued orders to his officers that "the exigencies of the public service" required "rigid economy in the consumption of forage" (Special Orders No. 20, Headquarters, Department of North Carolina, October 24, 1863, Miscellaneous Papers, MC).

8. Richmond *Daily Dispatch*, September 22, 1863. No supporting evidence has been found to show that the Davises attended the wedding or that the Lees sent a fruitcake.

9. Special Orders No. 226, September 23, 1863, *OR* 29 (2):746.

10. Pickett, *What Happened to Me*, 136; see also Pickett, *Pickett and His Men*, 326. George Rable, in *Civil Wars*, 72, describes Confederate women trying to "maintain a semblance of stability by preserving as much of traditional family life as possible" in the face of separation, death, and suffering. The Victorian ideal of womanhood and marriage made wives the moral superior of their husbands. Shirley Leckie notes that

in the Custer marriage, which had many parallels to the Picketts', Armstrong believed his wife, Libby, would make him a "better man" (*Elizabeth Bacon Custer*, 36, 45).

11. Pickett, *What Happened to Me*, 141. For general discussion of Confederate women seeking ways to feel less "useless" in war, see Faust, *Mothers of Invention*, 9–29, and Massey, *Bonnet Brigades*, 26, 30–42.

12. For earlier versions of this discussion of Pickett in North Carolina, see Gordon-Burr, "'Until Calm Reflection,'" 19–45, and Lesley Gordon, "Seeds of Disaster." The impact of the Civil War on North Carolina communities has been the subject of several recent studies. These include Escott, *Many Excellent People*; Durrill, *War of Another Kind*; and Paludan, *Victims*. See also Bardolph, "Confederate Dilemma," and Honey, "War within the Confederacy," 77. Honey credits North Carolina with the "sharpest internal opposition to the Confederacy of all the Southern states during the war."

13. Jenkin's brigade, one of those detached from Pickett's division before Gettysburg, was transferred to John Bell Hood's division. See Freeman, *Lee's Lieutenants*, 3:223–24.

14. Samuel Cooper to George E. Pickett, September 26, 1863, *OR* 29 (2):752.

15. President Davis had requested that Pickett's division join Longstreet to support Braxton Bragg's Army of Tennessee in the western theater. See Freeman, *Lee's Lieutenants*, 3:223.

16. George E. Pickett to Samuel Cooper, October 5, 1863, *OR* 29 (2):773–74.

17. Samuel Cooper to George E. Pickett, October 15, 1863, ibid., 788.

18. These points included Petersburg, Virginia, and Kinston and Weldon, North Carolina. See Samuel Cooper to George E. Pickett, October 9, 1863, ibid., 778; George E. Pickett to Samuel Cooper, October 15, 1863, ibid., 789; and George E. Pickett to Samuel Cooper, October 16, 1863, ibid., 790.

19. George E. Pickett to Samuel Cooper, October 21, 1863, ibid., 798; Indorsement of Samuel Cooper [to James Seddon], October 23, 1863, ibid.; James A. Seddon to Samuel Cooper, October 24, 1863, ibid.

20. This large Federal advance was to meet George Meade's crossing of the Rapidan, which resulted in the Mine Run campaign. See Robert E. Lee to J. D. Imboden, November 25, 1863, ibid., 846–47, and Current, ed., *Encyclopedia of the Confederacy*, 3:1043

21. George E. Pickett to Samuel Cooper, November 25, 1863, *OR* 29 (2):847; George E. Pickett to James A. Seddon, November 26, 1863, ibid., 848. Seddon admitted that Pickett's force was "less than I had supposed" and advised him to move other units within the department to protect Petersburg (James A. Seddon to George E. Pickett, November 26, 1863, ibid.).

22. LaSalle put a different spin on her husband's discontent, asserting that George foresaw enemy attacks on Petersburg and repeatedly stressed the city's vulnerability to Richmond officials, at first by telegram, then in person. She wrote that the secretaries of war and navy promised support, but "these promises, for causes unknown[,] were not fulfilled, and subsequent events showed their importance" (*Pickett and His Men*, 325–26). Here again LaSalle used an opportunity to present her husband as a prophet, a man unappreciated and overlooked by his contemporaries.

23. George E. Pickett to Samuel Cooper, October 21, 1863, *OR* 29 (2):797–98; George E. Pickett to Samuel Cooper, November 3, 1863, ibid., 818.

24. Barrett and Yearns, eds., *North Carolina Civil War Documentary*, 43.

25. Mrs. L. J. Johnson to cousin, August 22, 1863, in ibid., 48.

26. Joel R. Griffin to George E. Pickett, December 15, 1863, *OR* 29 (2):872–73. The 62nd Georgia Cavalry was just one of a hodgepodge of troops included in Pickett's department. Units from Alabama, Louisiana, North Carolina, and Virginia were also under his jurisdiction. See "Abstract from Return of the Department of North Carolina, Major General George E. Pickett, C.S. Army, Commanding, for the month of February 1864; headquarters Petersburg, Va.," *OR* 33:1201.

27. E. A. Wild to John T. Elliot, December 17, 1863, *OR*, ser. 2, 11:847; Joel R. Griffin to E. A. Wild, January 1864, in Moore, *Rebellion Record*, 8:304–5.

28. Pickett admitted that reports may be exaggerated and that perhaps slaveowners might object to his plan of taking away their slaves, "but," he maintained, "I think the case of emergency," and that Butler was capable "to commit any outrage" (George E. Pickett to Samuel Cooper, December 15, 1863, *OR* 29 [2]:872, and George E. Pickett to Samuel Cooper, December 15, 1863, ibid., 873). Pickett's reaction fit Everard H. Smith's argument that "the ideology of the Old South was an ethic of white male power, created by the dominant race, gender and class for the dual purpose of protecting slavery and preserving the status quo" ("Chambersburg," 448).

29. George E. Pickett to J. R. Griffin, December 15, 1863, *OR* 29 (2):874. He declared Yankees "heathen" in his telegram to Samuel Cooper, December 15, 1863, ibid., 873.

30. Described in Joel R. Griffin to E. A. Wild, January 1864, in Moore, *Rebellion Record*, 8:304–5.

31. Ibid., 301.

32. Joel R. Griffin to George E. Pickett, [December] 19, [1863], *OR* 29 (2):883. Griffin also reported to Pickett that an officer's wife and "other ladies, were arrested, tied, and placed in jail at Elizabeth City, and carried in irons to Norfolk; even their feet tied. Negroes killed a child in Camden County, committing all other kinds of excesses."

33. George E. Pickett to Samuel Cooper, December 20, 1863, ibid., 881–82. Eleven days later, Pickett notified Cooper that he needed to see the adjutant general in person to "get some advice and assistance about the North Carolina affairs" (George E. Pickett to Samuel Cooper, December 31, 1863, ibid., 897).

34. Enclosure dated January 13, 1864, signed by "subscribers of State of North Carolina, Pasquotank, County," *OR*, ser. 2, 6:846.

35. Robert E. Lee to George E. Pickett, January 20, 1864, Seth Barton Compiled Service Record, RG 109, NA. LaSalle, in *Pickett and His Men*, 331, credited George with the plan "which was approved of and applauded by both Lee and Beauregard, and was guarded with the strictest secrecy." There is no basis for this statement; Lee planned the attack with the help of native North Carolinian Robert Hoke. See Barefoot, *General Robert F. Hoke*, 106–7.

36. LaSalle referred to "General Ransom's home" but did not indicate if this was Matt or Robert Ransom, who were brothers and both generals. She also claimed that she and George briefly took refuge with a Baptist minister in Pickett, *What Happened*

to Me, 135–36; see also Pickett, "Wartime Story of General Pickett," *Cosmopolitan* 56 (May 1914): 768. It is unclear exactly to what location LaSalle referred when she described a village where the "hotel was impossible and the community was of Union sentiment," but it seems likely she meant somewhere in North Carolina, possibly Goldsboro. Quote from *What Happened to Me*, 136.

37. Pickett, *Pickett and His Men*, 332.

38. Details of the attack were gathered from Davis, *Jefferson Davis Constitutionalist*, 8:543; Loyall, "Capture of the *Underwriter* at New Bern," 137, 143; Freeman, *Lee's Lieutenants*, 3:335; Faust, ed., *Historical Times Illustrated Encyclopedia*, 524; Burgwyn, *Captain's War*, 119–20; Report of the Battle of New Bern, George E. Pickett to Samuel Cooper, February 15, 1864, *OR* 33:92–94; Report of the Battle of New Bern, Robert Hoke to W. Taylor, February 8, 1864, ibid., 95–97; and Report of the Battle of New Bern, Seth M. Barton to Charles Pickett, February 21, 1864, ibid., 97–99.

39. George E. Pickett to Samuel Cooper, February 3, 1864, *OR* 33:1145.

40. Davis, *Jefferson Davis Constitutionalist*, 6:169.

41. Robert E. Lee to Robert F. Hoke, February 11, 1864, *OR* 33:1160–61.

42. See Robert E. Lee to George E. Pickett, January 20, 1864, ibid., 1102–3; R. E. Lee to W. H. C. Whiting, January 20, 1864, ibid., 1103; and Robert E. Lee to Robert F. Hoke, January 20, 1864, ibid., 1103–4.

43. Report of the Battle of New Bern, George E. Pickett to Samuel Cooper, February 15, 1864, ibid., 94.

44. Barton demanded a court-martial investigation to clear his name of any wrong-doing. Lee endorsed this proposal, and a court of inquiry assembled in early March to investigate. Inexplicably, the War Department canceled the special order for the court a few weeks later. However, during its brief investigation, the court did request a copy of Lee's orders to Pickett, but no other records have surfaced to shed light on the court's findings. See Report of the Battle of New Bern, George E. Pickett to Samuel Cooper, February 15, 1864, *OR* 33:93–94; George E. Pickett to Robert E. Lee, February 15, 1864, ibid., 92; Seth M. Barton to Theodore O. Chestney, February 21, 1864, ibid., 97; Report of the Battle of New Bern, Seth M. Barton to Charles Pickett, February 21, 1864, ibid., 97–99; and Special Orders No. 54, section XXIV, March 5, 1864, Letters Received, Adjutant and Inspector General's Office, and W. Gordon McCabe to W. H. Taylor, March 12, 1864, Barton Compiled Service Record, RG 109, NA; see also Freeman, *Lee's Lieutenants*, 3:335, 144 n.

45. Report of the Battle of New Bern, George E. Pickett to Samuel Cooper, February 15, 1864, *OR* 33:94.

46. Lonn, *Desertion during the Civil War*, 214.

47. Henry M. Shaw was colonel of the 8th North Carolina Infantry, listed in Robert K. Krick, *Lee's Colonels*, 314–15, as killed in action near New Bern, February 1, 1864.

48. John J. Peck to George E. Pickett, February 11, 1864, *OR* 33:866–67.

49. This previous hanging stirred controversy and anger against Pickett by Union officials. See Samuel Spear to Benjamin F. Butler, January 16, 1864, *OR*, ser. 2, 6:845–46; Benjamin Butler to Henry Halleck, January 17, 1864, ibid., 845; and Benjamin Butler to Henry Halleck, January 20, 1864, ibid., 858.

50. John J. Peck to George E. Pickett, February 13, 1864, *OR* 33:867.

51. George E. Pickett to John J. Peck, February 16, 1864, ibid., 867–68. Staff officer Walter Harrison explained Pickett's denial of the story's reliability by stating: "It was never known, of course, by whom he [Col. Shaw] was shot, nor were any negro troops with us at New Bern" (Harrison, *Pickett's Men*, 120).

52. Hodijah Lincoln Meade to Richard Hodijah Lincoln Meade, February 21, 1864, Meade Family Papers, VHS.

53. George E. Pickett to John J. Peck, February 17, 1864, *OR* 33:868.

54. George E. Pickett to John J. Peck, February 27, 1864, in *Executive Document No. 98*, 39th Congress, 7.

55. John J. Peck to George E. Pickett, February 20, 1864, *OR* 33:868–69.

56. Proof of this is in the ledgers kept by the War Department, in Registers of Letters Received, Adjutant and Inspector General's Office, RG 109, NA.

57. George E. Pickett to Samuel Cooper, February 26, 1864, *Executive Document No. 98*, 39th Congress, 9.

58. Pickett's exact whereabouts throughout the hangings at Kinston are unclear. Walter Harrison claimed that after Pickett chose members for the court-martial he left for Weldon (Harrison, *Pickett's Men*, 119). He was in Weldon by February 8, but there is evidence that at some point he stayed in Goldsboro, some twenty to thirty miles from Kinston (see Thomas Clingman to Samuel Cooper, February 16, 1864, and George E. Pickett to Samuel Cooper, February 25, 1864, Letters Received, Adjutant and Inspector General's Office, RG 109, NA). See also George E. Pickett to Samuel Cooper, February 8, 1864, *OR* 33:1151. Pickett announced his return to his Petersburg headquarters in George E. Pickett to Samuel Cooper, February 9, 1864, ibid. It appears that one set of hangings occurred on February 5, 1864, a second group of men died on February 15, and a third hanging took place sometime between these two dates. See Chambers, *Diary*, 175, and Hall, "Atonement," 20.

59. Rev. John Paris, chaplain of the 54th North Carolina Infantry, wrote a long letter to the *North Carolina Presbyterian* detailing the hangings. Hall reproduces a portion of this letter in "Atonement," 20. Paris also preached to Hoke's brigade in a sermon entitled "A Sermon: Preached Before Brig.-Gen. Hoke's Brigade, at Kinston, N.C., on the 28th of February, 1864, By Rev. John Paris, Chaplain Fifty-Fourth Regiment, N.C. Troops, Upon the Death of Twenty-Men, Who Had Been Executed in the Presence of the Brigade for the Crime of Desertion." In the sermon, Paris derided the twenty-two hanged soldiers who had "yielded to mischievous influence, and from motives or feelings base and sordid, unmanly, and vile, resolved to abandon every principle of patriotism, and sacrifice every impulse of honor" (Hall, "Atonement," 7).

60. This description is based on *New York Times*, March 11, 18, 1864; New Bern *North Carolina Times*, March 9, 1864; Gaines, "Fayette Artillery," 96–97; Chambers, *Diary*, 175; Harrison, *Pickett's Men*, 116–19; Hall, "Atonement," 19–21; David Johnston, *Four Years a Soldier*, 290; and witness testimony in *Executive Document No. 98*, 39th Congress, 15–47, 53–87.

61. The exact number of unclaimed bodies is unclear. According to the testimony of Catherine Summerlin and Isaiah Wood, relatives and friends managed to claim most of the twenty-two bodies. However, as Summerlin recounted, "The wives of

some, within Union lines, could not get their bodies." See *Executive Document No. 98*, 39th Congress, 28, 33.

62. Ibid., 27–28.

63. Ibid., 28–30.

64. Ibid., 30–31. See below for more on Pickett's postwar trial for these executions.

65. Butler, *Correspondence*, 3:479–80.

66. Bardolph, "Confederate Dilemma," pt. 2, 205–9.

67. *Executive Document No. 98*, 39th Congress, 49–50.

68. Pickett quoted by Blunt King, a private in the 10th North Carolina Infantry, during his sworn testimony, in *Executive Document No. 98*, 39th Congress, 80. King added that Pickett told another soldier, "Every God-damned man who didn't do his duty, or deserted, ought to be shot or hung."

69. LaSalle did know of the hangings, because she plagiarized whole portions of Walter Harrison's *Pickett's Men* in *Pickett and His Men*; but while Harrison included a passage describing and defending Kinston, she was silent. Later, when the federal government sought to indict George for war crimes and they fled to Canada, LaSalle maintained that their exile was due to the government's desire to punish her husband for leaving the army prematurely before his resignation was formally approved. See Pickett, *What Happened to Me*, 201–2; Harrison, *Pickett's Men*, 116–20; and Gallagher, "Widow and Her Soldier," 335–36.

CHAPTER ELEVEN

1. Braxton Bragg to George E. Pickett, April 12, 1864, *OR* 51 (2):857; see also Braxton Bragg to Robert Hoke, April 12, 1864, ibid., 857–58. Earlier and partial versions of this chapter appear in Lesley Gordon, " 'Assumed a Darker Hue' " and "Seeds of Disaster."

2. Hoke's victory won him major generalship. See Boatner, *Civil War Dictionary*, 78, 650; Schiller, *Bermuda Hundred Campaign*, 18; and Current, ed., *Encyclopedia of the Confederacy*, 2:780. LaSalle alleged that her husband masterminded the capture of Plymouth but urged Richmond to abandon the attack because the expedition would leave Petersburg vulnerable. After he hastily visited Richmond to plead his case once more, she claimed, "He found that in the face of all argument, in spite of all warning, the expedition to Plymouth had been ordered forward" (Pickett, *Pickett and His Men*, 337–38).

3. Grant's overall plan is described in Grant, *Personal Memoirs*, 2:127–32, 134, 138–41, 146–48, and "Report of Lieut. Gen. Ulysses S. Grant, U.S. Army, commanding Armies of the United States, including operations March, 1864–May, 1865," Ulysses S. Grant to E. M. Stanton, July 22, 1865, *OR* 46 (1):11–21. See also Boatner, *Civil War Dictionary*, 247, and William Glenn Robertson, *Back Door to Richmond*, 14–16.

4. George E. Pickett to Samuel Cooper, November 7, 1863, *OR* 29 (2):827; George E. Pickett to James Seddon, November 26, 1863, ibid., 848; George E. Pickett to Samuel Cooper, December 31, 1863, ibid., 897; Harrison, *Pickett's Men*, 121. In Pickett, *What Happened to Me*, 138, LaSalle also described her husband's attempts to inform the War Department of Petersburg's vulnerability, but, she wrote, Confederate authorities disregarded his warnings.

5. J. F. Milligan to George E. Pickett, April 13, 1864, *OR* 51 (2):858; William Glenn

Robertson, *Back Door to Richmond*, 45–46; quote from Braxton Bragg to George E. Pickett, April 14, 1864, *OR* 51 (2):861.

6. See various dispatches exchanged between Pickett and Bragg in *OR* 51 (2):861–64. In other instances, Pickett had been more than willing to vent his judgment; for example, see George E. Pickett to Samuel Cooper, January 6, 1864, *OR* 33:1067–68, and George E. Pickett to Samuel Cooper, November 7, 1863, *OR* 29 (2):827.

7. Braxton Bragg to George E. Pickett, April 16, 1864, *OR* 51 (2):863–64.

8. George E. Pickett to Braxton Bragg, April 17, 1864, ibid., 865.

9. Freeman, *Lee's Lieutenants*, 3:451; William Glenn Robertson, *Back Door to Richmond*, 48, 65–66; Schiller, *Bermuda Hundred Campaign*, 53, 55–56; Special Orders No. 90, April 18, 1864, *OR* 33:1292; Roman, *Military Operations*, 2:542.

10. George E. Pickett to Samuel Cooper, April 24, 1864, Letters Sent, Adjutant and Inspector General's Office, RG 109, NA; James Longstreet to Charles S. Venable, May 1, 1864, *OR* 36 (2):940; Samuel Cooper to George E. Pickett, May 4, 1864, ibid., 950.

11. George E. Pickett to Samuel Cooper, May 17, 1864, Letters Received, Adjutant and Inspector General's Office, RG 109, NA; Schiller, *Bermuda Hundred Campaign*, 59; William Glenn Robertson, *Back Door to Richmond*, 66.

12. George E. Pickett to Samuel Cooper, May 4, 1864, *OR* 36 (2):951.

13. Ibid.; George E. Pickett to Samuel Cooper, May 5, 1864, ibid., 955–56.

14. George E. Pickett to Samuel Cooper, May 5, 1864, 3:00 P.M., ibid., 957.

15. Freeman calls the night of May 5, "in a word, a black night for George Pickett" (*Lee's Lieutenants*, 3:456); see also George E. Pickett to Samuel Cooper, May 5, 1864, *OR* 36 (2):958.

16. Hill lacked an official assignment. See Special Orders No. 3, May 5, 1864, *OR* 36 (2):960.

17. John M. Otey to George E. Pickett, May 6, 1864, *OR* 36 (2):965. Robert Schiller adds, "Beauregard, like Bragg[,] seemed to have little confidence in Pickett's abilities" (*Bermuda Hundred Campaign*, 74).

18. James Seddon to Braxton Bragg, May 7, 1864, Bragg Papers, PL.

19. William Glenn Robertson, *Back Door to Richmond*, 66–67; Schiller, *Bermuda Hundred Campaign*, 78; George E. Pickett to Samuel Cooper and P. G. T. Beauregard, May 6, 1864, Received 3:35 A.M., *OR* 36 (2):964; George E. Pickett to Samuel Cooper May 6, 1864, Received 5:20 A.M., ibid., 965; George E. Pickett to Samuel Cooper, Received 9:10 A.M., ibid.

20. In *Pickett and His Men*, 340, LaSalle observed, "Notwithstanding the repeated warning of Pickett, the government was totally unprepared and the country at large completely surprised. Thus the world heeds its clear-visioned seers, now, who tell of evil because they must, not more than in the olden days when the sorrowful Cassandra wandered sadly and alone in the sacred laurel grove of Apollo and poured forth her mournful plaint for a nation that would not see."

21. Ibid., 138.

22. Pickett, ed., *Heart of a Soldier*, 123. As with all of the published Pickett letters, it is unclear if these were entirely LaSalle's words or his. Given George's earlier concern with protecting the inhabitants of the Northern Neck, particularly the women, it is entirely plausible that he expressed such worries. She may have rephrased his thoughts to make them more dramatic to her readers.

23. Pickett, *Pickett and His Men*, 341.

24. Pickett, *What Happened to Me*, 139.

25. Pickett, ed., *Heart of a Soldier*, 125; emphasis in original.

26. George E. Pickett to Samuel Cooper, May 17, 1864, Letters Received, Adjutant and Inspector General's Office, RG 109, NA.

27. Gorgas, *Diary*, 100.

28. P. G. T. Beauregard to Braxton Bragg, May 11, 1864, *OR* 51 (2):920; see also Dowdey, *Lee's Last Campaign*, 238; William Glenn Robertson, *Back Door to Richmond*, 112.

29. Schiller, *Bermuda Hundred Campaign*, 165; William Glenn Robertson, *Back Door to Richmond*, 128.

30. Dowdey, *Lee's Last Campaign*, 233.

31. H. A. Carrington to Charlotte Elizabeth Carrington, May 12, 1864, Carrington Family Papers, VHS.

32. Pickett, *What Happened to Me*, 140.

33. Braxton Bragg to George E. Pickett, May 19, 1864, Letters Sent, Adjutant and Inspector General's Office, RG 109, NA. LaSalle wrote, "Petersburg being protected, my Soldier had time to remember he had been ordered to report for duty elsewhere" ("Wartime Story of General Pickett," *Cosmopolitan* 56 [May 1914]: 769). In *Pickett and His Men*, 345–46, she claimed that they left Petersburg on her birthday, May 16.

34. Dowdey, *Lee's Last Campaign*, 231, 247; Alexander, *Military Memoirs*, 530.

35. Thomas J. Howe, *Petersburg Campaign*, 1–3.

36. George E. Pickett to Robert E. Lee, May 21, 1864, Pickett Family Typescript Notebook, VHS; see also Freeman, *Lee's Lieutenants*, 3:497. Pickett was temporarily placed with the Third Corps, and he reported to A. P. Hill near the North Anna River on May 22. Within a week he was back with the First Corps.

37. George E. Pickett to G. Moxley Sorrel, May 28, 1864, *OR* 36 (3):843–44; see also "Diary of the First Army Corps," *OR* 36 (1):1058.

38. Sommers, *Richmond Redeemed*, 1–2; Thomas J. Howe, *Petersburg Campaign*, 3–10.

39. Freeman, *Lee's Lieutenants*, 3:532; quote from 627; Bell, *11th Virginia Infantry*, 52; "Official Diary of First Corps," 491–94, 503–4.

40. Blair Burwell to Jenny Pickett Burwell, May 26, 1864, Burwell Family Papers, EGSL.

41. Thomas J. Howe, *Petersburg Campaign*, 79–80.

42. Robert E. Lee to R. H. Anderson, June 17, 1864, reproduced in Pickett, *Pickett and His Men*, 350.

43. Charles Pickett to Henry T. Owen, October 14, 1881, Owen Papers, VHS. Freeman writes, "Pickett's men advanced as if the hill at Mrs. Clay's Farm were another Cemetery Ridge" (*Lee's Lieutenants*, 3:532).

44. Quoted in Bell, *11th Virginia Infantry*, 52.

45. See map in Sommers, *Richmond Redeemed*, 6.

46. Pickett, *Pickett and His Men*, 357; see also Pickett, *What Happened to Me*, 141.

47. Pickett, *What Happened to Me*, 141.

48. James Barrow quoted in James I. Robertson, *18th Virginia Infantry*, 31.

49. Pickett, *Pickett and His Men*, 364–65; Divine, *8th Virginia Infantry*, 31. A

typical day on the lines is described in George E. Pickett to W. H. Taylor, August 28, 1864, Venable Papers, SHC. See also Harrison, *Pickett's Men*, 66, 135; Osmun Latrobe to George E. Pickett, January 3, 1865, *OR* 46 (2):1008; Osmun Latrobe to George E. Pickett, January 4, 1865, ibid., 1014; W. H. Taylor to John C. Breckenridge, March 13, 1865, ibid., 1308; Osmun Latrobe to John F. Edwards, March 14, 1865, ibid., 1312; Osmun Latrobe to E. Taylor, March 14, 1865, ibid.; Osmun Latrobe to C. W. Field, March 14, 1865, ibid., 1313; and Bearss and Calkins, *Battle of Five Forks*, 10, 20–21.

50. Freeman, *Lee's Lieutenants*, 3:627; Thomas J. Howe, *Petersburg Campaign*, 73.

51. Pickett, *Pickett and His Men*, 362–64.

52. Pickett, *What Happened to Me*, 143.

53. Pickett, *Pickett and His Men*, 361.

54. Pickett, *What Happened to Me*, 144–45. An abbreviated form of this story is included in *Pickett and His Men*, 360–61, but LaSalle left out any mention of her picking up the head.

55. Historians disagree over motivations behind postwar Lost Cause ideology. Charles Reagan Wilson's *Baptized in Blood* argues that the Lost Cause became a civil religion for white southerners to cope with defeat. Gaines Foster, in his *Ghosts of the Confederacy*, on the other hand, asserts that mythmaking served as a transitory ideology to enable white southerners to come to terms with not only defeat but also the onset of market capitalism. See also Connelly and Bellows, *God and General Longstreet*, and Silber, *Romance of Reunion*.

56. Pickett, *Pickett and His Men*, 343.

57. According to an inspection on February 28, 1865, 5,967 men were listed as "present for duty," 8,073 men and officers were "aggregate present," and 6,151 men were "present effective for the field" ("Abstract from Returns of the Army of Northern Virginia, commanded by General Robert E. Lee, C.S. Army, February 24–March 1, 1865," *OR* 46 [1]:388); see also R. E. Lee to John C. Breckenridge, February 28, 1865, *OR* 46 (2):1265; W. H. Taylor to Robert E. Lee, March 8, 1865, ibid., 1292–93; Divine, *8th Virginia Infantry*, 31; Osmun Latrobe to W. H. Taylor, March 21, 1865, *OR* 46 (3):1332; and Robert E. Lee to John C. Breckenridge, March 27, 1865, ibid., 1353–54. In *R. E. Lee*, 4:25–26, Freeman estimates about 5,139 men in the division. Quote from Walter Harrison to George E. Pickett, November 14, 1864, Fairfax Papers, VHS.

58. Confederate Inspection Book No. 171, January 1, 1863–January 31, 1865, 4, 8, 9, 11, SHC.

59. Robert E. Lee to James Longstreet, January 19, 1863, Fairfax Papers, VHS.

60. U. S. Grant to Philip Sheridan, March 30, 1865, *OR* 46 (3):325; Freeman, *R. E. Lee*, 4:22; Boatner, *Civil War Dictionary*, 282; Harrison, *Pickett's Men*, 135–36; Pickett's Report of the Battle of Five Forks, reprinted in Pickett, *Pickett and His Men*, 393.

61. James Longstreet to W. H. Taylor, March 27, 1865, *OR* 46 (3):1357.

62. James Longstreet to Robert E. Lee, March 28, 1865, ibid., 1360; Boatner, *Civil War Dictionary*, 282; Bearss and Calkins, *Battle of Five Forks*, 13.

63. Freeman, *Lee's Lieutenants*, 3:658; see also Freeman, *R. E. Lee*, 4:30–31.

64. Charles Pickett to Osmun Latrobe, March 30, 1865, Lee Headquarters Papers, VHS.

65. M. M. Lewis to Osmun Latrobe, March 31, 1865, ibid.

66. Pickett's Report of the Battle of Five Forks, reprinted in Pickett, *Pickett and His Men*, 394.

67. McCabe's journal in Armistead C. Gordon, *Memories and Memorials*, 163.

68. Pickett's Report of the Battle of Five Forks, reprinted in Pickett, *Pickett and His Men*, 394; Freeman, *Lee's Lieutenants*, 3:657–59; Faust, ed., *Historical Times Illustrated Encyclopedia*, 220.

69. Pickett's Report of the Battle of Five Forks, reprinted in Pickett, *Pickett and His Men*, 395. See also Bearss and Calkins, *Battle of Five Forks*, 46, and Freeman, *R. E. Lee*, 4:35.

70. Pickett's Report of the Battle of Five Forks, reprinted in Pickett, *Pickett and His Men*, 395; see also Hutter, "Eleventh at Five Forks Fight," 359, and Freeman, *Lee's Lieutenants*, 3:660.

71. Pickett, *Pickett and His Men*, 386; emphasis in original. In *Lee's Lieutenants*, 3:661, 41 n, Freeman notes that although there is no copy of this telegram in the *OR*, "there is no reason to question its authenticity. It has verisimilitude." Walter Harrison, in *Pickett's Men*, 138, also referred to Lee telegraphing Pickett to "hold Five Forks at all hazards and to prevent if possible, the enemy form striking the South Side Railroad."

72. Pickett's Report of the Battle of Five Forks, reprinted in Pickett, *Pickett and His Men*, 395.

73. Robert E. Lee to John C. Breckenridge, April 1, 1865, *OR* 46 (1):1263–64; Freeman, *Lee's Lieutenants*, 3:662, 43 n.

74. Harrison, *Pickett's Men*, 138–39.

75. Letter of Thomas L. Rosser in Philadelphia *Weekly Times*, April 5, 1895; Walker, *Life of . . . Richard Heron Anderson*, 225–26; Boatner, *Civil War Dictionary*, 283; Thomas L. Rosser to James Longstreet, October 22, 1892, in personal collection of Matt Masters; Freeman, *Lee's Lieutenants*, 3:667–68. Thomas T. Munford, a Confederate brigadier general at Five Forks, recounted one of his staff being unable to find Pickett in "Unpublished Sketch of Five Forks," in Walker, *Life of . . . Richard Heron Anderson*, 227.

76. Pickett's Report of the Battle of Five Forks, reprinted in Pickett, *Pickett and His Men*, 395. The shad bake was not made public until 1886, when Tom Rosser first told of the luncheon in an article appearing in the Philadelphia *Weekly Times*. See also Freeman, *R. E. Lee*, 4:40, 79 n, and Freeman, *Lee's Lieutenants*, 3:668, 70 n, 669. The time of the Federal attack was around 4:00 P.M., meaning that Pickett, Rosser, and Lee had lunched for three hours. In "Unpublished Sketch," in Walker, *Life of . . . Richard Heron Anderson*, 226, Munford claimed that the lunch lasted four hours.

77. Quoted in Freeman, *Lee's Lieutenants*, 3:664.

78. Philadelphia *Weekly Times*, April 5, 1895.

79. Bearss and Calkins, *Battle of Five Forks*, 83–84, 86, 90.

80. Frank S. Robertson, "Memoirs," 18–19. See also Testimony of Fitzhugh Lee in Warren Court of Inquiry, in "Five Forks," Daniel Papers, AL; Freeman, *Lee's Lieutenants*, 3:669; and Munford, "Unpublished Sketch," in Walker, *Life of . . . Richard Heron Anderson*, 227.

81. Sheridan's Federals had initially swarmed across White Oak Road too far east of Pickett's main line, but after some confusion, Sheridan regrouped his attacking

troops. See Bearss and Calkins, *Battle of Five Forks*, 93, and Faust, ed., *Historical Times Illustrated Encyclopedia*, 261–62.

82. Pickett's Report of the Battle of Five Forks, reprinted in Pickett, *Pickett and His Men*, 395.

83. David Johnston, *Four Years a Soldier*, 390.

84. Griggs, "Thirty-Eighth Virginia," 231.

85. Bearss and Calkins, *Battle of Five Forks*, 113.

86. Pickett faced approximately 50,400 Federals at Five Forks. See Faust, ed., *Historical Times Illustrated Encyclopedia*, 261.

87. Freeman, *Lee's Lieutenants*, 3:665–66.

88. Pickett's Report of the Battle of Five Forks, reprinted in Pickett, *Pickett and His Men*, 395; Freeman, *R. E. Lee*, 4:40, 79 n.

89. Pickett, "The First United States Flag," 19–22; quote from 21.

90. Pickett, *What Happened to Me*, 164–65. See also Pickett, "My Soldier," 567, and Current, ed., *Encyclopedia of the Confederacy*, 3:1331.

91. LaSalle repeatedly wrote of the Lincoln-Pickett friendship. A typical example is in Pickett, "My Soldier," 567–68. Historians and contemporaries alike have dismissed the Lincoln connection, but it did make its way into Ida Tarbell's *Life of Abraham Lincoln*, 2:287–88. A contemporary's denunciation of this issue is in George Anson Bruce to Margaret Heth Vaden, April 11, 1928, Bruce Family Papers, VHS. Bruce refers to "contradictory accounts" regarding Pickett ever even meeting Lincoln and accuses LaSalle of making up stories about the friendship. See also George Anson Bruce to Benjamin Pierson Owen, December 27, 1927, and George Anson Bruce to Margaret Heth Vaden, April 22, 1928, ibid.; Gallagher, "Widow and Her Soldier," 337; Patterson, *Lincoln in American Memory*, 92; and Landrum, "General Who Studied Law in Quincy."

92. Freeman, *Lee's Lieutenants*, 3:688; Chris Calkins, "Appomattox Campaign," in Current, ed., *Encyclopedia of the Confederacy*, 1:45–47.

93. T. G. Barham Typescript, F&S.

94. James I. Robertson, in *18th Virginia Infantry*, 33, estimates that Pickett had about 2,000 men left. Harrison, in *Pickett's Men*, 153, puts the number at 2,200. William R. Aylett, "Pickett's Division," Aylett Family Papers, VHS.

95. Henry A. Wise, "The Career of Wise's Brigade," *Southern Historical Society Papers* 25 (1897): 18.

96. W. H. Palmer to W. H. Taylor, June 24, 1911, Taylor Papers, VSL.

97. Freeman, *R. E. Lee*, 4:112; "Tabular statement of officers and men of the Confederate Army paroled at Appomattox Court-House," OR 46 (1):1277; Freeman, *Lee's Lieutenants*, 3:750. In *Pickett's Men*, 66–67, Harrison estimated 800. See signed paroled prisoner's pass for T. P. Wallace, April 10, 1865, Armistead-Blanton-Wallace Papers, VHS.

98. Mosby, *Memoirs*, 381–82; Freeman quotes another version in *R. E. Lee*, 4: 112.

99. James Longstreet, "Introduction," in Pickett, *Pickett and His Men*, xii–xiii.

CHAPTER TWELVE

1. Pickett, *What Happened to Me*, 185.

2. Ibid., 186. Union General E. O. C. Ord described Pickett as one of "many

prominent and formerly wealthy citizens . . . [who were] asking me what they shall do to make their bread, expressing their great desire to co-operate with this Government if they can have peace and protection" (E. O. C. Ord to E. M. Stanton, April 19, 1865, *OR* 46 [3]:835).

3. George E. Pickett to Andrew Johnson, June 1, 1865, Johnson Papers, LOC. Interestingly, George's uncle Andrew Johnston personally presented this letter to Johnson on June 6. It was not uncommon for officers like Pickett to make such requests, and in many cases Johnson granted them pardons, to the extent that he angered Radical Republicans. See Faust, ed., *Historical Times Illustrated Encyclopedia*, 12, and Browning, *Diary*, 2:32.

4. George E. Pickett to Andrew Johnson, June 1, 1865, Johnson Papers, LOC. Pickett also took an oath of allegiance to the United States on June 15, 1865, but at least initially, this oath meant nothing without a specific pardon from Johnson. See Record from Office of Provost Marshall, Richmond, Virginia, June 16, 1865, Johnson Papers, LOC.

5. Pickett, *What Happened to Me*, 200–203; quote from 202. Thousands of ex-Confederates fled the United States for Europe and South America, some fearing Reconstruction, others feeling disgust and disappointment with Confederate defeat, and others merely seeking adventure or business opportunity. Daniel Sutherland, who offers the best overview of this phenomenon to date, notes that those individuals who left only temporarily went to Canada and that very few actually feared for their lives as George Pickett did. Those who sought permanent exile went to Mexico, Brazil, Venezuela, or other Latin American locations where they could have slaves and try to recreate southern slaveholding society. Jubal Early, John Breckenridge, and William Preston were other ex-Confederates who spent some or all of their exile in Canada. See Sutherland, *The Confederate Carpetbaggers*, 10–28.

6. Pickett, *What Happened to Me*, 207.

7. Ibid., 216.

8. Ibid., 233.

9. Bardolph, "Confederate Dilemma," pt. 2, 207; Testimony of John B. Neathery, *Executive Document No. 98*, 39th Congress, 61–63; Eugene Grissom to John A. Campbell, November 23, 1865, ibid., 58; Joseph Holt Report, December 12, 1865, ibid., 47–48. There is evidence that the investigation began as early as June 1865 in a sworn and notarized statement of Walter Harrison to Andrew Johnson, June 15, 1865, Browning Papers, Illinois State Historical Library, Springfield, copy in Pickett Family Typescript Notebook, VHS, and editor's note to George E. Pickett to Andrew Johnson, June 1, 1865, Bergeron, ed., *Papers of Andrew Johnson*, 8:165, 3 n. On June 19, 1865, Secretary of War Edwin Stanton notified Johnson, "General Pickett stands charged with the unlawful hanging of twenty [sic] citizens of North Carolina, and the case is now under investigation in North Carolina" (Edwin Stanton to Andrew Johnson, June 19, 1865, *Executive Document No. 11*, 7).

10. Several former Confederate officers cited Pickett as the highest ranking officer with the authority to order such action. See *Executive Document No. 98*, 39th Congress, 74, 75, 77.

11. Joseph Holt to Edwin M. Stanton, December 30, 1865, ibid., 53–55.

12. Pickett, *What Happened to Me*, 250.

13. Ibid., 261.

14. Ibid., 261–70; Pickett, *Pickett and His Men*, 67–85. LaSalle recounted the Montreal experience in private conversation with Arthur Inman's wife, Evelyn, in 1926 (recorded in Inman, *Diary*, 2:328). Proof of the Picketts borrowing money while in Canada is from diary entry, October 10, 1865, Lee Diary, SHC; Levin, *"This Awful Drama,"* 173; and Andrew Johnston to George E. Pickett, July 29, 1865, fragment only, Pickett Family Typescript Notebook, VHS.

15. Diary entries for June 6, 16, November 3, 1865, in Browning, *Diary*, 2:32, 34, 48. Browning was a former Kentucky lawyer, Illinois senator, and political adviser to Presidents Lincoln and Johnson, and a friend of Andrew Johnston. He successfully obtained pardons for George's uncle Andrew, his brother Charles, his sister Jenny, and his cousin and former staff member William Symington. Browning once referred to the Johnstons (Pickett's mother's family) as "very estimable" and who "seem to live happily together" (*Diary*, 1:212–13; 2:34, 38, 46). See also editor's notes included with George E. Pickett to Andrew Johnson, June 1, 1865, Bergeron, ed., *Papers of Andrew Johnson*, 8:165, 3 n.

16. It is not known if LaSalle's sickness was due to the stress of living in exile, or a specific ailment. George was clearly concerned when he wrote a friend a few months later: "She has I am sorry to say suffered much during the winter." For this and other evidence of her poor health, see George E. Pickett to Benjamin Starke, March 16, 1866, Pickett-Starke Letters, OHS, and George E. Pickett to [Samuel Barron], December 8, 1865, Barron Papers, AL.

17. George E. Pickett to Ulysses S. Grant, March 12, 1865, Amnesty Papers, RG 94, NA; emphasis in original; Ulysses Grant to Andrew Johnson, March 16, 1866, *Papers of Ulysses S. Grant*, 16:120–22; Hall, "Atonement," 21.

18. George E. Pickett to Benjamin Starke, March 16, 1866, Pickett-Starke Letters, OHS. Portions of this letter are written in Chinook.

19. Pickett, *What Happened to Me*, 202. E. P. Alexander wrote Pickett in 1867: "I have seen how hotly our Yankee friends have been after you, but trust they will simply have to take it out in hate. They would doubtlessly like to murder you, but fortunately for us all the Old Army officers are not dead in honor and have too much power to be run over. So I hope we will all come out alright" (Edward Porter Alexander to George E. Pickett, January 16, 1867, Pickett Family Typescript Notebook, VHS).

20. Henry Stanberry to Andrew Johnson, July 26, 1866, Bergeron, ed., *Papers of Andrew Johnson*, 10:740–41.

21. William H. Doherty to Joseph Holt, July 16, 1866, *Executive Document No. 11*, 5. Holt attached his endorsement to Doherty's letter, recommending that Pickett be immediately arrested and tried, in Joseph Holt to E. D. Townsend, "Indorsement," July 21, 1865, ibid.

22. Henry Stanberry to Andrew Johnson, December 6, 1866, ibid., 6; see also William G. Moore to M. Stitt, December 5, 1866, and House of Representatives Resolution, December 3, 1866, 39th Congress, 2nd Session, both in Amnesty Papers, RG 94, NA.

23. Edwin Stanton to Andrew Johnson, December 10, 1866, *Executive Document No. 11*, 3. In July, the War Department had stated that Pickett had not been brought to

trial because of a lack of evidence needed from "rebel sources" (E. D. Townsend to Edwin M. Stanton, July 27, 1866, ibid.).

24. Faust, ed., *Historical Times Illustrated Encyclopedia*, 12; editor's notes to George E. Pickett to Andrew Johnston, June 1, 1865, Bergeron, ed., *Papers of Andrew Johnson*, 8:165, 3 n.

25. Pickett, "My Soldier," 569.

26. George E. Pickett to Benjamin Starke, March 16, 1866, Starke-Pickett Letters, OHS.

27. For more on his various postwar financial endeavors, see James Tilton to George Pickett, March 5, 1874, Pickett Family Typescript Notebook, VHS; Pickett, "My Soldier," 569; Freeman, *Lee's Lieutenants*, 3:771; George E. Pickett to [James Gordon], February 5, 1869, Pickett Papers, HHL; and George E. Pickett to George A. Martin, May 11, 1871, Martin Papers, SHC. George also accepted a pseudomilitary position as special agent for the Virginia state militia in the early 1870s. LaSalle later tried to gain recompensation for her husband's brief service but apparently failed. See James Kemper to J. Hoge Taylor, July 11, 1879, and James Kemper to Benjamin Barbour Johnson, February 5, 1880, Kemper Family Papers, VHS. LaSalle's allegation that he turned down a nomination for governor is highly suspect, not only because of George's apparent disregard for politics but also because of his unpopularity that seemed to carry over from his Civil War days.

28. Pickett, *What Happened to Me*, 201.

29. For example, see George E. Pickett to William Roane Aylett, January 14, 1867, Aylett Family Papers, VHS. See also Reardon, "The Image of 'Pickett's Charge,'" 146–47, and *Pickett's Charge*, 86, for discussion of why he did not join the "early Lee bloc." For more on his avoidance of politics, see Freeman, *Lee's Lieutenants*, 3:771, and Walter C. Newberry, "New Union Dedication for Memorial Day," *Confederate Veteran* 9 (June 1901): 258.

30. George E. Pickett, "Address Delivered to This Company upon Completion of a Flag by the Ladies of Richmond," n.d., Pickett Papers, HHL; emphasis in original, capitalization standardized by author. LaSalle admitted that this speech represented "perhaps the only writing in existence by the General about the battle, since his original report to Lee on the battle was destroyed at Lee's request" (LaSalle Corbell Pickett to Henry Huntington, October 6, 1925, Pickett Papers, HHL).

31. Details of this often repeated story are from Mosby, *Memoirs*, 380–81; John S. Mosby to Eppa Hunton, March 25, 1911, Mosby Papers, VHS; and Freeman, *Lee's Lieutenants*, 1:xxiii–xxiv.

32. Corbell was born in 1865 or 1866 and died at the age of eight sometime in 1874, but little more is known about him. According to LaSalle, he was talented artistically and musically, precocious and angelic. When he was only three years old, he expressed "a strong aversion to colored people," which proved problematic, LaSalle explained, in finding him a nurse. See Pickett, *What Happened to Me*, 315–20, 340–52.

33. George E. Pickett to "My Dear Friend," December 14, 18[?], Pickett Family Typescript Notebook, VHS. In another letter, George wrote a friend that he was "still in bed and very weak" (George E. Pickett to I. H. Carrington, December 29, 1868, Carrington Papers, PL).

34. George E. Pickett to "My Dear Friend," December 14, 18[?], Pickett Family

Typescript Notebook, VHS. Other examples of her poor health are included in George E. Pickett to Charles Ellis Jr., May 18, 1875, Munford-Ellis Papers, PL, in which George referred to her being "troubled with that uncomfortable feeling on her left side," and George E. Pickett to Benjamin Starke, November 20, 18[?], Pickett-Starke Letters, OHS, in which he mentioned LaSalle suffering from a sore throat and croup. LaSalle apparently did have at least one nurse to help with the children. See Pickett, *What Happened to Me*. 314.

35. George E. Pickett to Benjamin Starke, March 16, 1866, Pickett-Starke Letters, OHS.

36. W. Heth to George E. Pickett, March 23, 1869, Pickett Family Typescript Notebook, VHS.

37. George E. Pickett to Collier Cabell, March 4, 1869, Cabell Family Papers, VHS. See also George E. Pickett to Benjamin Starke, March 16, 1866, Pickett-Starke Letters, OHS, where he expresses similar sentiments. It is also revealing that he frequently used military imagery in his postwar correspondence. He spoke of a "council of war," conducting a "campaign," and "winter quarters," in George E. Pickett to James Kemper, September 12, 187[?], Kemper Papers, AL; and in George E. Pickett to Simon Buckner Bolivar, June 7, 1869, Pickett Papers, HHL, he spoke of "conducting a vigorous campaign" and "mak[ing] an active campaign" when he referred to selling insurance.

38. James Tilton to George E. Pickett, March 5, 1874, Pickett Family Typescript Notebook, VHS.

39. Pickett, ed., *Heart of a Soldier*, 189.

40. LaSalle did not give an actual date of Corbell's death (or birth), but one of the letters published in *Heart of a Soldier* and in the Inman Papers, JHL, referring to Corbell's death in the recent past, is dated January 1874. LaSalle may have changed the date of his death to Easter to enhance her Christlike portrait of him. See George E. Pickett to LaSalle Corbell Pickett, January 1874, typescript letter, Inman Papers, JHL; also published in Pickett, ed., *Heart of a Soldier*, 208–9, with no date. Interestingly, Inman chose to omit this letter from *Soldier of the South*. For LaSalle's detailed description of Corbell's death, see Pickett, *What Happened to Me*, 340–51.

41. Pickett, "My Soldier," 569–70. His obituary listed his cause of death as "gastric fever," and his death certificate stated the cause as abscess of liver. Dr. Jack K. Welsh, in correspondence with the author, explained that such abscesses took two forms, bacterial or amebic. Welsh wrote, "In general, those caused by bacteria can be metastic—from some source outside of the liver—or secondary to disease of the biliary system. Either one can produce symptoms (fever, pain, debility, and possible jaundice) for weeks to years, before death" (Jack K. Welsh to Lesley Gordon-Burr, September 5, 1994, in possession of author). See also Welsh, *Medical Histories*, 172, and "Obituary," Richmond *Daily Dispatch*, July 31, 1875.

42. Quoted in Reardon, *Pickett's Charge*, 82.

43. *Atlanta Daily Constitution*, August 3, 1875.

44. Ibid.; Reardon, *Pickett's Charge*, 80–81; Richmond *Daily Dispatch*, July 31, August 2, 3, 1875.

45. Reardon, "The Image of 'Pickett's Charge,' " 48, and *Pickett's Charge*, 82–83; Richmond *Daily Dispatch*, October 14, 1916; *Atlanta Daily Constitution*, October 26,

1875; *Atlanta Daily Herald*, October 26, 1875; Dabney, *Richmond*, 232; Hollywood Cemetery Souvenir, MC.

46. LaSalle Corbell Pickett to James T. Pickett, February 9, 1878, Meany Papers, UWL.

47. Pickett, *What Happened to Me*, 363.

48. James Tilton to James Tilton Pickett, November 10, 1875, Meany Papers, UWL. LaSalle implied in her autobiography that her kindness toward Union prisoners during the war helped her obtain and keep this position. See *What Happened to Me*, 156. See also Willard and Livermore, eds., *Woman of the Century*, 571.

49. For discussion of the impact of war on southern white women's status, see Scott, *Southern Lady*; Faust, *Mothers of Invention*; Rable, *Civil Wars*; and Friedman, *Enclosed Garden*.

50. LaSalle Corbell Pickett to James Tilton Pickett, February 9, 1878, Meany Papers, UWL; Pickett, *Literary Hearthstones*, 253.

51. James Tilton to James Tilton Pickett, November 10, 1875, Meany Papers, UWL.

52. Jessie Knight Grisdale to [?], n.d., Pickett Collection, WSCM. James's foster family, the Collinses, were apparently quite devoted to him and wanted to keep him under their care. In the fall of 1865, Tilton assured James's foster father that he would see Pickett and "advise him to let you keep the boy always" (James Tilton to John Collins, September 26, 1865, Meany Papers, UWL).

53. James T. Pickett Diary, quoted in unpublished biography by Thomas Bibb, Pickett Collection, WSCM.

54. Bibb biography, Pickett Collection, WSCM.

55. Biographical information is from James T. Pickett to Catherine Collins, November 24, 1883, January 8, 1885, May 14, 18[?], Meany Papers, UWL; Jessie Grisdale Knight to [?], n.d., A. L. Callow to Jessie Grisdale Knight, April 11, 1933, and Jessie Grisdale Knight to T. W. Bibb, April 12, 1933, Pickett Collection, WSCM; and Edson, *Fourth Corner*, 115–25. In June 1880, James was living with nine white men in a Mason County boardinghouse and his occupation was listed as "employee of lumber man." The 10th U.S. Census, 1880, Mason County, Washington Territory, also claims that he was unemployed for two months of the census year.

56. Edson, *Fourth Corner*, 123. LaSalle's original letters to James have not surfaced, but a scattering of typescript copies exist at the University of Washington and are reprinted in Edson's book. James's foster mother did not want Professor Meany to have possession of any of her adopted son's papers, but somehow Meany managed to attain them.

57. Examples include LaSalle Corbell Pickett to James T. Pickett, February 9, 1878, and LaSalle Corbell Pickett to "My Dear Son," May 2, 18[?], Meany Papers, UWL.

58. LaSalle Corbell Pickett to [James T. Pickett], May 2, 18[?], ibid.

59. W. D. Campbell to Jessie Grisdale Knight, April 18, 1933, Pickett Collection, WSCM.

60. H. C. McReavy to Jessie K. Grisdale, August 19, 1933, ibid.

61. Ibid.; Edson *Fourth Corner*, 119, 125.

62. Binns, *Laurels Are Cut Down*, 10.

63. LaSalle Corbell Pickett to [James T. Pickett], May 2, 18[?], Meany Papers, UWL. James commented on LaSalle's continued poor health in James T. Pickett to

Catherine Collins, April 6, 1884, ibid.; original in possession of Pickett House, Bellingham, Washington. Additional evidence of her continued poor health is from LaSalle Corbell Pickett, "General George E. Pickett's Service on San Juan Island," *Seattle Post-Intelligencer*, March 3, 1907.

CHAPTER THIRTEEN

1. Pickett, *Pickett and His Men*, 89. Gallagher discusses her plagiarism of Harrison in "Widow and Her Soldier," 329–44.

2. Pickett, *Pickett and His Men*, v.

3. James Longstreet, "Introduction," in *Pickett and His Men*, xi–xii. Many wives of Civil War generals and politicians pursued literary careers and became "professional widows." Examples include Helen Longstreet, Mary Anna Jackson, Varina Davis, and Libbie Custer.

4. LaSalle Corbell Pickett to Fannie C. Ryals, August 11, 1899, MC. The book's popularity led Lipincott to put out a new illustrated edition of *Pickett and His Men* in 1912. A sampling of favorable reviews appears in an advertisement for her books in *Confederate Veteran* 25, no. 5 (May 1917): 240. See also *The Literary Digest* 47 (September 27, 1913): 536; *The Bookman* 37 (July 1913): 564; *Dial* 54 (June 13, 1913): 513; and LaSalle Corbell to Edmond S. Meany, November 7, 1912, Meany Papers, UWL.

5. Pickett, *What Happened to Me*, 30, 74.

6. Pickett, *Ebil Eye*, 145.

7. Pickett, *What Happened to Me*, 1–33, 74; Scott, *Southern Lady* 4; Farnham, *Education of the Southern Belle*, 75.

8. In 1928, Margaret Heth Vaden wrote: "I have inquired about Mrs. Pickett the widow of my cousin and hear that she lives comfortable in Washington with a companion. I reckon she must have accumulated a nice little sum from her books" (Margaret Heth Vaden to George Anson Bruce, May 18, 1928, Bruce Family Papers, VHS).

9. George Anson Bruce to Margaret Heth Vaden, April 22, 1928, ibid. Mention of Pickett lecturing in Boston for the "Keith Vaudeville management" is in "Something about Entertainment," clipping from unnamed newspaper, 1910, BC.

10. Reardon, *Pickett's Charge*, 62–213; Kinsel, "From Turning Point to Peace Memorial." For more on reunionism and memory, see Silber, *The Romance of Reunion*, and Foster, *Ghosts of the Confederacy*.

11. *New York Times*, July 5, 1887.

12. Ibid.; Reardon, *Pickett's Charge*, 97–102.

13. LaSalle Corbell Pickett to Lida Perry, February 28, 1889, Pickett Papers, PL.

14. LaSalle Corbell Pickett to Lida Perry, May 21, 1906, Civil War Documents, Accession II, ML. Perry was evidently a distant cousin of George's.

15. Gallagher discusses her plagiarism and these controversial letters in "Widow and Her Soldier," 329–44. Letters at the Virginia Historical Society and Brown University do not match George's handwriting and appear to be forgeries.

16. Pickett, *Kunnoo Sperit and Others*, xiv, xvi.

17. Alderman and Harris, eds., *Library of Southern Literature*, 15:343. For discussion of Gilded Age writers and northern interest in the "plantation tradition," see

Flusche, "Private Plantation," 38; Foster, *Ghosts of the Confederacy*, 7; Silber, *Romance of Reunion*, 2, 122–23; and Connelly and Bellows, *God and General Longstreet*, 49.

18. Charles E. Hooker and O. O. Howard quoted in Slayton Lyceum Bureau brochure, Meany Papers, UWL.

19. Quoted in National Chautauqua Bureau brochure, Inman Papers, JHL.

20. Editorial in *Carolina and the Southern Cross* 2, no. 4 (July 1914). George Anson Bruce threatened to expose the falsity of her Lincoln-Pickett stories but opted not to do anything. See George Anson Bruce to Benjamin Pierson Owen, December 27, 1927, Bruce Family Papers, VHS. Gallagher also discusses the slim chance of veterans attacking her in "Widow and Her Soldier," 343–44.

21. Brooks, "To Mrs. LaSalle Corbell Pickett," 175.

22. "Mrs. Pickett and Her Books," 237.

23. Pickett, *Literary Hearthstones*; Pickett, *Across My Path*, 5–7, 64, 95–97.

24. LaSalle Corbell Pickett to Mrs. M. E. Knight, December 3, 1911, Pickett Collection, WSCM. Compare to Pickett, *Bugles of Gettysburg*, 20–21, and *What Happened to Me*, 34–35.

25. Leckie, *Elizabeth Bacon Custer*, xxiii.

26. LaSalle Corbell Pickett to Edmond S. Meany, October 7, 1904, Meany Papers, UWL; LaSalle Corbell Pickett to O. G. Wall, January 26, 1907, reprinted in the *Seattle Post Intelligencer*, March 3, 1907; quote from LaSalle Corbell Pickett to Edmond S. Meany, November 7, 1912, Meany Papers, UWL.

27. LaSalle Corbell Pickett to Mrs. Edward J. Parker, March 31, 1911, Pickett Papers, HQAC.

28. LaSalle Corbell Pickett to Robert Burwell, May 29, 1911, Burwell Papers, EGSL.

29. LaSalle Corbell Pickett to Selma Lewisohn, May 22, 1925, Pickett Papers, HHL.

30. Ibid. Further evidence of her failing health and money troubles comes from a collection of letters Pickett wrote Henry Huntington from 1925 to 1927. In these she referred to her poor health and expressed gratitude for his financial assistance. See LaSalle Corbell Pickett to Henry E. Huntington, October 6, 29, 1925, [January 1926], and March 5, 1926, Pickett Papers, HHL.

31. This exchange is based on Evelyn Inman to Arthur Crew Inman, November 22, 1926, in Inman, *Diary*, 2:327–28. Additional details from Selma Lewisohn to Joseph Duveen, n.d., Pickett Papers, HHL, and "Obituary," *New York Times*, March 23, 1931.

32. Selma Lewisohn to Joseph Duveen, n.d., Pickett Papers, HHL. Examples of "Mother Pickett," in undated obituary in United Daughters of the Confederacy, Virginia Division, Boydton, Mecklenburg Co., Chapter No. 157, Scrapbook, 1913–57, VHS. She called herself "Mother Thine" in LaSalle Corbell Pickett to Selma Lewisohn, May 22, 1925, Pickett Papers, HHL.

33. Pickett, *Across My Path*, 126–27. See also Brantley, *Feminine Sense*, 141–44, 157–58, 163–64, for discussion of southern women writing memoirs and autobiography and the influence of Romanticism. Brantley focuses on Katherine Anne Porter and Lillian Hellman, who seemed to share LaSalle Pickett's insistence of "truth in art."

34. Pickett, *Across My Path*, 112.

35. Pickett, *What Happened to Me*, 185.

36. Quoted in Fitts, "Pickett's Wife to Be Reburied," 1. In 1931, the Junior Hollywood Memorial Association apparently tried a compromise by offering to bury

both Picketts in the officers' section, but the family refused the offer. The Pickett family fully supported (and participated in the memorial service marking) LaSalle's re-interment in 1998. Details of the 1931 controversy are from *Washington Post*, March 29, 1931; *New York Times*, March 29, 1931; and Mitchell, *Hollywood Cemetery*, 137–38.

37. Undated obituary in United Daughters of the Confederacy, Virginia Division, Boydton, Mecklenburg Co., Chapter No. 157, Scrapbook, 1913–57, VHS. Quote from obituary in the *Washington Post*, March 23, 1931, which included the following description of this final book: "It contained reminiscences of the hazardous journey she made with her small son to Canada at the end of the Civil War to join her husband, who fled there in exile."

BIBLIOGRAPHY

PRIMARY SOURCES
Manuscript Collections
Atlanta, Ga.
  Emory University
    James Longstreet Papers
Bellingham, Wash.
  Bellingham Public Library
    Fort Bellingham, Verticle File
      Joseph K. F. Mansfield, "Report of the Inspection of Fort Bellingham in
        December 1858" (copy of original)
    Pickett House, Verticle File
  Washington State Archives, Regional Branch
    Whatcom County Deed Records
  Western Washington University
    Center for Pacific Northwest Studies
      Howard E. Buswell Collection
      P. R. Jeffcott Collection
Carbondale, Ill.
  Morris Library, Southern Illinois University
    Civil War Documents
Chapel Hill, N.C.
  Louis Round Wilson Library, University of North Carolina
    Southern Historical Collection
      Edward Porter Alexander Papers
      Confederate Inspection Book, 1863–65
      Bryan Grimes Papers
      Edwin Gray Lee Diary
      James Longstreet Papers
      George A. Martin Papers
      Raphael J. Moses Papers
      John Paris Papers
      Glenn Tucker Papers
      Charles S. Venable Papers
Charlottesville, Va.
  Alderman Library, University of Virginia
    Samuel Barron Paper
    John W. Daniel Papers
    James Kemper Papers
Concord, N.H.
  New Hampshire Historical Society
    John B. Bachelder Papers

Durham, N.C.
  William R. Perkins Library, Duke University
    Braxton Bragg Papers
    I. H. Carrington Papers
    Monroe Fulkerson Cockrell Papers
    John Adams Elder Papers
    Richard L. Maury Papers
    Munford-Ellis Papers
Fredericksburg and Spotsylvania National Military Park, Va.
  T. G. Barham Typescript
  Prillaman Family Letters
Hampton, Va.
  Edwin C. Cotten Private Collection
    Corbell Family Bible Page
Olympia, Wash.
  Washington State Capital Museum
    James Tilton Pickett Collection
Portland, Oreg.
  Oregon Historical Society
    Pickett-Starke Letters
Providence, R.I.
  John Hay Library, Brown University
    Arthur Crew Inman Papers
Quincy, Ill.
  Brenner Library, Quincy University
    Landry Genosky Papers
  Historical Society of Quincy and Adams County
    George E. Pickett Papers
Richmond, Va.
  Museum of the Confederacy
    Ed Baird Papers
    George K. Griggs Diary
    Henry Heth Papers
    Miscellaneous Papers
    James Thomas Petty Diary, 1862–63
    G. Moxley Sorrel Diary
  Virginia Historical Society
    Armistead-Blanton-Wallace Papers
    Aylett Family Papers
    Bruce Family Papers
    Cabell Family Papers
    Carrington Family Papers
    Cocke Family Papers
    Collier Family Papers
    John W. Daniel Papers
    Dearing Family Papers

John Walter Fairfax Papers
Gregory Family Papers
Heth Family Papers
Kemper Family Papers
Osmun Latrobe Diary, typescript
Robert E. Lee Headquarters Papers
Robert E. Lee Papers
Meade Family Papers
John Kirkley Mitchell Papers
John S. Mosby Papers
Henry T. Owen Papers
Pickett and Maynard Account Book
Pickett Family Typescript Notebook
Charles Pickett Papers
United Daughters of the Confederacy Scrapbook
John Dudley Whitehead Papers
Virginia State Library
Minge Family Genealogical Papers
Henry T. Owen Papers
Report of the Board of Visitors to the United States Military Academy, 1842
Walter Herron Taylor Papers (microfilm)
San Juan Island, Wash.
Michael Vouri Private Collection
George E. Pickett Papers
San Marino, Calif.
Henry E. Huntington Library
George and LaSalle Pickett Papers
Seattle, Wash.
University of Washington Libraries
Manuscripts and University Archives Division
Edmond S. Meany Papers
Springfield, Ill.
Illinois State Historical Library
Orville H. Browning Papers
Washington, D.C.
Library of Congress
Andrew Johnson Papers
National Archives
Record Group 94
Adjutant General's Office, United States Army, 1800–1860
Amnesty Papers
Returns from Regular Army Infantry Regiments, June 1821–December 1916
Record Group 107
Office of the Secretary of War, 1801–70
Record Group 109
Adjutant and Inspector General's Office, Confederate States Army, 1861–65
Compiled Service Records of Confederate General Officers and Staff Officers

West Point, N.Y.
   United States Military Academy Archives
      "Circumstances of Parents of Cadets," 1842–43
      George W. Cullum Papers
      Library Circular Collections, 1842
      George E. Pickett Papers
      Record of Special Requests for Library Materials, 1840–50
      Register of Delinquencies, Class of 1846
Williamsburg, Va.
   Earl Gregg Swem Library, College of William and Mary
      Baird Family Papers
      Robert A. Bright Papers, Southall Papers
      Burwell Family Papers
      Joseph E. Johnston Papers
      Overton Family Papers

Newspapers

Atlanta Constitution
Atlanta Daily Herald
Daily Alta Californian
The (Fayetteville) *North Carolina Presbyterian*
Memphis *Commercial Appeal*
New Bern *North Carolina Times*
New York Times
North Carolina Presbyterian
Olympia *Pioneer and Democrat*
Philadelphia *Weekly Times*
Quincy Herald-Whig
Quincy Daily Whig
Raleigh *Daily Confederate*
Richmond *Daily Dispatch*
Richmond Dispatch
Richmond *Times*
Richmond Times-Dispatch
Richmond Whig and Public Advertiser
San Juan Islander
Seattle Post-Intelligencer
Southern Illustrated News
Washington Post
Whatcom County *Northern Light*

Government Documents

Executive Document No. 8. House of Representatives, 30th Congress, 1st Session.
Executive Document No. 98. House of Representatives, 36th Congress, 1st Session.
Executive Document No. 11. House of Representatives, 39th Congress, 2nd Session.

Executive Document No. 98. House of Representatives, 39th Congress, 1st Session.
Executive Document No. 1. Senate, 30th Congress, 1st Session.
Executive Document No. 96. Senate, 34th Congress, 1st Session.
Executive Document No. 10. Senate, 36th Congress, 1st Session.
The Official Atlas of the Civil War. Compiled by Calvin D. Cowles. Washington, D.C.: Government Printing Office, 1891–93.
Report of the Board of Visitors to the United States Military Academy, 1842. Washington, D.C.: Government Printing Office, 1842.
U.S. Census Office. 5th Census of the United States, 1830: Population Schedule, Henrico County, Va.
——. 6th Census of the United States, 1840: Population and Slave Schedules, Nansemond County, Va.
——. 7th Census of the United States, 1850: Population and Slave Schedules, Dinwiddie County, Va.
——. 7th Census of the United States, 1850: Population and Slave Schedules, Henrico County, Va.
——. 7th Census of the United States, 1850: Population and Slave Schedules, St. Mary's Parish, La.
——. 8th Census of the United States, 1860: Population and Slave Schedules, Nansemond County, Va.
——. 8th Census of the United States, 1860: Population Schedule, San Juan Island Precinct, Washington Territory.
——. 10th Census of the United States, 1880: Population Schedule, Mason County, Washington Territory.
War of the Rebellion: A Compilation of the Official Records of the Union and Confederate Armies. 128 vols. Washington, D.C.: Government Printing Office, 1880–1901.

Printed Diaries, Memoirs, Papers, and Reminiscences

Alexander, Edward Porter. *Fighting for the Confederacy: The Personal Recollections of General Edward Porter Alexander.* Edited by Gary Gallagher. Chapel Hill: University of North Carolina, 1989.
——. *Military Memoirs of a Confederate: A Critical Narrative.* 1907. Reprint, New York: Da Capo Press, 1993.
The Annals of War Written by Leading Participants, North and South. Philadelphia, Pa.: The Times Publishing Company, 1879.
Archer, James J. "The James Archer Letters: A Marylander in the Civil War." Edited by C. A. Porter Hopkins. *Maryland Historical Magazine* 56 (1961): 72–93, 125–49, 352–83.
"Army Officers Report on Indian War Treaties." *Washington Historical Quarterly* 19 (April 1928): 134–41.
Bachelder, John B. *The Story of the Battle of Gettysburg.* Boston: John P. Ball, 1904.
Bain, Hope. "Quotations from the Diary of the Reverend Hope Bain." *A History of Universalism in North Carolina.* N.p.: Universalist Convention of North Carolina, 1968.

Barrett, John G., and W. Buck Yearns, eds. *North Carolina Civil War Documentary.*
Chapel Hill: University of North Carolina Press, 1980.

Basler, Roy P., ed. *Collected Works: The Abraham Lincoln Association, Springfield,
Illinois.* 9 vols. New Brunswick, N.J.: Rutgers University Press, 1953.

Bergeron, Paul N., ed. *The Papers of Andrew Johnson.* Vols. 8 and 10. Knoxville:
University of Tennessee Press, 1989, 1992.

Bishcoff, William N. Introduction to *We Were Not Summer Soldiers: The Indian War
Diary of Plympton J. Kelly, 1855–1856,* by Plympton Kelly. Tacoma: Washington
State Historical Society, 1976.

Bleser, Carol K., ed. *The Hammonds of Redcliffe.* New York: Oxford University Press,
1981.

Bright, Robert A. "Pickett's Charge." *Southern Historical Society Papers* 31 (1903):
228–36.

Brooks, Fred Emerson. "To Mrs. LaSalle Corbell Pickett." *Confederate Veteran* 11, no.
4 (1903): 175.

Browning, Orville Hickman, *The Diary of Orville Hickman Browning.* 2 vols. Edited
by Theodore Calvin Pease. Springfield, Ill.: Illinois State Library, 1925–33.

Buel, Clarence C., and Robert U. Johnson, eds. *Battles and Leaders of the Civil War.*
4 vols. New York: The Century Co., 1884–88.

Burgwyn, William H. S. *A Captain's War: The Letters and Diaries of William H. S.
Burgwyn, 1861–1865.* Edited by Herbert M. Schiller. Shippensburg, Pa.: White
Mane Publishing Co., 1994.

Butler, Benjamin F. *Autobiography and Personal Reminiscences of Major-General
Benj. F. Butler; Butler's Book.* Boston: A. M. Thayers, 1892.

——. *Private and Official Correspondence of Gen. Benjamin Butler, during the Period
of the Civil War.* 5 vols. Norwood, Mass.: Jessie Ames Marshall, 1917.

Chambers, Henry A. *Diary of Captain Henry A. Chambers.* Edited by T. H. Pearce.
Wendell, N.C.: Broadfoot Bookmark, 1983.

"Confederate Military History." *Confederate Veteran* 7, no. 10 (October 1899): 459.

Conner, James. *Letters of General James Conner, C.S.A.* Edited by Mary Conner
Moffet. Columbia, S.C.: R. L. Bryan, 1950.

Cowan, Andrew. "Repulsing Pickett's Charge." *Civil War Times Illustrated* 3 (August
1964): 27–29.

Crimmins, M. L., ed. "W. G. Freeman's Report of the Eighth Military Department."
Southwestern Historical Quarterly 51 (July 1947–April 1948): 54–58, 167–74, 252–
58, 350–57; 52 (July 1948–April 1949): 100–108, 227–33, 349–54, 444–47; 53 (July
1949–April 1950): 71–77, 202–8, 308–19, 443–73.

Davis, Jefferson. *Jefferson Davis Constitutionalist: His Letters Papers and Speeches.*
Edited by Dunbar Rowland. 10 vols. Jackson, Miss.: J. J. Little & Ives Co., 1923.

Dawson, Francis W. *Reminiscences of Confederate Service, 1861–1865.* Edited by Bell
Irvin Wiley. Baton Rouge: Louisiana State University Press, 1980.

Domschcke, Bernhard. *Twenty Months in Captivity: Memoirs of a Union Officer in
Confederate Prisons.* Edited by Frederick Trautmann. London: Association of
University Presses, 1987.

Dooley, John. *John Dooley, Confederate Soldier, His War Journal.* Edited by Joseph T.
Durkin. Georgetown: Georgetown University Press, 1945.

Easley, D. B. "Saw Pickett 'Riding Grandly Down.'" *Confederate Veteran* 38 (April 1938): 133.

Fitzhugh, E. C. "Letter to I. I. Stevens, April 5, 1857." *Washington Historical Quarterly* 31 (October 1941): 403.

Fremantle, Arthur J. Lyon. *Three Months in the Southern States*. London: William Blackwood and Sons, 1863.

Gaines, E. W. "Fayette Artillery: The Movement on New Berne Thirty-Three Years Ago." *Southern Historical Society Papers* 25 (1897): 288–97.

Gardner, William Montgomery. "Memoirs of Brigadier-General William Montgomery Gardner." Edited by Elizabeth McKinne Gardner. Memphis *Commercial Appeal*, 1912.

Glisan, Rodney. *Journal of Army Life*. San Francisco: A. L. Bancroft and Co., 1874.

Gorgas, Josiah. *The Civil War Diary of General Josiah Gorgas*. Edited by Frank Vandiver. University, Ala.: University of Alabama Press, 1947.

Grant, Ulysses S. *The Papers of Ulysses S. Grant*. Edited by John Simon. Vols. 1–. Carbondale, Ill.: Southern Illinois University Press, 1970–.

———. *Personal Memoirs of U. S. Grant*. 2 vols. New York: Charles L. Webster, 1885.

Griggs, George K. "The Thirty-Eighth Virginia (Steuart's Brigade) at Battle of Five Forks." *Southern Historical Society Papers* 16 (1888): 231.

Grimes, Bryan. *Extracts of Letters of Major General Bryan Grimes to His Wife*. Raleigh, N.C.: Edwards Broughton and Co., 1883.

Haller, Granville O. *San Juan and Secession*. 1897. Reprint, Seattle, Wash.: Shorey Books Store, 1967.

Harrison, Walter. *Pickett's Men: A Fragment of War History*. New York: D. Van Nostrand, 1870.

Haskell, John Cheves. *The Haskell Memoirs*. Edited by Gilbert E. Govan and James W. Livingood. New York: G. P. Putnam's Sons, 1960.

Hawkins, Rush C. *An Account of the Assassination of Loyal Citizens of North Carolina for Having Served in the Union Army*. New York: J. H. Folan Printer, 1897.

Hoke, Jacob. *The Great Invasion of 1863*. Dayton, Ohio: W. J. Shuey, 1887.

Hotchkiss, Jedediah. *Make Me a Map of the Valley: The Civil War Journal of Stonewall Jackson's Topographer*. Edited by Archie P. McDonald. Dallas: Southern Methodist University Press, 1973.

Howard, McHenry. *Recollections of a Maryland Confederate Soldier and Staff Officer under Johnston, Jackson, and Lee*. Baltimore: Williams and Wilkins, 1914.

Hubbs, Paul K. "Pickett's Landing on San Juan and the Cutler Incident." *San Juan Islander*, October 22, 1909.

———. "San Juan Contest." *Seattle Post-Intelligencer*, June 4, 1892.

Hunter, Alexander. *Johnny Reb and Billy Yank*. New York: The Neale Publishing Co., 1905.

Hunton, Eppa. *Autobiography of Eppa Hunton*. Richmond: William Byrd Press, 1933.

Hutter, J. Risque. "The Eleventh at Five Forks Fight." *Southern Historical Society Papers* 35 (1907): 357–62.

Inman, Arthur Crew. *The Inman Diary: A Public and Private Confession*. Edited by Daniel Aaron. 2 vols. Cambridge, Mass.: Harvard University Press, 1985.

———, ed. *Soldier of the South: General Pickett's War Letters to His Wife.* Boston: Houghton Mifflin Co., 1928.

Irby, Richard. *Historical Sketch of the Nottoway Grays.* Richmond: J. W. Fergusson and Son, 1878.

Johnston, David. *Four Years a Soldier.* Princeton, W. Va.: n.p., 1887.

Johnston, Joseph E. *Narrative of Military Operations.* 1874. Reprint, Bloomington: Indiana University Press, 1959.

Jones, J. B. *A Rebel War Clerk's Diary at the Confederate States Capital.* 2 vols. 1866. Reprint, New York: Old Hickory Bookshop, 1935.

Kirk, Ruth, and Carmela Alexander. *Exploring Washington's Past.* Seattle: University of Washington Press, 1990.

Lane, Lydia Spencer. *I Married a Soldier, or Days in the Old Army.* 1893. Reprint, Albuquerque, N. Mex.: Horn and Wallace, 1964.

Lee, Robert E. *Lee's Dispatches to Jefferson Davis, 1862–1865.* Edited by Douglas Southall Freeman. New York: G. P. Putnam's Sons, 1957.

———. *The Wartime Papers of R. E. Lee.* Edited by Clifford Dowdey and Louis H. Manarin. New York: Bramhall House, 1961.

Lewis, John H. *Reminiscences from 1860–1865.* Washington, D.C.: Peake and Co., Publishers, 1895.

Longstreet, James. *From Manassas to Appomattox: Memoirs of the Civil War in America.* Edited by James I. Robertson Jr. 1896. Reprint, Bloomington: Indiana University Press, 1960.

Loyall, B. P. "Capture of the *Underwriter* at New Bern, North Carolina, February 2, 1864." *Southern Historical Society Papers* 27 (1899): 136–44.

McCabe, William Gordon. "Defense of Petersburg." *Southern Historical Society Papers* 2 (December 1876): 257–306.

McCulloch, Robert. "The High Tide at Gettysburg." *Confederate Veteran* 21 (October 1913): 473–76.

McPherson, J. R. "A Private's Account of Gettysburg." *Confederate Veteran* 6 (April 1898): 148–49.

Martin, Rawley. "Colonel Rawley Martin's Account." *Southern Historical Society Papers* 32 (1904): 183–89.

Maury, Dabney H. *Recollections of a Virginian in the Mexican, Indian and Civil War.* New York: Charles Scribner and Sons, 1894.

Maxey, Samuel Bell. "George E. Pickett." *Annual Reunion of the Association of the Graduates of the United States Military Academy.* West Point, N.Y.: USMA, 1876.

Mayo, Joseph C. "Pickett's Charge at Gettysburg." *Southern Historical Society Papers* 34 (1906): 327–35.

Montague's Richmond Directory and Business Advertiser for 1850–1851. Richmond, Va.: Hill Directory Company, 1850.

Moore, Frank. *The Rebellion Record: A Diary of American Events with Documents, Narratives, Illustrative Incidents, Poetry, Etc.* 11 vols. New York: D. Van Nostrand, 1865.

Morgan, W. H. *Personal Reminiscences of the War of 1861–65.* Lynchburg, Va.: J. P. Bell Co., 1911.

Morrison, James L., ed. *The Memoirs of Henry Heth*. Westport, Conn.: Greenwood Press, 1974.

Mosby, John S. *Memoirs of Colonel John S. Mosby*. Edited by Charles W. Russel. Boston: Little Brown and Co., 1917.

"Mrs. Pickett and Her Books." *Confederate Veteran* 24, no. 5 (May 1917): 237.

"Official Diary of First Corps, A.N.V., While Commanded by Lieutenant-General R. H. Anderson, May 7–31st, 1864; June 1st–Oct. 18, 1864." *Southern Historical Society Papers* 7 (October–November 1879): 491–94, 503–12.

Paris, Rev. John. *A Sermon: Preached before Brig.-Gen. Hoke's Brigade, at Kinston, N.C., on the 28th of February, 1864, by Rev. John Paris, Chaplain Fifty-Fourth Regiment, N.C. Troops, upon the Death of Twenty-Men, Who Had Been Executed in the Presence of the Brigade for the Crime of Desertion*. Greensborough, N.C.: A. W. Ingold & Co., 1864.

Peck, William A., Jr. *The Pig War and Other Experiences of William Peck*. Edited by C. Brewster Coulter and Bert Webber. Medford, Oreg.: Webb Research Group, 1993.

Phillips, Ulrich B., ed. *The Correspondence of Robert Toombs, Alexander H. Stephens, and Howell Cobb*. 1913. Reprint, New York: Da Capo, 1970.

Poague, William. *Gunner with Stonewall*. Edited by Monroe F. Cockrell. Jackson, Tenn.: McCowat-Mercer Press, 1957.

Robertson, Frank S. "Memoirs." *Bulletin of the Washington County Historical Society* (1986): 18–19.

Roman, Alfred. *The Military Operations of General Beauregard in the War between the States, 1861–1865*. 2 vols. New York: Harper, 1884.

Sherman, William T. *Memoirs of General William T. Sherman*. 2 vols. New York: Appleton and Co., 1875.

Shotwell, Randolph Abbot. *The Papers of R. A. Shotwell*. Edited by J. G. De Roulhac Hamilton. 3 vols. Raleigh: North Carolina Historical Commission, 1929.

Sims, Benjamin Haggason. "Diary of Benjamin Haggason Sims." In *Confederate Letters and Diaries, 1861–1865*, edited by Walbrook D. Swank, 187–97. Shippensburg, Pa.: Bird Steed Press, 1992.

Sorrel, G. Moxley. *Recollections of a Confederate Staff Officer*. 1905. Reprint, Dayton, Ohio: Morningside, 1978.

Stevens, Isaac I. "Letters of Isaac I. Stevens." Edited by Ronald Todd. *Pacific Northwestern Quarterly* 31 (1940): 403–59.

Stiles, Robert. *Four Years under Marse Robert*. New York: The Neale Publishing Co., 1903.

Taylor, Walter Herron. *Lee's Adjutant: The Wartime Letters of Colonel Walter Herron Taylor, 1862–1865*. Columbia: University of South Carolina Press, 1995.

Tocqueville, Alexis de. *Democracy in America*. Translated by George Lawrence. Edited by J. P. Mayer. New York: Doubleday and Co., Inc., 1969.

Trimble, Isaac Ridgeway. "The Civil War Diary of General Isaac Ridgeway Trimble." *Maryland Historical Magazine* 17 (March 1922): 1–20.

Turnley, Parmenas Taylor. *Reminiscences of Parmenas Taylor Turnley: From the Cradle to Three Score and Ten*. Chicago: Donahue and Henneberry, 1892.

Viele, Teresa Griffin. *Following the Drum: A Glimpse of Frontier Life*. 1858. Reprint, Lincoln: University of Nebraska Press, 1984.

Wise, John S. *The End of an Era*. Boston: Houghton Mifflin Co., 1900.

Withers, Robert Enoch. *Autobiography of an Octogenarian*. Roanoke, Va.: The Stone Printing and M.F.G. Co. Press, 1907.

Wood, William Nathaniel. *Reminiscences of Big I*. Edited by Bell Irvin Wiley. Jackson, Tenn.: McCowat-Mercer Press, 1956.

Woodward, C. Vann., ed. *Mary Chesnut's Civil War*. New Haven: Yale University Press, 1981.

Young, Jesse Bowman. *The Battle of Gettysburg: A Comprehensive Narrative*. New York: Harper and Brothers Publishers, 1913.

Youngblood, William. "Unwritten History of the Gettysburg Campaign." *Southern Historical Society Papers* 38 (January–December 1910): 312–18.

SECONDARY SOURCES
Books

Alderman, Edwin Anderson, and Joel Chandler Harris, eds. *Library of Southern Literature*. New Orleans: The Martin and Hoyt Co., 1907.

Ambrose, Stephen E. *Duty, Honor, Country: A History of West Point*. Baltimore: Johns Hopkins University Press, 1966.

Bachelder, John B. *The Story of the Battle of Gettysburg*. Boston: John D. Ball, 1904.

Banner, Lois W. *American Beauty*. New York: Alfred A. Knopf, 1983.

Barrett, John G. *The Civil War in North Carolina*. Chapel Hill: University of North Carolina Press, 1963.

Barefoot, Daniel. *General Robert F. Hoke: Lee's Modest Warrior*. Winston-Salem, N.C.: John F. Blair, Publisher, 1996.

Bauer, K. Jack. *The Mexican War, 1846–1848*. 1974. Reprint, Lincoln: University of Nebraska Press, 1992.

Bearss, Edwin, and Chris S. Calkins. *The Battle of Five Forks*. 2nd ed. Lynchburg, Va.: H. E. Howard, 1985.

Bell, Robert T. *11th Virginia Infantry*. Lynchburg, Va.: H. E. Howard, 1985.

Binns, Archie. *The Land So Bright*. 1939. Reprint, Corvallis: Oregon State University Press, 1992.

——. *The Laurels Are Cut Down*. New York: Literary Guild of America, 1937.

——. *Northwest Gateway: The Story of the Port of Seattle*. Garden City, N.Y.: Doubleday and Co., 1946.

Blackman, Margaret B. *During My Time: Florence Edenshaw Davidson, a Haida Woman*, rev. ed. Seattle, Wash.: University of Washington Press, 1992.

Bleser, Carol, ed. *In Joy and in Sorrow: Women, Family, and Marriage in the Victorian South, 1830–1900*. New York: Oxford University Press, 1991.

Boatner, Mark M., III. *Civil War Dictionary*. New York: David McKay, 1959.

Boelscher, Marianne. *The Curtain Within: Haida Social and Mythical Discourse*. Vancouver: University of British Columbia Press, 1988.

Brantley, Will. *Feminine Sense in Southern Memoir*. Jackson: University Press of Mississippi, 1993.

Busey, John W., and David G. Martin. *Regimental Strengths and Losses at Gettysburg.* Highstown, N.J.: Longstreet House, 1986.

Bynum, Victoria. *Unruly Women: The Politics of Social and Sexual Control in the Old South.* Chapel Hill: University of North Carolina Press, 1992.

Calkins, Chris M. *The Battles of Appomattox Station and Appomattox Court House, April 8–9, 1865.* Lynchburg, Va.: H. E. Howard, 1987.

Carhart, Edith Beebe. *A History of Bellingham, Washington.* Bellingham: Argonaut Press, 1926.

Castel, Albert. *Winning and Losing in the Civil War: Essays and Stories.* Columbia: University of South Carolina Press, 1996.

Clinton, Catherine, and Nina Silber, eds., *Divided Houses: Gender and the Civil War.* New York: Oxford University Press, 1992.

Coddington, Edwin B. *The Gettysburg Campaign: A Study in Command.* New York: Charles Scribners and Sons, 1968.

Coffman, Edward M. *The Old Army: A Portrait of the American Army in Peacetime, 1784–1898.* New York: Oxford University Press, 1986.

Connelly, Thomas L. *The Marble Man: Robert E. Lee and His Image in American Society.* New York: Alfred A. Knopf, 1977.

Connelly, Thomas L., and Barbara L. Bellows. *God and General Longstreet: The Lost Cause and the Southern Mind.* Baton Rouge: Louisiana State University Press, 1982.

Cooke, John Esten. *A Life of Gen. Robert E. Lee.* New York: D. Appleton, 1871.

Cormier, Steven A. *The Siege of Suffolk: The Forgotten Campaign, April 11–May 4, 1863.* Lynchburg, Va.: H. E. Howard, 1989.

Craven, Avery. *The Coming of the Civil War.* 2nd ed. Chicago: University of Chicago Press, 1957.

Crute, Joseph, Jr. *Confederate Staff Officers.* Powhatan, Va.: Derwent Books, 1982.

Cullum, George W. *Biographical Register of Officers and Graduates of the U.S. Military Academy at West Point from Its Establishment.* 3rd ed. 3 vols. Boston: Houghton Mifflin Co., 1891.

Cunliffe, Marcus. *Soldiers and Civilians: The Martial Spirit in America, 1775–1865.* Boston: Little, Brown and Co., 1968.

Current, Richard N., ed. *Encyclopedia of the Confederacy.* 4 vols. New York: Simon and Schuster, 1993.

Dabney, Virginius. *Richmond: The Story of a City.* Garden City, N.Y.: Doubleday and Co., 1976.

———. *Virginia: The New Dominion.* Garden City, N.Y.: Doubleday and Co., Inc. 1971.

Dawson, Will. *The War That Was Never Fought.* Princeton: Auerbach Publishers, 1971.

Deans, James. *Tales from the Totems of the Hidery.* Chicago: International Folk-lore Association, 1899.

Divine, John. *8th Virginia Infantry.* 2nd ed. Lynchburg, Va.: H. E. Howard, 1984.

Dowdey, Clifford. *Lee's Last Campaign: The Story of Lee and His Men against Grant, 1864.* Boston: Little, Brown and Co., 1960.

———. *The Seven Days: The Emergence of Lee.* New York: Fairfax, 1978.

———. *The Virginia Dynasties.* Boston: Little, Brown and Co., 1969.

Durrill, Wayne. *War of Another Kind: A Southern Community in the Great Rebellion*. New York: Oxford University Press, 1990.

Edson, Lelah Jackson. *The Fourth Corner: Highlights from the Early Northwest*. Seattle, Wash.: Craftsman Press, 1968.

Ekirch, Arthur A., Jr., *The Civilian and the Military*. New York: Oxford University Press, 1956.

Elliot, Charles Winslow. *Winfield Scott: The Soldier and the Man*. New York: Macmillan Co., 1937.

Ellsworth, Eliot, Jr. *West Point in the Confederacy*. New York: G. A. Baker, 1941.

Elshtain, Jean Bethke. *Women and War*. New York: Basic Books, Inc., 1987.

Escott, Paul. *Many Excellent People: Power and Privilege in North Carolina, 1850–1900*. Chapel Hill: University of North Carolina Press, 1985.

Esposito, Vincent J., ed. *West Point Atlas of American Wars*. 2 vols. New York: Praeger, 1959.

Evans, Clement A., ed. *Confederate Military History*. 17 vols. 1899. Reprint, Wilmington, N.C.: Broadfoot Publishing Co., 1987.

Farnham, Christie Anne. *The Education of the Southern Belle: Higher Education and Student Socialization in the Antebellum South*. New York: New York University Press, 1994.

Faulkner, William. *Intruder in the Dust*. New York: Random House, 1948.

Faust, Drew Gilpin. *Mothers of Invention: Women of the Slaveholding South in the American Civil War*. Chapel Hill: University of North Carolina, 1996.

Faust, Patricia, ed. *Historical Times Illustrated Encyclopedia of the Civil War*. New York: Harper and Row, 1986.

Fellman, Michael. *Citizen Sherman: The Life of William Tecumseh Sherman*. New York: Random House, 1995.

——. *Inside War: The Guerrilla Conflict in Missouri during the American Civil War*. New York: Oxford University Press, 1989.

Fields, Frank E., Jr. *28th Virginia Infantry*. Lynchburg, Va.: H. E. Howard, 1985.

Foster, Gaines. *Ghosts of the Confederacy: Defeat, the Lost Cause and the Emergence of the New South, 1865–1913*. New York: Oxford University Press, 1987.

Fox-Genovese, Elizabeth. *Within the Plantation Household: Black and White Women of the Old South*. Chapel Hill: University of North Carolina Press, 1988.

Franklin, John Hope. *The Militant South, 1800–1861*. Cambridge, Mass.: Harvard University Press, 1956.

Frazer, Robert W. *Forts of the West; Military Forts and Presidios and Posts Commonly Called Forts West of the Mississippi River to 1898*. Norman: University of Oklahoma Press, 1965.

Freeman, Douglas Southall. *Lee's Lieutenants: A Study in Command*. 3 vols. New York: Charles Scribner's Sons, 1944.

——. *R. E. Lee: A Biography*. 4 vols. New York: Charles Scribner's Sons, 1934–35.

Friedman, Jean E. *The Enclosed Garden: Women and Community in the Evangelical South, 1830–1900*. Chapel Hill: University of North Carolina Press, 1985.

Gallagher, Gary, ed. *The Fredericksburg Campaign: Decision on the Rappahannock*. Chapel Hill: University of North Carolina Press, 1995.

——. *The Third Day at Gettysburg and Beyond*. Chapel Hill: University of North Carolina Press, 1994.

Genosky, Landry, Rev., ed. *The People's History of Quincy and Adams County, Illinois*. Quincy: Jost and Kiefer Printing Co., 1973.

Georg, Kathleen R., and John W. Busey. *Nothing but Glory: Pickett's Division at Gettysburg*. Hightstown, N.J.: Longstreet House, 1987.

Gibbs, George. *Dictionary of the Chinook Jargon, or Trade Language of Oregon*. New York: Cramoisy Press, 1863.

Gillialand, Miki. *Entering Bellingham*. Bellingham, Wash.: Bayside Press, 1989.

Glassley, Ray Hoard. *Indian Wars of the Pacific Northwest*. 1953. Reprint, Portland, Oreg.: Binfords and Mort, 1972.

Gordon, Armistead Churchill. *Memoirs and Memorials of William Gordon McCabe*. Vol. 1. Richmond, Va.: Old Dominion Press, 1925.

Gramm, Kent. *Gettysburg: A Meditation on War and Values*. Bloomington: Indiana University Press, 1994.

Gregory, G. Howard. *38th Virginia Infantry*. Lynchburg, Va.: H. E. Howard, 1988.

Hattaway, Herman, and Archer Jones. *How the North Won: A Military History of the Civil War*. Urbana: University of Illinois Press, 1983.

Henry, Robert Selph. *The Story of the Mexican War*. Indianapolis: The Bobbs Merrill, Co., 1950.

Hoke, Jacob. *The Great Invasion of 1863*. Dayton, Ohio: W. J. Shuey, 1887.

Howe, Henry. *Historical Collections of Virginia*. Charleston, S.C., 1845.

Howe, Thomas J. *The Petersburg Campaign: Wasted Valor, June 15–18, 1864*. Lynchburg, Va.: H. E. Howard, Inc., 1988.

Huntington, Samuel P. *The Soldier and the State*. Cambridge, Mass.: Harvard University Press, 1957.

Inventory of Early Architecture and Historic Sites, County of Henrico, Virginia, 1976.

Jeffcott, P. R. *Nooksack Tales and Trails*. Ferndale, Wash.: Sedro-Woolley Courier-Times, 1949.

Jenkins, William Sumner. *Pro-Slavery Thought in the Old South*. Gloucester, Mass.: Peter Smith, 1960.

Jensen, Les. *32nd Virginia Regiment*. Lynchburg, Va.: H. E. Howard, 1990.

Jervey, Edward D. *Prison Life among the Rebels: Recollections of a Union Chaplain*. Kent, Ohio: Kent State Universtiy Press, 1990.

Johannsen, Robert. *To the Halls of Montezuma: The Mexican War in the American Imagination*. New York: Oxford University Press, 1985.

Kammen, Michael. *Mystic Chords of Memory*. New York: Alfred A. Knopf, 1991.

Kirk, Ruth. *Washington State: National Parks, Historic Sites, Recreation Areas and Natural Landmarks*. Seattle: University of Washington Press, 1974.

Krick, Robert E. L. *The 40th Virginia*. Lynchburg, Va.: H. E. Howard, 1985.

Krick, Robert K. *Lee's Colonels: A Biographical Register of the Field Officers of the Army of Northern Virginia*. Dayton, Ohio: Morningside Bookshop, 1979.

Lebsock, Suzanne. *The Free Women of Petersburg: Status and Culture in a Southern Town, 1784–1860*. New York: W. W. Norton and Co., 1984.

Leckie, Shirley A. *Elizabeth Bacon Custer and the Making of a Myth*. Norman: University of Oklahoma Press, 1993.

Leonard, Elizabeth D. *Yankee Women: Gender Battles in the Civil War*. New York: W. W. Norton and Co., 1994.

Levin, Alexandria Lee. *"This Awful Drama": General Edwin Gray Lee, C.S.A. and His Family*. New York: Vintage Press, 1987.

Lewis, Ronald. *Coal, Iron and Slaves: Industrial Slavery in Maryland and Virginia, 1715–1865*. Westport, Conn.: Greenwood Press, 1979.

Linderman, Gerald. *Embattled Courage: The Experience of Combat in the American Civil War*. New York: The Free Press, 1987.

Longacre, Edward G. *Pickett: Leader of the Charge*. Shippensburg, Pa.: White Mane Publishing Co., 1995.

Longstreet, Helen D. *Lee and Longstreet at High Tide: Gettysburg in the Light of the Official Records*. Gainesville, Ga., 1904.

Lonn, Ella. *Desertion during the Civil War*. Gloucester, Mass.: Peter Smith, 1966.

Lowenthal, David. *The Past Is a Foreign Country*. Cambridge: Cambridge University Press, 1985.

Lystra, Karen. *Searching the Heart: Women, Men, and Romantic Love in Nineteenth-Century America*. New York: Oxford University Press, 1989.

McCabe, James. *The San Juan Water Boundary Question*. Toronto: University of Toronto Press, 1964.

McMurry, Richard M. *John Bell Hood and the War for Southern Independence*. Lexington: The University Press of Kentucky, 1982.

McPherson, James M. *Battle Cry of Freedom: The Civil War Era*. New York: Oxford University Press, 1988.

McWhiney, Grady. *Southerners and Other Americans*. New York: Basic Books, 1973.

McWhiney, Grady, and Perry Jamieson. *Attack and Die: Civil War Military Tactics and the Southern Heritage*. University: University of Alabama Press, 1982.

Managan, J. A., and James Walvin, eds. *Manliness and Morality: Middle-Class Masculinity in Britain and America, 1800–1940*. New York: St. Martins Press, 1987.

Manarin, Louis H. *A Guide to Military Organizations and Instillations in North Carolina, 1861–1865*. Raleigh: North Carolina Confederate Commission, 1961.

Massey, Mary Elizabeth. *Bonnet Brigades*. New York: Alfred A. Knopf, 1966.

——. *Ersatz in the Confederacy*. Columbia: University of South Carolina Press, 1952.

——. *Refugee Life in the Confederacy*. Baton Rouge: Louisiana State University Press, 1964.

Miller, J. Michael. *The North Anna Campaign: "Even to Hell Itself," May 21–26, 1864*. Lynchburg, Va.: H. E. Howard, 1989.

Mitchell, Mary H. *Hollywood Cemetery: The History of a Southern Shrine*. Richmond: Virginia State Library, 1985.

Mitchell, Reid. *The Vacant Chair: The Northern Soldier Leaves Home*. New York: Oxford University Press, 1993.

Moers, Ellen. *The Dandy: Brummell to Beerbohm*. New York: Viking Press, 1960.

Morris, George, and Susan Foutz. *Lynchburg in the Civil War: The City, the People, the Battle*. Lynchburg, Va.: H. E. Howard, 1984.

Morrison, Alfred J. *The Beginnings of Public Education in Virginia, 1776–1860*. Richmond: Bottom, Superintendent of Public Printing, 1917.

Morrison, James L. *"The Best School in the World": West Point in the Pre-Civil War Years, 1833–1860*. Kent, Ohio: Kent State University Press, 1986.

Murray, Keith. *The Pig War*. Tacoma, Wash.: Washington State Historical Society, 1968.

Newton, Steven H. *The Battle of Seven Pines, May 31–June 1, 1862*. Lynchburg, Va.: H. E. Howard, 1993.

Norton, Mary Beth. *Liberty's Daughters: The Revolutionary Experience of American Women, 1750–1800*. Boston: Little, Brown and Co., 1980.

Osterweis, Rollin G. *Romanticism and Nationalism in the Old South*. New Haven: Yale University Press, 1949.

O'Sullivan, Richard. *55th Virginia Infantry*. Lynchburg, Va.: H. E. Howard, 1989.

Paludan, Phillip Shaw. *Victims: A True Story of the Civil War*. Knoxville: University of Tennessee Press, 1981.

Patterson, Merrill D. *Lincoln in American Memory*. New York: Oxford University Press, 1994.

Piston, William S. *Lee's Tarnished Lieutenant: James Longstreet and His Place in Southern History*. Athens: University of Georgia Press, 1987.

Potter, Dorothy T., and Clifton W. Potter. *Lynchburg: "The Most Interesting Spot."* Lynchburg, Va.: Progress Publishing Co., 1976.

Powell, William S. *Annals of Progress: The Story of Lenoir County and Kinston, North Carolina*. Raleigh: State Department of Archives and History, 1963.

Pugh, David G. *Sons of Liberty: The Masculine Mind in Nineteenth-Century America*. Westport, Conn.: Greenwood Press, 1983.

Rable, George C. *Civil Wars: Women and the Crisis of Southern Nationalism*. Urbana: University of Illinois Press, 1989.

Reardon, Carol. *Pickett's Charge in History and Memory*. Chapel Hill: University of North Carolina Press, 1997.

Richards, Kent D. *Isaac I. Stevens: Young Man in a Hurry*. 1979. Reprint, Pullman: Washington State University Press, 1993.

Ripley, R. S. *The War with Mexico*. 2 vols. New York: Burt Franklin, 1849.

Roberts, Robert B. *Encyclopedia of Historic Forts*. New York: Macmillan Co., 1988.

Robertson, James I. *18th Virginia Infantry*. Lynchburg, Va.: H. E. Howard, 1984.

——. *General A. P. Hill: The Story of a Confederate Warrior*. New York: Random House, 1987.

Robertson, William Glenn. *Back Door to Richmond: The Bermuda Hundred Campaign, April–June 1964*. Newark: University of Delaware Press, 1987.

Rodenbough, Theodore F., and William L. Haskins. *The Army of the United States: Historical Sketches of Staff and Line with Portraits of Generals-in-Chief*. 1896. Reprint, Ann Arbor: University Microfilm, 1966.

Roth, Lottie Roeder, ed. *History of Whatcom County*. 2 vols. Chicago/Seattle: Pioneer Historical Publishing Company, 1926.

Rothman, Ellen K. *Hands and Hearts: A History of Courtship in America*. New York: Basic Books, 1984.

Rotundo, E. Anthony. *American Manhood: Transformations in Masculinity from the Revolution to the Modern Era*. New York: Basic Books, 1993.

Ryan, Mary P. *Women in Public: Between Banners and Ballots, 1825–1880*. Baltimore: Johns Hopkins University Press, 1990.

Schiller, Herbert. *The Bermuda Hundred Campaign: Operations on the South Side of the James River, Virginia, May 1864*. Dayton, Ohio: Morningside Books, 1988.

Schleifer, James. *The Making of Tocqueville's Democracy in America*. Chapel Hill: University of North Carolina Press, 1980.

Schlicke, Carl P. *General George Wright: Guardian of the Pacific Coast*. Norman: University of Oklahoma Press, 1988.

Scott, Anne Firor. *The Southern Lady: From Pedestal to Politics, 1830–1930*. Chicago: University of Chicago Press, 1970.

Sears, Stephen. *George B. McClellan: The Young Napoleon*. New York: Ticknor and Fields, 1988.

———. *To the Gates of Richmond: The Peninsula Campaign*. New York: Ticknor and Fields, 1992.

Selcer, Richard. *"Faithfully and Forever Your Soldier": Gen. George E. Pickett, CSA*. Gettysburg, Pa.: Farnsworth House Military Impressions, 1995.

Shaara, Michael. *The Killer Angels*. New York: Ballentine Paperback Edition, 1974.

Silber, Nina. *The Romance of Reunion: Northerners and the South, 1865–1900*. Chapel Hill: University of North Carolina Press, 1993.

Skelton, William B. *An American Profession of Arms: The Army Officer Corps, 1784–1861*. Lawrence: University Press of Kansas, 1992.

Smith, Justin H. *The War with Mexico*. 2 vols. New York: Macmillan Co., 1919.

Sommers, Richard J. *Richmond Redeemed: The Siege of Petersburg*. Garden City, N.Y.: Doubleday and Co., Inc., 1981.

Stewart, George. *Pickett's Charge: A Microhistory of the Final Attack at Gettysburg, July 3, 1863*. Boston: Houghton Mifflin Co., 1959.

Stowe, Steven M. *Intimacy and Power in the Old South: Ritual in the Lives of the Planters*. Baltimore: Johns Hopkins University Press, 1987.

Sutherland, Daniel. *The Confederate Carpetbaggers*. Baton Rouge: Louisiana State University Press, 1988.

Tarbell, Ida M. *The Life of Abraham Lincoln*. 2 vols. New York: Lincoln Memorial Association, 1900.

Taylor, William R. *Yankee and Cavalier: The Old South and American National Character*. Cambridge, Mass.: Harvard University Press, 1979.

Thomas, Emory M. *Bold Dragoon: The Life of J. E. B. Stuart*. New York: Harper and Row, 1986.

———. *The Confederate State of Richmond: A Biography of the Capital*. Austin: University of Texas Press, 1971.

———. *Robert E. Lee: A Biography*. New York: W. W. Norton and Co., 1995.

Trotter, William R. *Ironclads and Columbiads: The Civil War in North Carolina: The Coast*. Winston-Salem, N.C.: John F. Blair, 1989.

Tucker, Glenn. *High Tide at Gettysburg: The Campaign in Pennsylvania*. 1958. Reprint, Dayton, Ohio: Morningside Press, 1973.

———. *Lee and Longstreet at Gettysburg*. Indianapolis: Bobbs-Merrill Co., Inc., 1968.

Turberville, Daniel E., III. *Illustrated Inventory of Historic Bellingham Buildings, 1852–1915*. Bellingham, Wash.: Bellingham Municipal Arts Commission, November 1977.

Utley, Robert M. *Frontiersmen in Blue: The United States Army and the Indian, 1843–1865*. New York: Macmillan Co., 1967.

Van Den Brink, J. H. *The Haida Indians: Cultural Change Mainly between 1876–1970.* Leiden: E. J. Brill, 1974.

Walker, C. Irvine. *The Life of Lieutenant General Richard Heron Anderson of the Confederate States Army.* Charleston, S.C.: Art Publishing Co., 1917.

Wallace, Lee A., Jr. *1st Virginia Infantry.* Lynchburg, Va.: H. E. Howard, 1985.

——. *17th Virginia Infantry.* Lynchburg, Va.: H. E. Howard, 1990.

Warner, Ezra. *Generals in Blue: Lives of the Union Commanders.* Baton Rouge: Louisiana State University Press, 1964.

——. *Generals in Gray: Lives of the Confederate Commanders.* Baton Rouge: Louisiana State University Press, 1959.

Waugh, John C. *The Class of 1846: From West Point to Appomattox, Stonewall Jackson, George McClellan and Their Brothers.* New York: Warner Brother Books, 1994.

Wector, Dixon. *The Hero in America: A Chronicle of Hero Worship.* 1941. Reprint, New York: Charles Scribner's Sons, 1972.

Weems, John Edward. *To Conquer a Peace: The War between the United States and Mexico.* 1974. Reprint, College Station: Texas A & M University Press, 1988.

Weigley, Russell. *History of the United States Army.* New York: Macmillan Co., 1967.

Welsh, Jack K. *Medical Histories of Confederate Generals.* Kent, Ohio: Kent State University Press, 1995.

Wert, Jeffrey. *General James Longstreet, the Confederacy's Most Controversial Soldier: A Biography.* New York: Simon and Schuster, 1993.

Whites, LeeAnn. *The Civil War as a Crisis in Gender: Augusta, Georgia.* Athens: University of Georgia Press, 1995.

Willard, Francis E., and Mary A. Livermore, eds. *A Woman of the Century: Fourteen Hundred-Seventy Biographical Sketches Accompanied by Portraits of Leading American Women in all Walks of Life.* Chicago: Charles Wells Moulton, 1893.

Wilson, Charles Reagan. *Baptized in Blood: The Religion of the Lost Cause, 1865–1920.* Athens: University of Georgia Press, 1980.

Wilson, Clyde N. *Carolina Cavalier: The Life and Mind of James Johnston Pettigrew.* Athens: University of Georgia Press, 1990.

Wright, Marcus J. *General Officers of the Confederate Army.* New York: The Neale Publishing Co., 1911.

Wyatt-Brown, Bertram. *The Literary Percys. Family, History, Gender and the Southern Imagination.* Athens: University of Georgia Press, 1994.

——. *Southern Honor: Ethics and Behavior in the Old South.* New York: Oxford University Press, 1982.

Young, William A., Jr., and Patricia Young. *56th Virginia Infantry.* Lynchburg, Va.: H. E. Howard, 1990.

Articles

Bardolph, Richard. "Confederate Dilemma: North Carolina Troops and the Deserter Problem." Parts 1 and 2. *North Carolina Historical Review* 66 (January and April 1989): 61–86, 179–210.

——. "Inconstant Rebels: Desertion of North Carolina Troops in the Civil War." *North Carolina Historical Review* 41 (Spring 1964): 163–89.

Cashin, Joan. " 'Decidedly Opposed to the Union': Women's Culture, Marriage and Politics in Antebellum South Carolina." *Georgia Historical Quarterly* 78 (Winter 1994): 735–59.

Crimmins, M. L. "Experiences of an Army Surgeon at Fort Chadbourne." *West Texas Historical Association Year Book* 15 (October 1939): 31–39.

Earle, Elinor. "LaSalle Corbell Pickett." *United Daughters of the Confederacy Magazine* 53 (August 1990): 22.

Fisher, B. J. "Military Justice of the Texas Frontier." *The West Texas Historical Association Yearbook* 64 (1988): 123–39.

Gallagher, Gary W. "A Widow and Her Soldier: LaSalle Corbell Pickett as Author of the George E. Pickett Letters." *Virginia Magazine of History and Biography* 94 (July 1986): 329–44.

Georg, Kathleen R. "Where Was Pickett During Pickett's Charge?" *Civil War Quarterly* 11 (Winter 1987): 25–33.

Gordon, Lesley J. "The Seeds of Disaster: The Generalship of George E. Pickett after Gettysburg." In *Leadership and Command in the American Civil War*, edited by Steven Woodworth. Campbell, Calif.: Savas-Woodbury Publishers, 1995.

Gordon-Burr, Lesley J. " 'Until Calm Reflection Should Take the Place of Wild Impulse': George E. Pickett and the Hangings at Kinston, North Carolina, February 1864," *Proceedings and Papers of the Georgia Association of Historians* 12 (1991): 19–45.

Gorn, Elliot. " 'Gouge and Bite, Pull Hair and Scratch': The Social Significance of Fighting in the Southern Backcountry." *American Historical Review* 90 (February 1985): 18–32.

Hall, James O. "Atonement." *Civil War Times Illustrated* 19 (August 1980): 19–21.

Higginbotham, R. Don. "The Martial Spirit in the Antebellum South: Some Further Speculations in a National Context." *The Journal of Southern History* 58 (February 1992): 3–26.

Honey, Michael K. "The War within the Confederacy: White Unionists of North Carolina." *Prologue: Journal of the National Archives* 18 (Summer 1986): 75–93.

Jervey, Edward P. "Prison Life among the Rebels: Recollections of a Union Chaplain." *Civil War History* 34 (March 1988): 22–45.

Kinsel, Amy. "From Turning Point to Peace Memorial: A Cultural Legacy." In *The Gettysburg Nobody Knows*, edited by Gabor S. Boritt, 203–22. New York: Oxford University Press, 1997.

Kruman, Marc W. "Dissent in the Confederacy: The North Carolina Experience." *Civil War History* 27 (December 1981): 293–313.

Landrum, Carl. "An 1840s Resident of Quincy Recounts City's Early Days." *Quincy Herald-Whig*, August 15, 1993.

———. "From Quincy to Gettysburg." *Quincy Herald-Whig*, April 26, 1981.

———. "General Who Studied Law in Quincy." *Quincy Herald-Whig*, March 24, 1991.

McKay, Charles. "History of San Juan Island." *Washington Historical Quarterly* 3 (October 1907–July 1908): 290–93.

"Minge Family Register." *William and Mary Quarterly* 21 (Winter 1913–15): 31–32.

Olsen, Allee. "The Pickett House." *United Daughters of the Confederacy Magazine* 54 (August 1991): 26.

Palmer, Heather. "The Civil War Wedding of LaSalle Corbell." *Lady's Gallery* 1, no. 6 (n.d.): 53–54.

Patterson, Gerald A. "George E. Pickett: A Personality Profile." *Civil War Times Illustrated* 5 (May 1966): 18–24.

Selcer, Richard. "George Pickett: Another Look." *Civil War Times Illustrated* 33 (July–August 1994): 44–49, 60–73.

Smith, Everard H. "Chambersburg: Anatomy of a Confederate Reprisal." *American Historical Review* 96 (April 1991): 432–55.

Smith-Rosenberg, Carroll. "The Hysterical Women: Sex Roles and Role Conflict in Nineteenth-Century America." *Social Research* 39 (Winter 1972): 652–78.

Stivers, R. E. "Turkey Island Plantation." *Virginia Cavalcade* 14 (Autumn 1964): 41–47.

Tunem, Alfred. "The Dispute over the San Juan Island Water Boundary." *Washington Historical Quarterly* 23 (1932): 38–46, 133–37, 196–204, 286–300.

Dissertations, Theses, and Other Unpublished Sources

Adams, George Rollie. "General William Selby Harney: Frontier Soldier, 1800–1889." Ph.D. diss., University of Arizona, 1983.

Carmichael, Peter S. "The Last Generation: Sons of Virginia Slaveholders and the Creation of Southern Identity, 1850–1865." Ph.D. diss., Pennsylvania State University, 1996.

Flusche, Michael A. "The Private Plantation: Versions of the Old South Myth, 1880–1914." Ph.D. diss., Johns Hopkins University, 1973.

Gamble, Richard Dalzell. "Garrison Life at Frontier Military Posts, 1830–1860." Ph.D. diss., University of Oklahoma, 1956.

Gordon, Lesley Jill. " 'Assumed a Darker Hue:' Confederate Major General George E. Pickett, May 1863–May 1864." M.A. thesis, University of Georgia, 1991.

——. "Before the Storm: The Early Life of George E. Pickett." Senior Honors Thesis, College of William and Mary, 1987.

——. " 'Days of Darkness and Blood': George and LaSalle Pickett and the American Civil War." Ph.D. diss., University of Georgia, 1995.

The National Guard, State of Washington, "Collection of Official Documents on the San Juan Imbroglio, 1859–1872."

Piston, William S. "Lee's Tarnished Lieutenant: James Longstreet and His Image in American Society." 2 vols. Ph.D. diss., University of South Carolina, 1982.

Reardon, Carol Ann. "The Image of 'Pickett's Charge,' 1863–1913: Virginia's Gift to American Martial Tradition." M.A. thesis, University of South Carolina, 1980.

Sadlow, Jeane Louise. "Life and Campaigns of General George Edward Pickett." M.A. thesis, St. Johns University, 1959.

Strevey, Tracy Elmber. "Pickett on Puget Sound." M.A. thesis, University of Washington, 1925.

Tyndall, Clifford C. "Lenoir County during the Civil War." M.A. thesis, East Carolina University, 1981.

Vouri, Michael. "George Pickett and the Frontier Army Experience." Unpublished manuscript in possession of author.

——. "Raiders from the North: The Northern Indians and Northwest Washington in the 1850s." Unpublished manuscript in possesion of the author.

Wills, Brian Steel. "In Charge: Command Relationships in the Suffolk Campaign, 1863." M.A. thesis, University of Georgia, 1985.

Wolff, Alfred Young, Jr. "The South and the American Imagination: Mythical Views of the Old South, 1865–1900." Ph.D. diss., University of Virginia, 1971.

Books, Articles, and Short Stories Authored by LaSalle Corbell Pickett

Pickett, LaSalle Corbell. *Across My Path: Memories of People I Have Known.* 1916. Reprint, Freeport, N.Y.: Books for Libraries Press, 1970.

——. *The Bugles of Gettysburg.* Chicago: F. G. Browne and Co., 1913.

——. *Digging through to Manila.* Washington, D.C.: Press of Byron S. Adams, 1905.

——. *Ebil Eye.* Washington, D.C.: The Neale Co., 1901.

——. "The First United States Flag Raised in Richmond after the War." In *The Fourth Massachusetts Cavalry in the Closing Scenes of the War for the Maintenance of the Union*, edited by William B. Arnold, 19–22. Boston: n.p., n.d.

——. *Jinny.* Washington, D.C.: The Neale Co., 1901.

——. *Kunnoo Sperit and Others.* Washington, D.C.: The Neale Co., 1900.

——. *Literary Hearthstones of Dixie.* Philadelphia: J. B. Lipincott, Co., 1912.

——. "My Soldier." *McClure's Magazine* 30 (March 1908): 563–71.

——. *Pickett and His Men.* Atlanta: Foote and Davies, 1899.

——. "The Wartime Story of General Pickett." Parts 1–9. *Cosmopolitan* 55 (November 1913): 752–60; 56 (December 1913–May 1914): 33–42, 178–85, 332–39, 473–81, 611–22, 762–69; 57 (July–August 1914): 196–205, 369–77.

——. *What Happened to Me.* New York: Brentano, 1917.

——. *Yule-Log and Others.* Washington, D.C.: The Neale Co., 1900.

——, ed. *The Heart of a Soldier: As Revealed in the Intimate Letters of General George E. Pickett, C.S.A.* New York: Seth Moyle, 1913.

United Daughters of the Confederacy, 181

United States Army: and tension between professionals and volunteers, 20, 46; life on prewar frontier, 32–33; in Pacific Northwest, 42–65; and brevet system, 191 (n. 30), 197 (n. 38); and politics, 192 (n. 45); and drinking, 194 (n. 13). *See also* Military; Native Americans: and U.S. Army; Texas: and U.S. Army; United States Army Regular Troops; United States Military Academy; Women: as army officers' wives

United States Army Regular Troops: 4th Infantry, 47, 207 (n. 43); 6th Infantry, 24; 7th Infantry, 23; 8th Infantry, 18, 23, 24, 25, 32, 37, 192 (n. 39); 9th Infantry, 40, 41, 42, 43, 44, 198 (n. 45), 199 (n. 10)

United States Military Academy (West Point), 10, 11, 12–17, 18–19, 20, 23, 26, 28, 32, 33, 39, 46, 65, 78, 79, 80, 130, 153, 160, 187 (nn. 22, 24), 188 (n. 47), 188–89 (n. 51), 194 (n. 13), 203 (n. 4), 207 (n. 43), 218 (n. 24)

Vaden, Elizabeth Heth, 32, 37, 38
Vera Cruz, 19; siege of, 21, 23
Viele, Teresa, 35
Virginia, 4, 6, 7, 8, 15, 18–19, 20, 33, 34, 39, 40, 41, 63, 64, 65, 66, 68, 69, 78, 92, 98, 102, 113, 118, 124, 160, 162, 167, 168, 169, 172, 173, 178; secession of, 84, 207 (n. 50)
Virginia Military Institute, 78, 167, 169
Virginia troops, 73, 77, 93, 109, 224 (n. 26); 7th Infantry, 151; 8th Infantry, 78, 213 (n. 50); 9th Cavalry, 70; 9th Infantry, 99; 11th Infantry, 94, 218 (n. 39); 18th Infantry, 78, 85, 86, 89, 94, 143, 211 (n. 12); 19th Infantry, 78, 86, 88; 24th Cavalry, 99; 28th Infantry, 78; 40th Infantry, 72; 55th

Infantry, 208 (n. 22); 56th Infantry, 98
Vouri, Michael, 49

Waite, Carlos A., 24, 25
Ward, William N., 72, 73, 208 (n. 22)
Washington, D.C., 39, 62, 66, 67, 119, 141, 160, 161, 168, 177, 180
Washington Territory, 42–65. *See also* Pig War; San Juan Island, Wash. Terr.
West Point. *See* United States Military Academy
What Happened To Me (L. Pickett), 173
Whiting, W. H. C., 125
Wilcox, Cadmus M., 87, 113, 115, 120
Wild, Edward, 126, 127
Wilderness, battle of the, 141, 142
Wilkins, Margaret Minge, 34, 195 (n. 17)
Wilkins, Richard, 34, 195 (n. 17)
Williamsburg, battle of, 81–83, 84, 92
Wilson, Sara Evans, 175
Wise, George D., 167
Wise, Henry, 154
Withers, R. E., 89, 211 (n. 12)
Women: southern, 34, 75, 124, 145, 158, 168, 172, 173, 178, 194 (n. 16), 195 (n. 21); as army officers' wives, 34–35, 195 (n. 21, 22); and war, 76, 124, 168, 209 (nn. 34, 35, 36), 217 (n. 12), 218 (n. 36), 222 (n. 10); and marriage, 194 (n. 16); and education, 209 (n. 34); and gender ideals, 222 (n. 5), 222–23 (n. 10); as "professional widows," 238 (n. 3)
Wood, J. Taylor, 128, 129
Wool, John Ellis, 43–44, 198–99 (n. 9), 199 (n. 11)
Worth, William J., 21, 22, 25–26, 28, 190 (nn. 19, 25)
Wright, George, 25, 42, 44, 64, 65

Yakima War, 43–44, 199 (n. 11)
Yorktown, Va., 79, 80; siege of, 80–81
Youngblood, William, 116

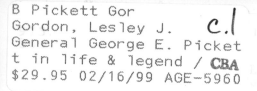